MAA AANKH

Volume I
Second Edition

Finding God the Afro-American Spiritual Way,
by Honoring the Ancestors and Guardian Spirits

Derric Moore

MAA AANKH

Volume I

Finding God the Afro-American Spiritual Way, by Honoring the Ancestors and Guardian Spirits

By Derric Moore

Published by:	Four Sons Publications
Contact:	1 SõL Alliance Co. P.O. Box 596 Liberal, KS 67905-0596 www.1solalliance.com

Copyright © 2013 Derric Moore

Edited by Sebastián Lalaurette

All rights reserved. No part of this publication may be reproduced or transmitted in any form or by any means, electronic or mechanical, including photocopying, recording or by any information storage and retrieval system, without written permission from the author, except for the inclusion of brief quotations in a review.

Includes bibliographical references and index.

Cover art and Illustrations by: Derric "Rāu Khu" Moore

Photos courtesy of Dreamstime.com

ISBN: 978-0-9855067-2-8
Printed in the United States of America

Dedication

To my family, those whose shoulders I stand upon and those whom have yet to come.

About the Author

Derric "Rau Khu" Moore grew up in a loving strong Christian household in Detroit, Michigan, surrounded by rich Christian folk traditions. He is a loving son, brother, husband, father, grandfather, uncle and cousin. He has studied religion, mysticism, metaphysics, folklore and spiritualism for over ten years. Educated as a chemical engineer, he is an academic instructor, poet, folk artist, graphic artist and urban shaman.

Table of Contents

PREFACE XI

PART I: THE SEARCH FOR GOD 1
WHAT A TIME YOU CHOSE TO BE BORN 2
BUCKIN' THE OLD WAY 10
EGYPT, THE MYSTERIOUS LIGHT OF THE EAST 14
ONE MIRACLE AT A TIME 20
LESSONS FROM MARTIN L. KING & MALCOLM X 22
LEARNING ABOUT THE SUPREME 25
COLLEGE DAYS 32
TASHA AND TIFFANY 38
LOSING SIGHT OF THE PRIZE 41

PART II: DISCOVERING THE SPIRITUAL PATH 43
BREAKING SPIRITUAL GROUND 44
THE PHILADELPHIA EXPERIENCE 50
A REAL SPIRITUAL MOMMA 56
HITTIN' ROCK BOTTOM 60
FLORIDA SUNSHINE BLUES 62
A BRIEF WALK WITH A CUBAN SAINT 71
THE CANDLE SHOP VISIT 88

PART III: LEARNING TO WALK ON MY OWN 91
IN THE STRANGE LAND OF OZ 92
HELP FROM A LIL' CUBAN SAINT 97
IYA AND THE CALLING 101
MY FRIEND, BEST FRIEND, GIRLFRIEND & WIFE 105
TRYING TO UNDERSTAND THIS QUEST 108
THE WHITE MAN'S RELIGION MYTH 118
VODU, GRIS-GRIS AND THE LOUISIANA PURCHASE 125
THE INFLUENCES OF SPIRITISM AND SPIRITUALISM 128
THE HOLINESS AND PENTECOSTALISM INFLUENCES 132
RELIGIOUS SYNCRETISM IN NORTH AMERICA 139
WHY I LEFT THE CHURCH 147
WHY ANCIENT KAMIT? 153

PART IV: BORN AGAIN 169
CROSSING OVER TO THE OTHER SIDE 170

THE AAKHU: ANCESTRAL SPIRITS 175
THE ANCESTORS SPEAK 177
ANCESTRAL HEALING 180
LUCK, GROWTH AND HEALING FROM THE DEAD 189
THE STORY OF RA AND OSET 194
THE KAMITIC HOLY GHOST 197
DISCOVERING MORE HIDDEN HANDS 201
THE MAA AANKH 213
THE STORY OF OSAR 224
THE POWER OF WHITENESS 232
WHAT CHA GOIN' TO DO? 234

PART V: BECOMING A VESSEL FOR GOD 239
ACCEPTING THAT HE WILL WORK IT OUT 240
ESOTERIC UNDERSTANDING OF ANCIENT KAMIT 243
CHILLOUT BABY 253
NETCHARU: THE INHABITANTS OF KAMTA 262
AAPEPU: THE INHABITANTS OF TASETT 270
TRYING THE SPIRIT 278
ASSISTANCE FROM NPU 282
THE BATTLE HAS JUST BEGUN, BABY 290
A VISIT FROM THE KING OF WHITENESS 295
TWO EYES ARE BETTER THAN ONE 299
WHO CALLED ME? 303

APPENDIX A: MAKING MAA AANKH WITH THE AAKHU & NETCHARU 307
APPENDIX B: THE 42 DECLARATIONS OF MAA 317
APPENDIX C: THE PRECIOUS BLOOD OF THE RAM (LAMB) 319
APPENDIX D: BIBLIOMANCY 322
APPENDIX E: GLOSSARY OF TERMS 326
APPENDIX F: SELECTED BIBLIOGRAPHY & RECOMMENDED READING 335
INDEX 341

Acknowledgement

Thanks to God for everything and most importantly for allowing me to see the beauty of life that He has created.

Thanks to my ancestors for the numerous sacrifices that were made in order for me to have life and enjoy the privileges that I have today. A special thanks goes out to my late grandparents who laid the foundation for their children, grandchildren and great-grandchildren to follow until their return.

Thanks to my father, mother and brothers for your unconditional love, concern, encouragement and support. Thanks to my good friend, my girlfriend, my wife, who encouraged me to pursue this project and has eagerly awaited for it to be finished. Thanks *Dulce* for listening, supporting and believing in me. Thanks to my in-laws who also showed me the importance and purpose of family.

Thanks to my best friend G, for standing by when you saw me taking a wrong turn, helping me to recover after I did, and telling me the truth even when I didn't want to hear it.

And finally, thanks to my godmother in Philadelphia, godfather in Florida, godsister in New York, Iya and all my teachers who have helped me along the way.

How to Use This Book

Although this book is a memoir, I have structured it as a guide into African American spirituality and thought, in order to give the reader a glimpse of how I used history, philosophy and mental sciences as a tool of healing and spiritual empowerment. To get the best out of this book it is strongly suggested that one simply keep an open mind, sit back and enjoy.

This book has been divided into five parts, which correspond to the stages of development, as well as the moments of the maa aankh.

- ❖ **Part 1**, "The Search for God," is about how I began this journey, from my childhood religious experience to my young adult years.
- ❖ **Part 2**, "Discovering the Spiritual Path," discusses the common misconceptions and obstacles I encountered when dealing with spiritual development.
- ❖ **Part 3**, "Learning to Walk On My Own," focuses upon how I went through a trial and error period of proving which philosophies and theories worked and didn't work for me.
- ❖ **Part 4**, "Born Again," deals with how to put in practice what one has learned once one has found the truth.
- ❖ **Part 5**, "Becoming a Vessel for God," means just that: once one learns a truth, one is supposed to use it to help others. This is done by living according to one's highest ideals about God, which is the highest form of worship: emulating God.

List of Illustrations

Figure 1: Ellegua - Orisha of the Crossroads 71
Figure 2: The Kongo Yowa Cross or Tendwa Kia nza-n' Kongo 204
Figure 3: KHEPERA - The Coming Into Existence RA 208
Figure 4: RA 209
Figure 5: RA ATUM - The Complete RA 210
Figure 6: AMUN RA - The Hidden RA 210
Figure 7: Maa Aankh Cosmogram 213
Figure 8: Crown of the Red Lands 217
Figure 9: Crown of the Black Lands 218
Figure 10: KAMTA & TASETT 222
Figure 11: Pschent (White & Red Crown) 231
Figure 12: Maa Aankh & Kamitic Crowns 231
Figure 13: Hedjet Crown & Djet Pillar 232
Figure 14: Maa Aankh and the Cycle of Life 254
Figure 15: Maa Aankh and the Flow of Rau 260

List of Tables

Supreme Mathematics 26
Supreme Alphabet 28
Supreme Mathematics, Kabala and the Paut Neteru 45
Types of Spirits per Allan Kardec 129
Table 1: Map of Upper and Lower Kamit 216
Divisions of the Spirit 245
Divisions of the Spirit and the Maa Aankh 250
Table 2: Nine Divisions of the Spirit 247

Disclaimer

The information contained in this book is intended to be educational and not for diagnosis, prescription, or treatment of any health disorder whatsoever. This information should not replace consultation with a competent healthcare professional. The content of the book is intended to be used as an adjunct to a rational and responsible healthcare program prescribed by a licensed healthcare practitioner. This is a book about faith. As such the author and publisher do not warrant the success any person would have using any of the exercises and techniques contained herein. Success and failure will vary. The author and publisher therefore are in no way liable for any misuse of the material contained herein.

To protect the identity and privacy of others, most of the names within this book have been adapted, modified and changed for confidentiality purposes. Any resemblance to real persons, living or dead is purely coincidental.

Preface

There is nothing more heartbreaking, disturbing, upsetting and discouraging than not knowing where you are supposed to go, who you are supposed to be or, what's the purpose of your life. This lack of self-direction and self-understanding, quiet as kept, is a serious problem because, when you don't know the answer to any of these questions, it can lead you down a path resulting in all sorts of health problems. Not to mention making choices and decisions that one will regret later on.

Without a clear picture of who we are, what we are doing here, what we are supposed to do or any explanation into the subject, it is hard for us to adjust and make changes when things go awry. We then view every trial, tribulation, obstacle and problem that occurs, from a destructive purpose as if some great force is plotting to destroy us. We even go so far as to believing that there is no hope and no God that cares for us.

Fortunately, we are not the first that have traveled down the road of self-discovery. There are numerous people before us that have felt the same way and understood that even though God is omnipotent and the source of everything, God is not in control of everything. God doesn't stop us from putting a cigarette in our mouth or drinking alcoholic beverages excessively. Some things man and woman have to learn how to do for themselves and just praying for peace, patience, self-control, anger management, a successful marriage, etc. is not enough. Something else had to be done, so these people that walked before us on the road to self-discovery discovered a better way and they left signs along the way or road maps as they traveled to find God, to help others to find where they were supposed to be in life as well.

Unfortunately, due to chauvinism, colonialism,

discrimination, racism and every other "ism" that has contributed to portraying non-western (Native American, African, etc.) traditions and practices as being primitive, backwards, silly, superstitious, evil, foolish, polytheistic, etc. the signs and road maps to self-discovery for most have been lost. As a result, when all of the Western medicine and westernized techniques, which focus primarily on the physical reality and not both (the physical and spiritual), fail to work, many of us are at a loss as to what to do next. Desperately, we scramble around looking for some type of solution or some sign to show us how to "fix" the problems in our life, when all of our physical resources have been exhausted.

Thankfully, the ones that left the signs and created the road maps are not easily removed. Our ancestors and guardian angels continue to guide and inspire us even if we are too "sophisticated" for them. They know that no matter how high we become life has a way of humbling us through hardships, trials, tribulations, obstacles, and other experiences. So, they patiently wait for us to come to them but this time they wait for us to show some initiative and interpret the signs. Interpreting the signs and reading the road maps that our ancestors left requires knowledge and not just knowledge based upon our intellect, but knowledge of the spiritual realm. Obtaining access into this mystical realm requires that one use their imagination to understand such signs as dreaming of fish, seeing a particular bird such as one fly in their house or witnessing a particular phenomenon in nature.

As a result, a Western "trained" mind describes events that occur in nature that he cannot logically explain arrogantly as a "freak of nature". A non-western "trained" mind describes events that she cannot explain as signs from God, angels, ancestors or the spirits, or simply the language of the Spirit.

Learning the language of the Spirit and how to use it to improve one's life, especially if one has been raised in a westernized society, is an adventure. It is what I had to do in order to find God, overcome obstacles that were in my way and improve my life. Like many that have walked before me, I tried to fix my life by following the advice and suggestions of others (or reading thousands of books), which many times led me further away from God and made me more frustrated. But it was an experience I had to undergo in order to learn how to go within.

It was only after years of reading, studying and learning that I finally submitted. That's when I was given a sign that connected me back to my ancestral past, helped me to better understand myself, understand how to connect to God and gave me purpose in life. Using my experience as a guide to understand how certain patterns unfolded, I began to see that nothing happens by accident or by coincidence. Everything that occurs in our life happens for a reason but the only way to see this is by not becoming depressed, upset and remorseful about our experiences. Instead focus on trying to understand the meaning behind them.

History, I found, is full of examples of individuals that had to overcome great obstacles in order to become great men and women, but how most great men and women overcame these obstacles is always presented as a mystery. This is because it is a learning experience that is not taught in a classroom and there is no graduation from, yet you will learn things that no one else may have ever known before, until you leave this earthly existence. This path that I had taken in order to find answers to questions denied to me in my youth has led to me having some ups and downs. I have also had a number of questionable moments where I have made some serious and regrettable mistakes, which led to me almost losing my life, as I wandered in search of God and a cultural home, hoping one day to be welcomed with open arms and to hear someone tell me welcome home. I will not lie to you. It was frightening, in fact downright scary at times, but it was so rewarding in the end because that's how I discovered the grace, mercy, power and wisdom of God lies within me. It was through these various obstacles that I found God, my ancestral home and true liberation from the mental, physical and spiritual chains of bondage.

    Presented within these pages, is my story and the system that was taught to me by my ancestors on how to improve my life. I present it here not as the absolute truth and the cure all to all of the ills that exist in society. No system has all of the answers and is the cure all to everything. I present it as my truth, based upon my theory and my experience, and I hope and pray that it can help you as it has benefited me.

Peace, blessings and prosperity, be upon you.

Derric Moore

January 1, 2010

Part I:
The Search for God

No matter how long the Night,
the Day is sure to come.

—Kongo Proverb

What a Time You Chose to Be Born

How I came into the world should have been a sign that there were going to be a lot of problems and I was going to be different. According to my mother I was in the right position and then shortly before delivery I turned upside down and was born breeched. My mother claimed that every since that day I have been backwards. I jokingly interpreted, unknowing what was in store for me, that I got a peek of the things to come and decided to return from whence I had come from (the heavens).

Whatever the case, I was born the eldest son of four boys to a young couple in Detroit, Michigan, in the early 1970s. My father worked as a telephone repairman during the day and as an Apostolic Pentecostal assistant pastor at night and the weekend. My mother was an elementary school teacher and a devout Christian songstress.

Aside from the fact that my father was either always working to provide for his family or attending to church business, I had a pretty good childhood. Like most kids back in the day, my brothers and I had chores, but since my mother was my grandparents' eldest child out of nine children and had seven – as she would say "rusty" brothers (my brothers knew them as the Mighty Seven, since we had to wrestle them in order to earn their respect), we weren't raised that it was a woman's job to do anything. So, my brothers and I alternated on doing the dishes. We all had weekend chores as well. I was responsible for cleaning the bathroom and the kitchen, while my younger brother did the dusting. So every Saturday morning, as I was taught, two capfuls of Pine-Sol were dropped into a plastic bucket and warm water was added. I eventually would try to do my chores on Friday night so that I could watch the double horror features that would come on late Friday night and the kung fu flicks that came on Saturday morning undisturbed. Among my favorite martial arts films were *The Kid with the Golden Arms*, *The Five Deadly Venoms*, and

Shogun the Assassin, where the samurai Lone Wolf tells his son Cub that he must decide (by fate) to either live or die by choosing a sword (for life) or a ball (for death). In the end, Saturday morning would end up being the day I did most of my chores.

Since my father worked as a telephone technician or was busy tending to church business, my mother, for the most part, was the one that my brothers and I usually relied upon to help us with our homework and other issues when growing up. She helped us with everything, it seems, but she didn't take any mess from us either. She stood up to us boys with a belt or the dreaded switch in her hand. She always told us, when she gave us a spanking, that she loved us and was spanking us so that we understood what we were doing was wrong, and that our wrongful behavior hurts us and everyone involved. My mother's theory, just like my grandparents' theory, was that she would rather spank us and go to jail for rearing us right, than allow us to go to jail or be killed for not being reared correctly. This was the old school way and it was enforced by the men. My father backed my mother up and my grandfather backed my grandmother up and so on and so on. One hated to get a whooping from their father, grandfather, uncle or any man for that reason.

    Now, it wasn't that my father wasn't a good father, but he was either working on the job or working for the church, which took up a lot of his time. Occasionally, my father, I remember, would help me with my math and science homework. In fact, it was because of him that I won first place in several science fairs. But my father had basically, in my young, mind built up a reputation of not being around. When my brothers and I finally saw my father it was either late at night or early in the morning, and it seemed for a few minutes. As a result, my mother was the one that we saw most of the time in the house. She was the one that we relied upon the most. My mother, it seemed, was the one that had for the most part the most authority and the most influence in our house, but she respected and loved my father, who always got the big piece of chicken (smile).

    Given that my mother was a teacher, my brothers and I were always learning something, because she made sure that there was plenty of educational material around the house. My father also was an avid reader and when he wasn't busy working he was reading horror books, science fiction novels, or books related to the church. But again, since my mother had the most influence in our house it seemed, we lived by her rules, which were enforced by our distant father so much so, that in the summer, when most of the children were out playing from sunrise to sunset, from sunrise to noon, my brothers and I attended my mother's school in the house.

My mother's school during the summer was at our kitchen table after eating breakfast. Every summer, so that we didn't forget what we learned during the school year and would be ready when school started in the fall, we had to read a magazine, newspaper or something in addition to give a book report, along with do our mathematics. I hated at the time following this routine, but when it finally kicked in that I had to do it every summer, years later, I would learn that the reason my mother made my brothers and I do this was because my grandmother, who didn't finish school but loved to learn, followed this routine and benefited from it. She in turn made my mother do the same thing, which most likely led to my mother graduating and going on to college to become a teacher, so it was my brothers and my turn now. Accepting that this was my summer fate, I remembered the book I chose to do a book report on one summer, which became my favorite childhood book (and one of my mothers') was Homer's *Illiad* and the *Odyssey*. Anyway, we followed this routine every summer and for a month we were given a break just before school started.

During that month break, my father, after working so hard for a full year, would take us all on vacation. We would either go across the river to Canada, Chicago, Orlando or some other place to meet our relatives for a family reunion. Then, when the school year started back up, we would start doing the same thing all over again.

It was also during the regular part of the year that my mother forced my brother and I to take piano lessons at an early age, but I stopped going as soon as I started learned how to play the trumpet. I wanted to give up piano lessons anyway because I was tired of practicing my Schaums music book. I didn't know at the time that that little yellow book helped me to learn how to read music. Anyway, when I picked up the trumpet I soon learned about the world of jazz, but I would soon put this down because music wasn't my first passion. My first love was drawing and painting because through it I was able to draw and paint another world. In fact, I would actually get so deep into my artwork that I had to be forced to take a break and go outside and play. It was through artwork and music I could express myself but artwork (or my doodling) was the only tool that I could take with me and allowed me to escape the boringness of church.

Like many African American youths during that time, I went to church all my life. Everything in my parents' home revolved around church or God first then family. Growing up in our house wasn't real bad because we could listen to anything (as long as it wasn't real loud) any day of the week except on Sunday. Sunday was considered God's Day in our home and it was the day we spent most of our time at church. If my brothers and I would argue on Sunday afternoon, we were made to go back to church and forced to sit on the front pew to get the devil out of us. After sitting on the front pew for several years because of arguing and fighting with each other, eventually we learned to be quiet and at least act like we loved each other until Monday.

There were a lot of things that my parents and their church friends did that I really enjoyed. For one, I was quite fond of the old call and response hymns that weren't recorded on most gospel albums, but the entire congregation knew. These songs were traditional hymns that were passed down from preceding generation like, *Got Good Religion, Lead Me, (I like) The Old Time Way, God's Been Good to Me, Hold on to God's Unchanging Hand* and *Drive Old Satan Away*. I also liked the songs sung by our choir, especially the ones that were written by Edwin and Walter Hawkins.

One thing I liked was that even though our church was relatively large (one of the largest in the city), everyone seemed to know each other like a family. I liked that our church also had quite a few elders. Many of these elders you could see had been through a lot and lived to talk about them. One day I had wanted to listen to some of their stories because you could see that they had a lot of power and wisdom within them, but I never got a chance to do it.

Some of the other things that I enjoyed were going to church on New Years Eve and giving thanks to God for a blessed year, which they called Watch Meeting Night. Then after service was over people would gather and eat in order to have a happy New Year.

Then there were some things that my parents and their friends were real secretive about and rarely talked about in front of us children. The way these older people mysteriously talked about some of these subjects made me almost believe that being an adult meant also being a member of a secret society. This was because some of the subjects that the adults spoke about didn't directly coincide with the church's beliefs.

For instance, when some babies were born that seemed to have a lot of personality, the older people would say that the child was an old soul. When there was a thunderstorm we children were told to be or play quietly and not to use the telephone because God was talking and/or fighting the devil. I remember when I was younger also being told not to whistle inside the house because it brought ill to the home.

There were other things that the adults did that seemed quite strange. Like interpreting dreams based upon signs that appeared in their dreams. Dreaming of fish for example was a sign that someone was pregnant. Another sign that someone was pregnant was if you dreamt of someone dying in your dream. There were other signs that existed that had many meanings, as well, but it seemed that not everyone knew them. There were however some people that had more knowledge of these signs than others because they were said to have been born with a veil (membrane) over their faces, thus allowing them to see certain things.

I remember that when I heard some of these things that the adults talked about, it made me think that some of these people had power like the people in the Bible. For instance, my mother told my brothers and I, when we got older of course, that she had four miscarriages each preceding the birth of her four sons. The only reason why she was able to carry my brothers and I full term was because she prayed to be able to do so. There was a secret thing that existed amongst the adults, I just knew it, because I could hear and see it in their expressions when they saw or heard certain things. Like when we past the brightly colored storefronts alongside 7-Mile Road, I discovered when I got older were candle shops or the Rev. Ike's commercials that would play on the AM dial after the Sunday morning church broadcast of someone saying, "Somebody put a ROOT on me." It was confirmed that the adults knew something or were at least up to something. But when I asked my mother, "What's a ROOT?", she told me it was nothing.

Another thing that convinced me that the adults were definitely into something was how my parents, after living in their home for 19 years, never had it burglarized until they moved.

It was these customs and practices, and several of the stories that I heard from my parents, grandparents, aunts, uncles and their friends what fascinated me, because the people that told them were able to overcome the odds that they were facing through what appeared to be magical means, like the people in the Bible. I remember when I asked my father how were people able to do some of the things that they did. I was told it was because of the Holy Ghost within them. I wanted to ask him to explain what he meant by these people having the Holy Ghost within them, but I didn't because by this time my father had appeared so distant to me, because of his work and obligations to the church, that he was like God to me, someone that was rarely seen. When he was seen in our house, during the regular part of the year, it seemed like in my young mind he was only there to chastise and issue a punishment for something that I had done wrong. This, however, didn't stop me from wanting to know everything, in fact it made me wish that I were like King Solomon, the wisest man in the Bible. Hopefully one day, I would be given a chance to make the wish like

Solomon and become a wise man as well.

Buckin' the Old Way

Now, I wasn't just asking about the Holy Ghost because I wanted to perform miracles per se, like some of these people I had heard testify in church had done. No, I wanted the Holy Ghost for a different reason, unimaginable to many of the adults in my life.

It began one night after hearing a hell bent sermon from a visiting evangelist to our family church. I tarried with several of my friends and other young people for the Holy Ghost to descend, so that I could receive the Holy Ghost and escape the rising crack cocaine epidemic that hit Detroit, Michigan and the rest of urban America in the 1980s. I was trying to get saved from the rising homicide rate, and the odds that were against me as a young black male. Since there weren't any jobs, because many Detroiters had put their faith in the automotive companies that had turned their back on them, unemployment combined with social ills led to the estimation that most African American males between the age of 12 and 17 wouldn't make it to our 18th, 21st or 25th birthday. So, that night I got "saved".

This, along with the regular pressures of school, made being *saved* extremely difficult because it was hard to turn the other cheek and not get bullied. Then again if you stood up for your self too strong you could either be killed by a rival or recruited to sell drugs because that was the favorable personality for selling drugs. I tried as best I could to turn the other cheek and not lose my Holy Ghost, but I did because I was not going to be punked!

Now, I wasn't bullied or punked because I was a nerd or academically challenged. It was because everyone knew that I was a PK (preacher's kid) and a lot of the kids thought I could easily be pushed around. I imagine now that I probably could have continued to be *saved* and still fought people off of me from another perspective, but I didn't. As a result, if someone talked about me or threatened me, I usually would ignore it. It was the old school way. But if they touched me I would try my best to kill them. I knew it wasn't right to feel that way but I did. To prevent myself from getting into those situations, I followed some advice my grandfather use to always tell his grandkids, which was, "Don't let your mouth get you into something your backside can't get you out of."

As a result, I usually would distance myself from situations that would provoke me to fight. Since I wasn't physically big, I couldn't play football, and I wasn't tall enough to play basketball, so I tried out for the swim team and tried to run track. Thankfully, I only had a few fights from the eighth grade all the way through high school but the situation made me wonder why didn't the *Holy Ghost* work for me. I wondered why I had to lose the *Holy Ghost* or this power in order to survive. Why didn't God fight my battles? I wasn't sure. But that's when I began questioning everything that I learned and was ever taught.

It was because I was really hurt that I had lost the Holy Ghost and backslid because I really did want to be saved. Again, it wasn't so much because I didn't want to go to heaven or hell. It was because I didn't want to be killed, since so many young guys were killing each other carelessly. I really wanted the power of God so that I didn't become a statistic because I knew that, if I didn't have it, it would only be a matter of time and I too would eventually be dead. The thought of dying from some reckless act of violence, which had already killed a lot of people that I knew in the church and school, always stayed fresh on my mind. The media made sure of it and it made me so angry because I had tried to do the right thing by getting saved. I didn't know how I lost the Holy Ghost but I lost it and I felt like I was being punished for doing so.

    This constant thought of death drove me into a mild depression, and made me want to commit suicide, but instead I wore black and other dark clothes all the time throughout most of my high school years. Since it was estimated that I was going to die anyway, even though I had tried to be saved but couldn't, I began to lose interest in living and started looking forward to dying. I spent most of my time either in the basement or hiding out in our garage alone where I would draw and lose myself in my artwork, angry at what seemed to be my catch-22 situation. I became so angry with God that I would deliberately try to offend God so that I could be struck down by lightning. Many times, thinking about my situation, I boldly lifted my right hand to the heavens and gave God my middle finger. I couldn't wait to stand before God to be judged, so I could tell Him how He screwed up and didn't give me any other choice but to fail in the situations that I was in. Eagerly I waited for the moment when I would die for my offenses, so that I could give God a piece of my mind.

    It wasn't long after that I began to hate church and the relationship with my father got worst because of his responsibility to the church and not to me. In fact I hated going to church so much that the night before I would take chocolate laxatives so that the next morning it would appear that I had an upset stomach, diarrhea and wouldn't have to go to church. When my family would leave for church, after going to the bathroom and making sure the coast was clear, I would turn on the television and watch all of the shows that I missed because of me going to church like *Sergeant Preston of the Yukon, Laurel and Hardy* or my favorite *Abbott and Costello Meet Frankenstein (1948)*, which always seemed to ironically come on Sunday morning when it was time to go to church. Other times when I did go, I along with some of my friends would wait for offering to be collected. Then while everyone was up and about, we would sneak out and go joy riding down downtown Detroit. Sometimes we would even go to other churches just to see the girls. Then, we would return back early enough to ask someone what scripture the preacher preached from in case our parents ever questioned us. When I couldn't get out of church, I would simply sit up in church and draw on the church bulletin or whatever piece of paper I could get my hands on.

I didn't care anymore. I was trying to be and live destructive because I was depressed, frustrated and angry with God. While looking for the way death was going to come knocking on my door. I hated church and everything about it. I loved my parents but I hated church. I really hated the fact that my father was a preacher and I hated even more when people said I was going to be a preacher. I was so angry, depressed and frustrated that I stopped listening to my favorite DJ at the time, The Electrifying Mojo, and began immersing myself in other music that I had heard played in the city. Funk, soul, blues, jazz my favorite artist (Prince) and this new thing called "rap" that I would sneak and listen to couldn't express my pain. Only the throbbing music of Chicago's house music and the grimy futuristic sounds of Detroit techno, along with the underground rock music of Midnight Oil, The Cult, Depeche Mode, The Cure, The Smiths, The Bauhaus, The Sexpistols, The Sugarcubes, Massive Attack and Björk seemed to express how I truly felt.

Then that's when it happened! It was while questioning everything that my Sunday school teachers taught me that the subject came up about the Egyptians worshipping idols. Now, I had heard that the Egyptians were idol worshippers before numerous times in the church, but for some reason, at this particular junction in my life, the thought of the Egyptians worshipping idols stuck out in my mind like a sore thumb. At the time I didn't know why I felt so indifferent about hearing that the Egyptians were idol worshippers but, later as time went along. It became apparent that the reason this subject about the Egyptians interested me so much was because the Egyptians symbolized somewhat what I wanted.

Egypt, the Mysterious Light of the East

Again, since both of my parents were very intelligent people and our basement was always full of reading material, along with the regular black publications of *Ebony* and *Jet* magazine, there were numerous *Reader's Digests* and *National Geographic* magazines, which indicated that the Egyptians were a very intelligent people. Besides the building of the magnificent pyramids, I learned that the Egyptians were knowledgeable in numerous subjects including astronomy and medicine. All of these advancements that these ancient people knew that mystified the modern scientific community sounded to me like a people that had the Holy Ghost, or at least the power of God, in order to accomplish so many things.

To tell me then, after learning about the various accomplishments that the Egyptians made, that they were idol worshippers simply didn't make any sense. This was because I was taught that idol worshippers were fools because they didn't know that there is only one God, but the Egyptians didn't seem like fools to me. Consequently, I began to think about all of the stories that I remembered being told about the Egyptians. I thought about how, according to my Sunday school lessons, the Egyptians enslaved the Children of Israel in order to build their society. Then I remembered other stories like that of Joseph the Dreamer being betrayed by his own brothers, imprisoned but later becoming a vizier to a pharaoh. I also remembered that after Jesus was born his parents fled with him to Egypt in order to escape King Herod's wrath.

I wondered if the Egyptians were idol worshippers and against God, why would they in one instance enslave a people, then in another instance help the people that they enslaved. It didn't make sense, like some other things in the Bible that I began to question, such as the Adam and Eve being the first people on the planet and their son Cain marrying some woman that should have been his sister. Something wasn't adding up, which made me believed that somewhere somebody got something wrong. Afraid to claim that the Bible was wrong for fear of being called a heretic, I believed that somebody most likely interpreted the Bible wrong, because I couldn't believe that the jealous God that I was taught about in Sunday school would allow the Egyptians to live for thousands of years, if they were idol worshippers.

Something, I thought, is not right, so naturally I asked around and tried to make sense of what I had just realized. The first person I asked was of course my father and then other *saints* (people in the church), but instead of listening to my logic my father and others whom I asked quoted scriptures and told me that, the Egyptians were idol worshippers and that's it. But I knew deep within that, that wasn't it and that the Ancient Egyptians knew God! Then I thought about all of the accomplishments and discoveries that I saw in the magazines. I knew that the Ancient Egyptians knew God I just needed proof! *If I only had proof...*

Since the saints wouldn't hear or even try to listen to my reasoning and would only listen to the Bible because it was the "Word of God", I wished that I could find evidence that the Ancient Egyptians didn't worship idols and/or believed in One God in the Bible. I didn't know how I was going to find this because I was not a Bible scholar and didn't know the Bible like most people, but I was willing to try to find an answer. So, I placed my hand over the Bible and asked the question. Then I opened the Bible and read the first section of scriptures that appealed to me, which was Jeremiah 44[1].

---

[1] I later discovered that this practice is known as bibliomancy. For more information on it see Appendix C.

Jeremiah 44 is about God telling the prophet Jeremiah, concerning all of the Jews, that after He delivered them from bondage and blessed them, they returned to their wicked ways, so He was going to punish them. I didn't know why I opened the Bible up to Jeremiah 44, but after I read it and thought about it for a while, two things came to me in regards to my query.

The first one was that God was angry with the Jewish people but said nothing about being angry with the Ancient Egyptian people for what they were doing (if they were worshipping idols), which made me think that God either didn't care what the Egyptians were doing, was pleased about what they were doing or wasn't pleased at all about their actions. Again the story of Joseph the Dreamer came to mind, which made me rationalize that God to some extent had to be either pleased or at least tolerated the Ancient Egyptians to allow His servant to serve with the people and for the holy family to find shelter there.

The second thing that came to mind after reading Jeremiah 44 was that the Jewish people were not practicing the religion of their ancestors. They were practicing or following somebody else's traditions that they probably didn't fully understand in the first place, which was probably why God was angry with them burning incense to a foreign goddess.

I wasn't sure, though, and this was just speculation. Then I heard a voice say, "STUDY EGYPT". For a second I ignored the suggestion because I thought I was simply talking to myself, but again the voice said, "STUDY EGYPT".

Now, they never really directly spoke about

spirits at our church. We were told that wicked spirits exist and occasionally some really bizarre people would wander in off the streets during church service. The pastor,, accompanied by several of the ministers in the pulpit would usually pour some blessed olive oil in their hands and pray over the person, asking God to drive the spirits of wickedness or "The enemy" out of the person and deliver them from evil. Most times they wouldn't even touch the person and instead they would pray to God to send the possessed person back into the streets. This, I discovered later, was because the pastor wasn't the laying of hands or exorcising type. There was another gentleman, an older minister in our church named Elder Gear, whom I really liked when I was younger, that I later found out did the exorcising. Whatever the case, I never really knew what or who the enemy was, because the devil was depicted as being red and having horns upon his head.

Consequently, when the voice told me to "STUDY EGYPT", I thought to myself, "Is this an evil spirit telling me to study the Egyptians whom I was told were evil, idol worshippers?" Then the voice, as if knowing my thoughts, spoke and said, "If Egypt was evil, why did Joseph and Mary flee with Jesus as a child to escape King Herod?"

I thought about the question and wondered why would the Savior of Humanity try to find refuge in an evil country. Why would the Egyptians even welcome strangers into their country, unless they weren't really strangers? It came to me that the Egyptians allowed Joseph, Mary and Jesus to seek refuge in their country because they most likely had similar beliefs, customs, practices or something.

Again the voice said "STUDY EGYPT" and

that's when I realized that I was speaking with a spirit that wasn't meant to harm me, which I believed to be God at the time. Then another thought popped into my head from Sunday school, as I remembered that Egyptians worshipped idols. That was the reason why Moses demanded that his people, the Children of Israel, be set free so that he could lead them to the Promise Land and give them the true laws of God, The Ten Commandments.

The voice then posed a question to me and asked, "If that was the case why didn't Moses give the Egyptians the Ten Commandments?"

"Hmmm," I thought, why didn't Moses give the Egyptians the Ten Commandments? These Commandments, which seemed to be basic common sense laws that the Children of Israel seemed to not know, like not to steal from each other, covet each other's wife or kill one another. Could it be that the Egyptians already knew these basic laws? Again, the voice said, "STUDY EGYPT", and from that moment on, I read and studied everything that I could find about the Ancient Egyptians, because it seemed like the only way I could learn how to use the power of God to improve my life was to learn how they did it. Many of the things that I liked to do, like drawing and painting; I for the most part did only in my spare time, because I didn't seem to have a purpose for these talents, at least not at the present time.

One Miracle at a Time

I came out of my depression when I was a junior in high school and began to get involved in various student affairs such as student government, math and science clubs and one of my personal favorites, track and field. I liked track and field because I liked to run. My father was a 100-yard dash man, so I ran a 100-yard, the 200-meter, 400-meter and 4 x 100. It was through track I learned about the importance of discipline as I conditioned my body through the winter months to run during the track season.

Now, I wasn't a perfect runner. In fact, in almost all of my events I never won first place and would always come in second and third. It use to upset me that I spent so much time training during the off season and still I didn't get the results that I wanted. Until one day, determined to come in first place, I decided to talk to my "nemesis", this sprinter I would usually race against whom came in first place. Since I always cross the finish line a fraction of a second behind him, I asked him what his secret to coming in first place was. And he told me that he would imagine crossing the finishing line first.

So one cold, dreary rainy afternoon, while sitting on the bus with my fellow teammates, I imagined crossing the finishing line first. I imagined the image several times until it was time for my event. Because I had a history of finishing second or third, my coach and fellow teammates didn't really bother about cheering me on. They didn't know what was going on in my mind. After dressing down and doing a few stretches and preparing for the 100, I took my place, ran my event and surprisingly I won!

My victory not only surprised me but it also surprised everyone including my opponent. My adversary, who told me about his secret being a good sport, congratulated me even though his teammates were upset with him for losing to me. I never forgot about this moment and had wished that my parents, especially my father, were there to witness it, but I understood why they weren't there. Immediately afterwards, I went back to crossing the finished line second, because I stopped imagining, and continued to do so for as long as I ran track.

As more and more socially conscious and fun rap groups appeared on the scene, like The Jungle Brothers, KRS 1 & BDP, Eric B. & Rakim, X-Clan, Gangstarr, The Poor Righteous Teachers, Black Sheep, Brand Nubians, Public Enemy, A Tribe Called Quest, and Arrested Development, I began to get a sense of personal purpose, of why I was living, at least to some degree. So, I applied for various scholarships and was awarded one, to my surprise, from a foundation named after the mayor of the city. Shortly after I graduated from high school, instead of going to college in Canada as I had originally planned, I went to college in Prairie View, Texas, to study chemical engineering with a few high school buddies Rich, good friend Aaron and my best friend G.

Lessons from Martin L. King & Malcolm X

Since it was estimated that most of the freshmen attending college would not be present the following semester or next year, I took rigorously to my books so that I wouldn't become a college drop out statistic. No one said it was going to be easy, and it wasn't: as we fought for financial assistance to pay for our out-of-state fees, and additional money for our expensive books, we struggled to complete the 18 credit hours per the semester. In the end, I established my first ever 3.5 GPA in my engineering discipline.

Along the way, I met a number of people from all over the world that indirectly helped me with my spiritual quest. Along with the various people I met from all over the country that was Christian, Muslim or Rastafarian. I became friends with people I met from Egypt, Pakistan and India. I also befriended a number of people that were from Jamaica, T&T (Trinidad & Tobago), and St. Lucia that introduced me to the music of Bob Marley, Burning Spear, Steel Pulse and the soca music of Machel Montano. Through the Rastafarians that attended my school, I learned the basics of drumming and how to let your mind guide the rhythm and speed that suits you. One particular brother that I became real cool with as a result was named J.T., a poli-sci major who was also an aspiring vegan.

I also became friends with people from the Ivory Coast, Liberia, Ghana and Kenya, including a number of people from Nigeria like my good friend Femi, who told me that many people of Africa were told lies about African Americans similar to the lies that Africans Americans were told about Africans. I remember Femi telling me that he used to look down on African Americans because he was told that African Americans were slaves and thought that they were better than Africans who were believed to be backwards. I remember he told me he discovered the truth and got a different perspective about what it meant to be black in America after he read *The Isis Papers: The Keys to Colors* by Frances Cress Welsing. He told me he never imagined people being terrorized because of the color of their skin. Apparently, I was so use to the phenomenon that it was like a given. It would be years later that I would truly understand what Femi was telling me and how it related to my own development.

Thanks to Femi, I learned more about how things were done in various parts of Africa. Even though Femi was a Christian he secretly told me that his family still gives libations to their ancestors. He secretly told me this because there was a Christian lady from the same tribe as him who also attended the college, and who thought that ancestor honoring was a backward practice. It appeared that just like African Americans were harassed, mocked and ridiculed for following certain cultural practices by our own, Africans were too.

Anyway, I appreciated Femi very much because besides telling me about Africa and Nigeria in particular. He showed me how to make some of the traditional dishes from Nigeria like fufu, egusi and palm kernel soup, while introducing me to the music of Fela Kuti, the godfather of Afro pop.

Now, in the beginning I wouldn't have become friends with all of these people from different faiths because I was raised in the church that "our way was the correct way and that everyone else's faith was wrong". Even though I wasn't an active member of the church many of the church's teachings still permeated throughout my life. Then, while in college, I read about the life of Dr. Martin L. King Jr. and the biography of Malcolm X by Alex Haley. Besides the historical contributions that these men made, they both impressed me because of their discipline, leadership abilities and oratory skills. I was truly impressed by Malcolm being a street thug who not only did a complete turn around but also was able to accomplish feats that some to this day would consider impossible. Like reading and studying a dictionary. That was amazing to me and for that reason alone, he got my respect.

Both Malcolm and Martin represented to me two men from different backgrounds that definitely wanted the same goal but had different approaches as to how to achieve it. In the end, they were both willing to work together from different fronts, which made them in my mind unite together as brothers for a common cause. It was after reading about the lives of these men that I began to question, where would these men have gone in the afterlife since they weren't Apostolic-Pentecostal as I was raised?

They were men that had done extraordinary work for God and their people, which made me come to the conclusion. That God doesn't care about what we believe or call ourselves. God doesn't care if we call ourselves Baptist, Catholic, Pentecostal, Christian, Muslim, whatever and God doesn't care about what we believe. Based upon the lives of Martin L. King and Malcolm X, God is only concerned about the work or we should say the heroic work we do here on earth for our family, friends, community and the world.

Learning about the Supreme

It was right about that time I became real good friends with a brother named Fred who was a Five Percenter. The Five Percent, also known as the Five Percent Nation or the Nation of Godz & Earthz (NGE), is an offshoot of the Nation of Islam founded in Harlem, New York, by Clarence 13X in 1964. The Nation of Godz and Earthz, like the Nation of Islam, is not like Sunni Islam, the largest denomination of Islam that I often heard others refer to as orthodox Islam. The NGE, like the NOI, was more of a culturally African form of Islam, created to help people escape the hegemony of white supremacy. This was very important for me to know because it clearly distinguished the difference between Arabic Muslims that in Fred's perspective promoted another form of racism by stating that one had to adopt Arabic cultural values and ideas, and those Muslims concerned with just promoting the tenets of Islam. It was through this understanding that I was introduced to the music of Malian artists Youssou N'Dour and the late Malian singer and guitarist Ali Farka Toure (10/31/39 –

3/7/06)².

The term Five Percent stems from the teachings of the Nation of Islam that 85% of the world population is ignorant or blind about the knowledge of self and God, while 10% of the population knows the truth but refuses to tell the truth and instead teach lies. The remaining 5% are called the poor righteous teachers because they do not believe in the teachings of the 10% and teach that God is the Blackman of Asia. This means that, because man was made in the image of God, we are supposed to be gods.

Fred told me that the term Blackman is not a reference to race but to anyone that comes from the planet Earth, which is referred to as being black in color and once upon a time called Asia, which is why although mostly blacks are in the NGE there are Latinos and Whites members in the group as well.

After introducing me to this concept and seeing that I was truly interested in learning more, Fred began to teach me Supreme Mathematics, which is a number system that corresponds to specific concepts that the Five Percent used to arrive at logical solutions to a problem.

Supreme Mathematics

1   **Knowledge** – To Know
2   **Wisdom** – Act Upon What You Know
3   **Understanding** – Understand What You Know
4   **Culture Freedom** – Make it a way of life

---

[2] Interestingly I saw a documentary on Ali Farka Toure who said that he learned how to play guitar by playing for the vodou

5	**Power (Refinement)**
6	**Equality**
7	**God and Perfection**
8	**Build/Destroy**
9	**Born**
0	**Cipher**

It was this unique way of looking at things that made me really think, before acting and doing anything. To apply the Mathematics for instance, Fred taught me that how it all relates is that you first do the **Knowledge** on a thing, which means to first observe, look and listen before acting. After you do the Knowledge you act upon what you know, which is **Wisdom**. Once you act upon what you know then you truly try to **Understand** it. After these steps are taken you put what you know, have acted upon and understand into action as a way of life, which is **Culture** that gives you **Freedom**. From Culture and Freedom you obtain **Power** and with Power you have the ability to make choices or have control in your life and not be a slave to a thing, hence equal to all people or **Equality**. You thereby become a God in your own right meaning one that has the ability to create life and light or **Build** and not spread evil or **Destroy**. One can then **Born** or bring a thing into the physical existence and thus make it a **Cipher** or complete.

    After learning Supreme Mathematics, Fred proceeded to teach me the Supreme Alphabet. It was after I had become familiar with the Supreme Alphabet that I began to realize that the rap group Poor Righteous Teachers and many early rappers were actually quoting Five Percent philosophy. This made the already socially conscious music I was listening to even more enjoyable, because unless you were familiar with the philosophy you didn't really know what the rapper was talking about, because they were rapping in code. It was sort of like the slaves would sing in code about their escape right in front of the slave owner. The slave master, assuming that the people had no culture, was at a lost of what the slaves were actually planning.

Supreme Alphabet

A   Allah: (Arabic word for God) and backronym for Arm + Leg + Leg + Arm + Head
B   Born or Bring: into Existence
C   Cee or See: means to understand something
D   Divine is the essence of the self
E   Equality: is to deal with the equality of all things
F   Father: another's education or further them along - through education, nutrition and well being
G   God: is the Original Man therefore the purpose on earth is to become a god or a perfect being
H   He/Her or He and She: has the power to Build and Destroy based upon their level of awareness. Together He through Her also has the power to birth a nation because She is a queen.
I   I or Islam: is our culture and not a religion, which is a bacronym that means I-Self-Lord-And-Master. Islam means peace, which is the only way for man, woman and child to live by cultivating peace
J   Justice or Divine Justice: is the reward or penalty for one's actions and ways. The reward for embracing Islam is love, happiness and peace, the penalty is stress, suffering and confusion
K   King or Kingdom: a true king is ruler over his kingdom
L   Love – Hell – Right: means you go through hell to make what you love right. Daily we are given the opportunity to either love Hell or Love Right. It is a crossroad situation we all must go through
M   Master: is one that controls the universe, which is the sun and Man. It also means one that has the ability to teach others with less skills but the true

master is Allah because Allah has 360 degrees of knowledge, wisdom and understanding.

N   Now – Nation – End: Now is the present time of the 85% to knowledge their True Culture and bring forth an end to the ways of the ten percent, in order to give rise to a mighty and strong nation

O   Cipher: is the completion of a circle, 360 degrees, and anything that is round such as a conversation between two or more that are equal

P   Power: is truth and the truth shall set you free because it is light, which shines or lights a way in darkness to Allah

Q   Queen: is the woman who is the mother of the universe. This is a woman that has knowledge of self and purest of all women, so she must be protected. She is the ultimate prize in war because without her there is no Islam.

R   Rule or Ruler: means God is the only ruler because he is the ruler of all

S   Self – Savior: one's own being or one who saves another

T   Truth or Square: Truth is light and light is the only thing that disperse darkness in the square of the universe, which is 360 degrees

U   You – Universe: means You are the verse because Man is the creator of the sun (man), moon (woman) and child (star).

V   Victory: is a great achievement that comes after war. This is when Man will get his freedom, justice and equality

W   Wisdom: means to act upon what you know. Since it comes after knowledge it is also the woman and the child is understanding

X   Unknown: As in algebra X represents the unknown, the 85% who are deaf, dumb and blind or have no knowledge of them self are also unknown or have no knowledge

Y   Why: "Why?" is the question that the 85% always ask they don't have any knowledge of their self and therefore no wisdom or understanding

Z   Zig-Zag-Zig: means to move from knowledge (man),

to wisdom (woman) and understanding (child)

Supreme Mathematics and Supreme Alphabet not only made me look at everything from a different perspective in order to find a deeper meaning to it. It truly was life changing because it made me feel privilege for being able to see things from a unique perspective, which made me also very combative and defensive. In a society that ridiculed everything that was African inspired as being foolish and superstitious, yet promoting the warp Darwin theory that only the strongest survived, I learned through the Five Percent that everything that we learned had to be backed up with logical and rational proof. This was necessary in order to shield our selves from the harassment and ridicule that what we learned for our self-development was foolish and superstitious. The Five Percent teachings basically helped me to develop a rhinoceros skin so as to not care what others believe and think, so long as I had proof that what I believed in helped me.

One of the things I found interesting about the backronym Allah was that in West Central Africa, the Kongo people had an initiation ceremony that was performed for boys. The young initiates were laid in a cross like formation called Diyowa, which corresponded to their head, two arms and feet[3]. This sign, I learned, was called the Sign of God. Now, I am not sure if this is where the concept came from, but what made it even more interesting was that this is possibly what the Kamitic ankh symbolized as well, the body of a human being, with the loop symbolizes

---

[3] *Religion and Society in Central Africa: The BaKongo of Lower Zaire* by Wyatt MacGaffey, pages 117 – 119.

the ascending conscious moving from the Underworld thus becoming an enlightened being or a true Child of God. But I wasn't sure. I had to do more science on the subject.

I loved the Five Percent teachings. The only problem that I had with it was that it seemed to take me further away from God by making me rely more and more upon my intellectual self. It wouldn't be long that I would trade inexperience and inner knowing for external logic and reasoning. I would have to find a way of integrating both in my daily living. I never fully joined NGE but I was very thankful to have learned the lessons.

Shortly after, guided by reasoning, I would be inspired to stop eating pork, beef, and chicken, and eventually become a vegan like J.T. Like many vegans, I tried to live as close to nature as I possible by not eating man made or animal by-products like monosodium glutamate (MSG), sugar, white flour and dairy. Instead, I tried to eat raw and natural foods like beans, legumes, nuts, whole grains and soy products like tofu because it was supposed to be healthier. We ate this way because it was believed that our African ancestors ate healthy, natural and nutritious foods before the arrival of the Europeans. Of course, we didn't actually know if they (ancient Africans) actually ate this way or not, but it was a theory that was widespread and practiced by many. So when confronted by someone that disputed what we were doing, my friends and I that made this dietary and lifestyle change would always say,

"This is what they did in Africa!"

I committed to the change because the vegan lifestyle

and diet demanded personal sacrifice but in the end it rewarded one with good, smooth skin, regular bowels and overall it just made me feel good. Like the 5% teachings, it made me feel special and unique, like I was in a special group, as people (from all walks of life) I met commented on how they wish they had the discipline to be a vegan. This vegetarian lifestyle soon became sort of like a passport to meet other people and try food from other cultures like Ethiopian, Indian and Asian cuisine. It was through this experience I learned that the one of the best ways to learn about others is through food.

College Days

The lives of Martin L. King Jr. and Malcolm X made me focus more on being "spiritual" rather than being "religious". During that time in between my classes and studying, I continued to read and study everything that I could find about the Ancient Egyptians. Thanks to the scholarly works of W.E.B. DuBois, Chiekh Anta Diop, George G.M. James, Carter G. Woodson, J.A. Rogers, Chancellor Williams, Arturo Alfonso Schomburg, John Henrik Clarke, Gerald Massey, Godfrey Higgins, T. Obenga, Ivan van Sertima, Yosef Alfredo Antonio Ben-Jochannan, Molefi Kete Asante, Leonard Jeffries, E. A. Wallis Budge and countless of other scholars, I learned a lot about the Ancient Egyptians that isn't documented in most history books. For instance, like the Ancient Egyptians never called themselves Egyptian, which is derived from the Greek word Aigyptos. They instead called themselves Khamitic, Kemetic or Kamitic, which meant people of the black lands (similar to the 5% teachings of the Blackman) because it was a pun on the fertile black soil as a result of Nile flooding. The Ancient Egyptians, I learned, had several names for themselves including Kamemu (Egyptian citizens) and Kamut (black people), which I learned from the dean of architecture.

I learned that there were all sorts of archeological, cultural and historical evidence supporting the argument that the ancient Kamites were black and brown skinned Africans. For instance, the Greek historian Herodotus as well as other writers stated that the ancient Kamities were black. To name them all would take us beyond the scope of this work. It is worthy to note that there are even numerous examples given in the Bible. For instance, according to Exodus 2:12-19, the Kamitic people educated Moses, who fled to Midian (Saudi Arabia) because he killed a Kamitic taskmaster that was maltreating a Hebrew. When he arrived there he chased away some shepherds that were bullying some young women there and helped them to attend to their flock. When the sisters told their father what had happened they identified Moses as being a Kamite, a brown skinned man, like the Kamites were.

As to how did the modern Egyptians become so fair skinned, according to the French historian, philosopher, orientalist and politician Count Constantin de Volney (1747 – 1820) it was through race mixing from conquering armies. Volney, upon discovering that the Ancient Egyptians were black states:

"... the ancient Egyptians were true Negroes of the same type as all native-born Africans. That being so, we can see how their blood, mixed for several centuries with that of the Romans and Greeks, must have lost the intensity of its original color, while retaining nonetheless the imprint of its original mold. We can even state as a general principle that the face (this is the Sphinx) is a kind of monument able, in many cases, to attest or shed light on historical evidence on the origin of the people.[4]"

Volney also states reflecting on the Ancient Egyptian monument that:

"... Just think that the race of black men, today our slave and the object of our scorn, is the very race to which we owe our arts, science, and even the use of our speech.[5]"

It was because of various scholars like Jacques Joseph Champollion-Figeac (1778 – 1867), the brother of Jean-Francois Champollion who deciphered the Rosetta Stone, that was one of the first to declare that black skin and wooly hair were not sufficient characteristics to adequately define black people, and other absurd, doubletalk and nonsense, that many were led to focus solely upon the origin and ethnicity of the Ancient Egyptians.

Some of the other things about the Kamitic people that I learned were that they invented the present-day calendar dividing the 365 days into 12 months. Many of the grooming items that we use today such as eyeliner, toothpaste, hair combs and scissors also have their origin in Ancient Kamit. As well as the

---

[4] Cheikh Anta Diop, The African Origin of Civilization: Myth or Reality, ed. and trans. Mercer Cook (New York: Lawrence Hill & Co., 1974) pg. 27.

[5] Ibid., pg. 28

advanced math and sciences such as astronomy, botany, calculus and geometry, which they regularly used in the construction of various edifices and the maintenance of their society.

I also learned that from the reign of Amenophis I, a sacred Kamitic text known today as "The Ebers papyrus" reveals that Kamitic people had knowledge of the anatomy and physiology of the heart. They knew how to take the pulse and had even mapped out the entire circulatory system.

Another Kamitic text from the 18th dynasty called "The Edwin Smith papyrus" indicates that the ancient Kamites had a profound knowledge of surgical procedures. This document also shows that the ancient Kamites had a rigorous method of diagnosing and treating a number of ailments.

Besides the various inventions that the Kamitic people created, what also made them unique is that they were one of the only societies in ancient times that allowed people to advance to a higher social class based upon merit. The Kamitic society was also one of the few societies in ancient times to allow women to have similar rights as men a feat still not accomplished in these contemporary times.

I learned that the word "Egypt" appears in the Bible about 750 times. The king of Egypt, which is commonly known in the Bible as "pharaoh", appears about 200 or so times. Another fact that is not publicized is that the Kamitic people did have a set of commandments that were known as the 42 Declarations of Maa[6] which, unlike the Ten

---

[6] See Appendix D

Commandments that commanded what a person should do or not do, were more like a guide, which allowed the ancient Kamites to use their commonsense. For instance, instead of commanding them not to kill, the 42 Declarations of Maa instructed the ancients Kamites not to kill but at the same time gave them the right to defend themselves from wrongdoers.

I also discovered that Moses learned everything he knew from the Kamitic people (Ancient Egyptians) according to Acts 7:20-22, which states:

"In which time Moses was born, and was exceeding fair, and nourished up in his father's house three months: And when he was cast out, Pharaoh's daughter took him up, and nourished him for her own son. And Moses was learned in all the wisdom of the Egyptians and was mighty in words and in deeds."

This was all pretty impressive for a people that were supposed to be idol worshippers. All of this strongly inspired and encouraged me to continue to learn about the Kamitic tradition in order to implement it into my life.

Inspired by the lives of W.E.B. DuBois, Dr. Martin L. King Jr., Adam Clayton Powell, Paul Roberson as well as my high school principal and my high school science teacher, I pledged the first African American Greek letter organization, Alpha Phi Alpha Fraternity, Inc. It was through my neophyte year in the fraternity that I learned a great deal about my organization as well as other collegiate organizations that were founded in beginning of the 20th century by African Americans. This made me have a great deal of respect for the founders to create organizations that would be so powerful to this day during a time when racism against people of color was so evident and high.

Being a brother in Alpha Phi Alpha made me also realize that the interest in Kamit and Afro-Centric studies from an African American perspective is part of a movement that began possibly around the end of slavery (if not earlier). Evidence can be seen in the fact that the founders (known as Jewels) of Alpha Phi Alpha Fraternity founded the fraternity in 1906 and chose to represent the organization with Kamitic images and symbols. Another example of this growing movement can be seen in the NAACP 1911 copy of the *Crisis* magazine, which depicted an Afro-Centric interpretation of one of the Upper kings of the Nile.

Later, I learned that the dean of architecture that many of my fraternal brothers had a lot of respect for, who taught me a lot about the Kamitic history before joining the fraternity, was a member of the Greek letter fraternity, Kappa Alpha Psi Fraternity, Inc. What I found quite interesting was how at my college campus, most of the members of the fraternal organizations stressed the importance of saying that they were a member of a Greek-lettered organization. This was to indicate that they knew who and what their true origins were. The Greek letters were simply used as a mask.

Thanks to many of the older fraternal brothers of my chapter and a few brothers from other Greek-letter organizations, I was encouraged to continue to study the Kamitic history. Amongst my peers, I was looked upon as being somewhat of a young authority on the subject that eventually led to me being asked to participate in various speaking engagements sponsored by other organizations. However, I knew that I didn't know a lot because most of what I knew was just historical facts that I had memorized or because of Supreme Mathematics and Supreme Alphabets led me to see things differently. Yet, on more than one occasion I was still asked to speak about what I had learned regarding Kamitic spirituality. This led me to having the fortunate opportunity and privilege to speak behind the late Temple of the Black Messiah minister Ishakamusa Barashango, who once praised me for having such a knowledgeable and strong interest in Kamitic spirituality at such an early age.

Now, when I turned 21, I bought some beer and tried to get drunk because I had made it! I was almost in the clear. I had beaten the odds and made it to 21, so I was going to celebrate. I had four more years to go and when I turned 25 I would really have an even bigger party for myself and give the media and their statistics the "bird", but in order to make it to 25 I needed something more. I needed something spiritual for real, because there was a pressure building up around me. It was mostly financial pressure because this chemical engineering program was for five years (at least) and most institutions only provided finances for four years. I was starting to wonder how I was going to pay for it all and if I could get a good job. I wasn't sure how things were going to work out, so I tried not to think about it and just be glad that I had made it to 21 years of age. Then I decided to share my enthusiasm with two good friends I had met while in school, Tasha and Tiffany. Afterall I had four more years to go.

Tasha and Tiffany

I became friends with Tasha and Tiffany because they

weren't like some of the women I met in college that complained about being disrespected, yet breakin' and shaking it down to the summer hit, *B**** Betta Have My Money* by AMG. No, they were different. Tasha, an education major, was a good friend that liked to study spiritual matters like I. She had already read about African American history and was just beginning to learn about the Kamitic people. Tasha and I became friends instantly because of our interests and became very close, but I fell in love with Tiffany, a pre-dental major, because, although she didn't share my views and interests, she came from a similar religious background as I had.

Tiffany was the eldest of three girls raised by a single mom. She was deeply religious most of the time but had some issues coping with some of the church's concepts. These issues weren't enough to change or challenge her faith as they did mine but it made her a comfort to talk to. From our conversations we became relatively good friends, dated for a year and then one day I proposed to her to be my wife, which she gladly accepted. It was through Tiffany I learned about the joys of being in love. She helped me to understand that you can't really fall in love, love is an emotion you can choose to control or not. But the troubles I had with connecting to God made me feel like I didn't want to live again. This combined with my mounting worries of how I was going to pay for my last years in college, and if I was going to be able to get a job as an engineer. Made me feel worse because I wondered how I could support this woman through her dental school and as my wife.

Tiffany tried to encourage me as best she could. Seeing me spiraling in a direction that she refused to go down, she tried to tell me how I used to act and the things I used to do. Not caring to hear what she said, I chalked up what she told me as her not wanting to be "spiritual" just like the saints that I debated with in the church. Not long after that, we broke off the engagement and parted ways.

It wasn't Tiffany's fault. I knew I needed something more to keep me from going down that depressive road and help me to overcome the financial bind that I was entering. I was tired of reading and hearing about what the Kamitic people had done. I was ready to apply it and I thought that if I would have become more spiritual, I could miraculously fix my problems. I desperately wanted to be an engineer and be able to help others, but I couldn't even help myself financially and was starting to wonder if I was even supposed to be an engineer. This was the main reason why I began having problems in my relationship with Tiffany because I was beginning to wonder how I could pay for it all. I mean it was a known fact it seemed that if you didn't finish your degree program at the right time. Many employers would just look right pass you. Not to mention that you had to have a certain grade point average and put up with pressure from your professors as well. It was all coming down on me like a ton of bricks. How could I support this woman, whom I deeply cared about and loved, if I couldn't finish on time, get a job or even support myself?

It was all just very sickening to me. I mean, I loved math and science since I was a kid. I had had an interest in chemistry since that time as well. I remember having a play chemistry set when I was younger and getting nothing but A's and B's in most of my math and science classes all the way into college. I had prepared for this moment to be an engineer and I was so close to graduating, but the picture was becoming clear that I might have to drop out. So, I wanted to know what the Kamitic people did in order to keep going spiritually. I wanted to know how they manifested the miracles in their lives, because I was truly in need of a miracle right now! I was tired of talking about being made in God's image and that I am supposed to be a god and having no proof to show for it. I was ready to put it to the test because I had no choice but to do so. I had to do it in order to finish my degree program and help others as I had planned.

Losing Sight of the Prize

I could no longer be like some of the people that I was meeting who were telling me, "You know the Ancient Egyptians were black" while chugging down a pint of gin and juice and smoking a blunt of marijuana. I felt like I had to "Show N Prove" that Kamitic spirituality was the real deal and the only way I could do this was putting it into practice to fix my financial situation. I had simply crossed that road of understanding that it was important, in fact great to know the history of the Kamitic and other African people. But, if we can't use this history as tool of spiritual empowerment it is basically a bunch of useless dates, facts and names.

So, to ease my mind, I would listen to traditional African music, Afro-Brazilian ritual music, Native American music or the Senegalese singer Baaba Maal, and just draw whatever came to mind. Then it happened: after four years of attending school for chemical engineering, I had to drop out because of finances. There were some financial institutions that were willing to give me an extra loan provided my parents would co-sign and put up some collateral; but I was not about to let them do that.

Accepting that I would not be returning to Texas the next semester to finish my degree program, I decided to get a job to save up some money and devote the rest of my time to hopefully mastering some of the Kamitic principles, so that when I did return I would have a clear mind and be a more "spiritual" person.

Of course, I didn't know what was in store for me. If someone would have told me that the quest for spirituality was going to be so hard, and that I would have to fight for this way of life because my view of African spirituality was actually romanticized by various theories I have heard. I might have taken the blue pill like the one offered to the character Neo in the *Matrix*.

Part II:
Discovering the Spiritual Path

God conceals himself from the mind of man, but reveals himself to his heart.

- African Proverb

Breaking Spiritual Ground

Returning back home, I found a fairly decent job in downtown Detroit. G, who had just recently graduated with his B.S. in electrical engineering, took a job downtown as well, several blocks from where I worked. So, since my father had an extra car, I would pick up G and drive to and from work everyday.

Now, the relationship between my father and I was for the most part on a hi-and good-bye basis. We never talked about anything because there was really nothing to talk about. Even though I didn't openly express it, I still had a lot of hatred for the church and his allegiance to it. Thinking I was old enough to come and go as I pleased, I staunchly refused to go to church and followed my parents' rules according to my choosing.

Determined to live (what I thought was) a spiritual life, G and I had joined several spiritual study groups that existed around the city. We tried to practice Yoga and Tai Chi because we were told that they would help us to become more spiritual. We also tried to help each other in understanding various subjects that we had encountered. For instance, I remember one time we had a serious discussion about the myth that the original language was Arabic, but we learned that it was the Kamitic hieratic and demotic scripts, which looked a little bit like Arabic, that were the oldest written language and not Arabic.

Another thing that I helped him to learn was Supreme Mathematics, which helped both of us to learn and understand a little bit about the Jewish mystical system called the Kabala. Later we learned from a friend from New York about a new type of

Kabala system, which was created by the Kamitic people called the Paut Neteru. The Paut Neteru also called the Kamitic Tree of Life according to Ra Un Nefer Amen I author of *Metu Neter: The Great Oracle of Tehuti and the Egyptian System of Spiritual Cultivation Volume 1*, is the inspiration behind the Kabala.

Supreme Mathematics, Kabala and the Paut Neteru

Supreme Mathematics	Kabala	Paut Neteru
	0. EinSof – The Limitless	0. Amen
1. Knowledge	1. Kether – Will	1. Ausar
2. Wisdom	2. Chochmah – Wisdom	2. Tehuti
3. Understanding	3. Binah – Understanding	3. Seker
4. Culture/Freedom	4. Chesed – Mercy/Love	4. Maat
5. Power	5. Gevurah – Justice	5. Herukhuti
6. Equality	6. Tiferet – Beauty	6. Heru
7. God	7. Netzach – Victory	7. Het-Heru
8. Build-Destroy	8. Hod – Splendor	8. Sebek
9. Born	9. Yesod – Foundation	9. Auset
0. Cipher	10. Malkuth - Kingdom	10. Geb

The various study groups that G and I were participating in led us to start reading more about the traditional African religions, since the Kamitic people were believed to be of African descent. Many of these study groups were all reading or at least referring back to the *Metu Neter*. While a couple of these study groups were focused upon studying classical and contemporary traditional African civilizations, it was through one group in particular that focused upon

African history and thought that we were encouraged to read *The Irritated Genie: An Essay on the Haitian Revolution* by Jacob H. Carruthers, about the loa/orishá Oggun in regards to Haiti's independence.

At the time most of what I was read I found to be very fascinating, but it was overshadowed by the groups' politics. It didn't take long for G and I to see that many of these spiritual study groups, like any other organization, had problems too. In factthe same problems that almost existed in the church, spiritual study groups had them as well, and they were worst. What made spiritual study group politics worst than the church was that at least the churches were unified under the umbrella of their belief in God. In many of the spiritual study groups we tried to participate in there were numerous beliefs. The only unifying factor ended up being the individual that appeared to have the most knowledge (information). The individual that had the most knowledge was able to hold sway over most of the people in the group. That individual in another one of the spiritual study groups that G and I participated in was this lady named Bertha.

Bertha was married with three children and had moved from Philly to Detroit. Her family all had Kamitic and Yoruba names, which G and I thought was pretty neat. Later we learned that she and her family had been dealing with various spiritual traditions for about 13 years or more. All in her family were vegans and they were cool to be around because we could actually have some stimulating conversations about history and culture without being accused of being heretics or against God as was the case in the church.

It was Bertha that taught us that the different

Kamitic divinities were divisions of the spirit and that they corresponded to the Yoruba orishás. Now, I didn't know anything about the divinities, orishás, the spirit or divisions of the spirit and I especially didn't know anything about God. At this point in my life I wasn't really sure if God existed because I was under the belief that God was a mystery created by the 10%. Anyway, I began trying to learn about the Kamitic divisions by learning about the orishás. Since everything that Bertha said sounded good to me and indicated that she apparently was more advanced than G and I, naturally we placed her upon a pedestal because it seemed she knew more than us. It wasn't long that we began receiving spiritual counsel from her and asking her advice on various situations in our life because she could also do readings. Then one day, after a year of becoming friends, the entire family all of a sudden just vanished from their house with no trace. I called, G called and we would go by their house to see if they were all right but nothing, no one was there.

After several months of missing, I got a call from Bertha that they had returned back to Detroit and that she and her family were at a truck stop. She and her husband, who was a truck driver, were getting a divorce and he had already left to catch his next load. Come to find out they had been having problems all along and he had wanted to leave for a while. Feeling pretty bad, I picked Bertha and her kids up and checked them into a hotel because they didn't have any money. They stayed at the hotel for a couple of weeks before going home because her husband had claimed that he was remodeling the place so she didn't have the key. When she finally got the house key from him, he left to catch another load so G and I ended up taking Bertha and her kids back home.

When we got to the house, there was a horrible odor that just burned our nostrils and everything that they had had been tore up, as if they had been robbed but nothing was taken. After killing the fleas, picking up around the place, moving furniture, feces and the garbage left on the floor, we discovered that the source of the odor was the family's dead cat and the six or so kittens that it gave birth to when they were gone. There were fleas, feces and dead kittens all over the house and if I had known what I know now, I would have left the situation right then, but I didn't. Instead, we all pitched in and cleaned up the place. Since they didn't have any money, I offered to turn on the lights, phone and water in my name because I had good credit and she didn't. Mistake #1!

Now, Bertha's husband rarely came back and when he called the two always got into arguments. She had always said that he was messing around on her, but there was nothing she could basically do about it since he was a truck driver. Apparently he stayed on the road trying to get money to fund the divorce and support whomever else he was with. Naturally the relationship I had with her moved from being just friends to something more intimate. It wasn't long after that I would end up losing the little job I had because of my needy friends soon to be family.

Then one day she told me that we were destined to find each other and that we were soul mates. Now, if anyone else would have told me that, I would have said they were crazy and moved on, but I bought what she was saying because I placed her on a pedestal and had high regard for her counsel. She was more "spiritual" than I was, had demonstrated her "spiritual" or "psychic" abilities time and time again, and what she was doing was what (in my mind) people from Africa had the ability to do. It was the "that's what people do in Africa" ideology that got me. Along with the fact that my father was really getting on my nerves with the church thing and trying to get me to abide by his rules in his house, even though I was a grown man (so I thought).

So, when Bertha suggested that I should move in with them, I jumped at the opportunity as soon as I could. The night I decided to leave, my father and I got into a heated argument. During the argument he told me that he didn't like the woman I was with because he believed that she was twisting my mind and making me do crazy things. Now that I had the courage to face him and any other saint, I told him that he was wrong because I had been involved in this spiritual thing for a while. The argument went on for several minutes and when it was finally over; my father had basically told me that if I wasn't going to follow their rules I had to leave.

Later, when Bertha said that she was tired of Detroit and wanted to move back to Philly, where there was an even larger spiritual community than Detroit, I naturally objected, because I didn't know anything about Philly and all of my family was in Michigan, whom she didn't get along with. But I went against my gut feeling and did what she said, hoping and believing that everything was going to miraculously be all right because as she had claimed we were "soul mates" and her psychic abilities claimed we were destined to be together.

G, of course, told me I was crazy but refused to comment any further, because he respected Bertha's "spiritual" integrity as well. Instead, he wished me luck and we left for Philly on the bus with suitcases of our stuff.

The Philadelphia Experience

Living in Philadelphia was an experience because my "spiritual soul mate" or Bertha was right; the spiritual community was bigger here than it was in Detroit. Bue I soon discovered that if you didn't follow the so-called spiritual regimen to the letter you were perceived as being a faker, charlatan, etc.

    Just as I suspected, when I got to Philadelphia I didn't know anyone except for the people that Bertha and her children knew. Initially, the plan was to stay with Bertha's grandmother who had a three-bedroom house in the Germantown-Mt. Airy section of town but that plan fell through because Bertha's grandmother was from the very, old school way of doing things. She believed in a lot of things that I only heard people use to believe in. For instance, she believed that if a man and woman stayed together they were supposed to be married, which I could understand. However, she had some other beliefs that were just bizarre to me coming from the multicultural, multiethnic and semi-international Detroit (which was across the river from Canada), such as the belief that light-skinned blacks were more beautiful than darker-skinned blacks. Bertha's grandmother also believed that women were supposed to stay home in the kitchen and be a "good bed warmer" for their husbands, which was completely different belief than what I was told regarding women by my mother, grandmother and aunts —not to mention my father, grandfather and uncles. Whatever the case, we didn't have anywhere to stay except for at Bertha's grandmother's house, so we respected her and her rules by sleeping in separate rooms, but everyday she gave us hell about not being married and being *too black*.

For me, it was very hard to get a job because I was usually overqualified and under qualified for the jobs I was applying for. I basically had too much education for most of the jobs that were posted in the Philadelphia job centers and not enough education because I didn't have my degree. I later learned that Bertha couldn't work for long hours because she had back problems from several car accidents she was involved in. All responsibility for money fell upon my shoulders. Fortunately, Bertha had ways of getting money but it was never enough.

So, we all hustled to the best of our abilities. I did little odd jobs from passing out flyers to running errands in between looking for a full-time job at the job centers, just to scrape up enough money to eat and give to Bertha's grandmother for staying in her home. But the constant demands that Bertha's grandmother put on us to live a Christian life-style, get married and stop being "stupid niggers", which is how she viewed us believing that by going to church we would be saved from our "nigger-dom" as she put it, was just too much.

The time came and Bertha, after speaking to various people in the spiritual community, found individuals that were willing to help us and give us shelter. It wasn't much but we were allowed to stay in some of the peoples' homes because we had similar beliefs and ideals. We moved from Bertha's grandmother's home and took up residence in one of the spiritual community member's home. Everything for a while was moving along smoothly but again with no money coming in made living there very difficult.

For one, it made us compromise our diet, because vegan food was quite expensive there. Several times, with no more than $20 between all five of us (two of us and her children), we had to decide if we should eat tofu, which cost around five to seven dollars not to mention the organic spices that we would have to purchase, and end up having a dollar or two left, or eat a cheese pizza or a cheese hoagie and have $10 to spare for me to use as fare to get to a job. Of course, we chose the latter, but there were consequences as a result of us doing so. The spiritual people we were staying with, instead of seeing it as a desperate means of survival, saw us as spiritual charlatans that simply spent our money on westernized junk food. It was tough but we were thinking about survival and the music done by the WU (Wu-Tang Clan) especially the Genius or GZA, with their urban grit, kung fu samples and added Five Percent philosophy, reminded me that it was a battle to live. I don't know if I would have made it.

The lack of money also kept us from participating in various lectures and other classes, like those offered on metaphysics, Yoga and Tai Chi. I had already taken these classes anyway, and had at once practiced Yoga because it was said to be spiritual, but I didn't see any purpose or real benefit of doing so right now. I was concerned about money.

Anyway, while others in the spiritual community were attending forums, lectures and other cultural events, I was either looking for a job or trying to get some rest after looking for a job all day. There were a lot of times when Bertha's kids and I did participate in some of the functions like Capoeira classes but after attending in our bummed out clothes and being ridiculed, we just were too embarrassed to continue. We stopped until we could hopefully get some money to buy some clothes. This of course didn't help matters, as we ended up being talked about and ridiculed even more by various people we had great admiration and respect for. To remedy the problem we were told sometimes to perform certain rites, which didn't make a lot of sense to me. For instance, I was once told not to have sex at all in order to get a job, but I simply couldn't understand how not having sex had anything to do with me getting a job. I understood that not having sex would raise my energy level because I vaguely remembered hearing how various entertainers and athletes would abstain before a performance or a big bout. In fact it was a brother that was an engineer that told me about the entire Tao of Sex and how it was similar to the old spiritual practices where people would fast from food and sexual activity in order to raise their spiritual power to fulfill a particular task. So, I understood the concept but what did this have to do with me getting a job?

I also remembered being told not to eat any sweets because men in traditional Africa don't eat sweets. Now, I would have gone along with this theory had I not met and knew other people from Africa that ate sweets. The people I had met from Africa didn't eat a lot of candy (like my grandparents and great aunts and uncles), but they occasionally ate sweets, so I knew that this was not true. This greatly disturbed me because I couldn't believe someone would tell someone this garbage without proper clarification, so naturally it made me question everything for now that I was told. It wasn't that I had problem giving up sweets because I didn't particularly eat candy or sweets anyway. It was the generalization that made me see how certain people, cultures, religions, etc. are idolized in North America for certain practices without proper understanding of why these practices are done in the first place. It made me wonder if I was guilty of following others like I hear of others doing.

    I remembered my friend Femi ate sweets, so why was I being told that men in Africa don't eat sweets was beyond me. The idea, I understood, was that eating too many sweets it lowers the metabolism, but this is what gets me. Sometimes people see one or two things that people do from other cultures and without full explanation and understanding they jump to the generalization that everyone does the same thing, and then they go and tell other people to do the same thing because "they do it in Africa" or "in China". That's bogus! I remembered being told that Arabic was the language of the original people because the Kamitic demotic script looks like Arabic but it's not Arabic.

    I was like "Thank God, I was not that naïve," but I was starting to see the dangers of not knowing certain facts, not equating it with my present situation yet. So, when people told me to do something that I didn't understand and they couldn't properly explain, I chalked it up as a practical myth that the individual learned or is repeating without having full knowledge or experience of, based upon my Five Percent training. Of course, because I was starting to think for myself again and didn't just blindly follow everything that someone told me was spiritual, cultural, from Africa, from China, etc. made me seem a bit rebellious to others, when in fact I just wanted people to properly explain why I should do something. I was already beginning to recognize that I was in Philadelphia because of following someone's "spiritual" advice that I was gravely regretting. Since, I was having problems getting a job and finding adequate living arrangements, I was not by any means going to add more salt to an already bleeding and gaping wound.

But that's not how the "spiritual people" saw it. To the "spiritual people", if you aren't perfectly healthy, working, etc. it is because you're not being "spiritual" enough. I once saw a young "spiritual" man condemn an older man for breaking the unofficial "spiritual code" by eating a chocolate candy bar and drinking orange juice. What the younger man didn't know was that the "older man" was a diabetic. This all made me think about what if I had to eat a piece of pork? Would I do it? And if I did, would I go to hell? I mean, I didn't eat pork, but what if? I was beginning to see that there is a big difference between being spiritual and living as an ascetic.

Not long after that, we were constantly accused of doing things like stealing and other unthinkable acts. Not everyone felt the same way but there was a growing movement to get us out because we appeared to be "spiritual charlatans". This naturally made my defenses go up, so I fought these accusations as best I could. I also did the best I could to get food for my family, since I guess no one could see that our physical needs were more important than our spiritual needs at the present time. It was hard because I still had troubles seeing that our physical needs were just as important as our spiritual needs. I very much wanted to be around these people because they were very accommodating, and still had similar beliefs and ideas that I had, but the pressure was overwhelming. With little to no money coming in, not attending various cultural functions and appearing to be a bit rebellious, we were eventually asked to leave.

A Real Spiritual Momma

Fortunately, we got some of the help we needed from a lady named Ms. B, whose youngest son Bertha's teenage son had befriended. Ms. B for the most part understood the pressure that we were under and understood why we were in the situation that we were in, because she once had to struggle on her own with three children against old and for new ideologies. It was because of her "spirits" Ms. B claimed that she was able to remain strong and resilient.

Ms. B was a practicing *palera* (priestess) of the Afro-Cuban Palo Mayombe tradition. She said that one of the reasons why we were having so many problems was that, before getting involved in different faiths, one must first have a firm rapport with their own spirits, because there are a lot of unscrupulous and unwise people when it comes to dealing with spiritual traditions. If you don't have a firm rapport, it is easy to get lost and take the wrong path.

Ms. B was a fascinating woman because she was the closest I had ever gotten to the Afro-Caribbean religion without a book. She wasn't your stereotypical spiritual woman that wore African garb all the time adorned with cowry shells like some of the "spiritual people" I saw do claiming to be spiritual and "holier than thou". Ms. B was flesh and blood, real, down the earth and sometimes just downright raw when she had to be. She told us that she had once upon a time tried to be spiritual when she was younger. She thought "spiritual culture" was good for some things but totally idealistic; as I caught her saying often when we talked about spirituality, "But you are missing something." This, in her opinion, was the reason why most spiritual people talk about Africa traditions but later you find them practicing Eastern philosophy, which is often practiced out of zeal, with no real practical knowledge. People from all walks have done this, Ms. B told us, but "You have to take care of the physical too!"

Like an old folk traditionalist, Ms. B always explained herself using stories, tales and myths. Just about everything she did was inspired by a myth. I once saw her stand up during a thunderstorm and yell Cabosille (the king is not dead) to the orishá Chango, so that he wouldn't strike her house. Every time she wanted to make a point she would usually begin by telling a tale and then explain her decision in the matter. Our situation reminded her of the tale about the Yoruba orishá Babaluaiye, who was chased out of town because he had an illness and a horrible odor, later to become a glorious king. Relating our situation to the orishá of illness she decided to let us use a room in her house that wasn't being occupied. She told us that she didn't have much but she would share what she did have, so long as we paid her back. To assist us, Ms. B's youngest son gave Bertha's boys clothes that he had outgrown, while a few dollars were spared to purchase clothes for Bertha's daughter and food.

Then she turned her attention on me and told me what I already knew: that I needed to get a job. She said that after I got settled we could address the spiritual issues that were troubling me, but first things first, get a job. She told me (which I already knew) that all the responsibility was on me because I was the man. A responsibility that I was willing to accept even though this family, technically speaking, was not my family. Ms. B. gave me a deadline to have some money coming in or else she would have to ask me to leave. But, when she saw that I was going out every morning looking for a job and still coming back empty handed, she began to talk to some people that she knew and pick my head to see what I could do. She later hooked me up with a local artist whom I was able to help for a little while. Then, one day out of nowhere, she sat me down and told me of a story of how women would use their personal items to get men. After telling me this she offered to perform a spiritual cleansing on me and presented me to her Lucero. I wasn't sure if the cleansing had worked on me or not but I did feel better as a result and was open to positive change.

I was *"a little special"* because I didn't understand what she was saying at the time about women using their special items. Part of the reason I couldn't do it was because I simply was never taught about it. My parents (like so many others, I later discovered) refused to tell me certain things based upon the belief that if I didn't know about it, I wouldn't believe in it and it wouldn't affect me. It was a form of sheltering, but life made me learn. Like later on, while staying in Ms. B's house, I learned that Ms. B's youngest son was a psychic. He had the ability to see certain things like Bertha but would use cards to help in get the details.

Now, I didn't care too much about prophecies and what psychics predicted because I was always told that I would be a preacher when I was kid but nothing else. So it didn't really interest me as much. It wasn't until I met Bertha and saw her predict some things that were pretty accurate that I started to listen to psychics and prophecies. Then, when I saw that Ms. B's son would make some pretty accurate predictions, I decided to pay attention to what he would say, especially since he wouldn't charge me. I hoped that maybe the information he would give me could help me to get a job. Then, one day, Ms. B's son told me that "A man is going to ask you to do something, but don't do it" and that was it. There were no other details. The next day Ms. B and her youngest son went out of town. Later that night, there was a knock on the door and Ms. B's oldest son asked me to get the door. When I opened the door I was met with a double barrel shotgun and told to get on the floor. The masked thugs quickly ran up into the house and robbed Ms. B's eldest son and then ran back out. We didn't know that he was selling marijuana and I for sure didn't know that he was the man Ms. B's youngest son was psychically informing me about. This left a bad taste in my mouth about most psychic phenomena, as Bertha scolded me for not following the vague psychic instructions that were given to me.

Now, the voice of the guy that robbed Ms. B's eldest son sounded very familiar. I didn't see his face but I knew just from the sound of his voice that I had seen him before. It was interesting that when they came in that they went straight to the room where Ms. B's son was at, which meant they knew where he was. This made me really focus on getting a job, but when I started thinking about how I was living out a garbage bag, trying to figure out how, when and where I was going to get my last meal. Sleeping on a cold floor in the back room of some lady's house with a woman (I was beginning to think, that I barely knew), and her children. That's when it hit me and I began to see how low I had sunk. I couldn't believe that I had let myself go this low and it happened so easily. That's when I heard a voice say, *"That's right...you're homeless."*

Hittin' Rock Bottom

That day, instead of trying to get a job, I focused upon just trying to get some money to get out of this situation. I had tried to do things the right way. I registered with various job centers, submitted a number of applications all over the place, and still nothing. I had applied for jobs that I could do and jobs that I wasn't even qualified for and still nothing. I had even applied for a job that I wouldn't dare do unless it was my last resort, such as a volunteer fireman, etc. I did everything that I thought I knew how to do and still nothing. So Bertha suggested that I talk to some people that she knew in order to get me in-touch with some other people so that I could get some money by selling drugs.

Of course, I knew better, but I desperately needed some money at the time and selling drugs seemed like my only chance of getting some money. Despite the plight I had to go through just to escape the crack epidemic in Detroit, I was willing to compromise my principles to sell drugs. I didn't want to but I had to do something because I just couldn't see any way out of the situation that I was in. It was so easy to get into selling drugs and so easy to make the product... the street chemist had explained to me the purpose of using baking soda together with the cocaine, something I had to go to college to learn in biochemistry.

I rationalized that I would only sell drugs for a little while then "get out", but I saw images of the movie *New Jack City, Sugar Hill* and James F. Cagney

Jr.'s (July 17, 1899-March 30, 1986) role as Cody Jarrett, who boldly professes in *White Heat,* on top of a gigantic storage tank before dying, "Made it, Ma...Top of the world!" All reminded me that there is no getting out once you get in. The only way to get out was death; it was the code every young African American male in Detroit, my generation knew that was first drafted by Young Boys Incorporated (a.k.a. YBI).

The thought crossed my mind to just ditch Bertha and her kids, who would have probably had a better chance living with her grandmother without me. However, I wanted to be a positive role model for Bertha's kids and show them that just because you don't like things as a man you don't run. The thought also crossed my mind to just return home and give up on this spiritual pursuit thing, but I was determined to be spiritual. I was determined to find the answers to the questions that haunted me in my youth, so that my spirituality wasn't just intellectual or a chore. Then Bertha told me that she was pregnant, even though she claimed that she had had her tubes tied previously. I had not choice but to stay. I didn't know how I was going to make matters work, but I had to find a way, and the only way I knew to make quick money was to sell drugs.

Standing on the corner, looking down an empty street that seemed to lead to nowhere, with a pocket of little baggies, a voice said to me,

"You don't want to go down that road, do you?" and I answered "No". I then took the little baggies that I had and discreetly opened them up and dumped them into the sewer.

That's when I witnessed my first miracle,

because after I made the decision not to get involve in drugs, Bertha mysteriously got some money and we decided to go to Atlantic City. In Atlantic City, she won around 2500 dollars playing the $5 slot machines. When we came back to Philadelphia she gave some money to Ms. B and a little to her grandmother and then we moved to Jacksonville, Florida, where the cost of living wasn't as high. We laughed and talked about how she mysteriously won the money. She put it off as luck but something deep within me knew that it wasn't luck but something much deeper. I just was afraid to say it aloud out of fear of appearing overtly religious and being ridiculed as sounding like a Christian. I consider this my first miracle because it was the first time I truly saw how when you are at the end of the rope something miraculous occurs. I just had to do what my favorite Detroit DJ, the Electrifying Mojo, used to say: "Tie a knot. Keep hanging. Keep remembering that ain't no-body bad like you."

Still, I did not see the whole picture and concluded that the reason I had so many problems in Philadelphia was that what I had previously learned was simply not practical. In order to make it, I believed that I really had to apply myself so I wouldn't have in Florida the financial difficulties that I had in Philadelphia. So, I returned vigorously to the books and continued to read and study more mystical and metaphysical writings in order to connect to God, as the Kamitic people had done.

Florida Sunshine Blues

No one tells you that the Sunshine State, like California, is also a land of lost and misplaced dreams. So in Florida, I began to have similar problems of getting jobs, and as a result we ended up living in

what I later discovered was a skid row, drug infested motel full of druggies and homeless people.
Determined not to continue to live like this, I began to think about my experiences in Philadelphia. I changed my thinking and stopped focusing on what I didn't want and focused on what I can do. This change of thinking led me to find some pretty easy odd jobs that I could make enough money from to pay our weekly motel fee.

For example, one time, while walking down the street, I met a storeowner that paid me to paint a mural on the side of his storefront. From him, I met another business owner that paid me to do a mural for his company. I didn't know why I was able to get these odd jobs but I didn't try to understand why at the time, because I was just focused on getting money, so I continued to work wherever I could. This, of course, led me to doing all sorts of jobs that I would never have imagined I would do, like telemarketing sales, driving a taxi, selling cars, and security work. This drive eventually led me to being a convenience store clerk and taking a job as an administrative assistant because, contrary to what people thought, I could speak English, think, type and use a computer, which was shocking to the whites at the numerous temporary job agencies. Later, when a number of the Floridians learned that I was from Michigan, they called me a Yankee. *Wow, still upset about losing the Civil War.*

Anyway, my jobs led to us moving into an apartment, then finally into a house. I worked hard and gave my paychecks to Bertha, who, come to find out, wasn't pregnant at all. Because we needed the money, I worked full-time as an administrative assistant during the day, and then I would come home, sleep for a few hours and go to my second job as a midnight shift convenience store clerk. When 7 o'clock rolled around in the morning, I would go to my first job, and start all over again. At the convenience store I would eat the readily available junk food as dinner during my night shift, because Bertha rarely cooked or cleaned anything, because she claimed her back hurt or that she was sick. So many nights, I would go to work hungry and drink the free beverage provided by the store, a deadly caffeinated mixture of cappuccino-hot cocoa-espresso, just to stay awake.

However, I was making money, but it still wasn't enough money, as I signed my paychecks over to Bertha to pay the bills. Then one day, when I wanted to buy a bean burrito before heading off to my second job and asked Bertha for some money, we got into a real, ugly argument. I couldn't believe it. I was arguing about her giving me some five dollars to buy two bean burritos so that I wouldn't pass out on the job! That's when I stopped signing my checks over to her and instead cashing them first, taking a little money out for bus fare and my personal use, then giving her the rest. With Bertha still refusing to cook on a daily basis for the only person that was working in a household of five, fast food bean burritos became my best friend because it was cheap. Having no choice, I also began eating fish and seafood, because we lived on the coast and it was relatively inexpensive.

Then, as I was tired of walking, one day we decided to save up some money and buy a car. We had $500 that we managed to save to put down on a car. Since I was working two steady jobs, we figured the payments at a used car lot would be fairly decent. So I went down the street from where we were living and bought a used car with weekly payments of $50 for six months. The car was great; the only problem was that we didn't have enough money to get auto-insurance, but the dealership didn't seem too worried about it either and let us get the car.

Now, it was Thursday and I got paid on Friday, which meant I could get auto insurance the next day, but I just didn't feel good about driving an uninsured car. Of course, I thought the worst: what if we're in an accident and hurt someone seriously? Then we would have to pay out of the pocket. So, carefully, I drove our new car slowly as legally possible. When Bertha asked what I was doing and I told her my concerns, she scolded and called me every name in the book except a child of God, before finally declaring that I was just stupid for thinking the way I was. It didn't, however, deter me from driving more cautiously than usual.

The next day, Friday, I took the car to work, relieved that I didn't have to take the bus anymore. I got my paycheck then I drove home. That's when it started raining. As usual, the exits were backed up with cars waiting to exit off the highway, so I pulled in line. Then, the rain started coming down real bad and drivers in Florida, for some reason, didn't get the hint to slow down. The next thing I know is that I looked in the rearview mirror and saw a pickup truck trying to screech to a stop after going 80 miles per hour in the rain. BAM! That's right, the young naval officer totaled my brand new used car and I got a citation for not having any insurance, which I was going to get today.

The good thing was that no one was hurt and our new used car was totaled, so it was paid off by the other driver's insurance. I just couldn't believe that what I was worried about actually happened. This made me wonder if God likes Murphy's Law, or if God, like the Greek gods of old, just hover over the earth molding the lives of the little clay figures on earth for their entertainment. I wasn't sure but it convinced me that what we think definitely influences our physical reality. It wasn't too long after that I got a job in sales, which gave me access to a number of positive thinking books that I began to read. Anyway, I wasn't sure how the accident occurred, but Bertha sure was upset by it and blamed the whole thing on me and my thinking.

By this time, Bertha was really starting to get on my nerves, so much so that the little time that we saw each other all we did was argue. In just a short while our arguments progressively became no-holds-barred verbal fights, where we said anything about the other no matter how hurtful or scornful it was. It was during one of our cat-dog fights that the thought began to cross my mind that the reason she wouldn't cook or clean wasn't because of back pain and illness, but because she just didn't care about me and was lazy. The back pain and other sickness were simply excuses to get out of doing anything.

I saw what her grandmother believed and I could just imagine how growing up in a household like that would make anyone resentful about cooking and cleaning, but I wasn't her grandmother. Then, I remembered in my parents' house it was no persons' duty or responsibility to cook and clean, it was everybody that did it. Both my parents cooked and they cooked well. I remember my mother told my brothers and me, the reason we needed to learn how to cook, clean and even sow for ourselves was so that we didn't have to depend upon anyone for our survival except for ourselves. I remember my mother numerous times would tell us that there was nothing more pitiful than seeing a man go hungry because he is waiting for someone to cook for him, since he can't cook. My mother was determined that that wouldn't be my brothers and mine issue.

My brothers and I learned how to cook at an early age. In fact, I was in high school the first time I began cooking and it wasn't because it was my responsibility. It was because I was the first person home, so put some meat or beans on the stove. Simply put, it was convenience and consideration (or love) that dictated at my parents' house, which person was supposed to cook.

Sure, I could have come home from my first full-time job and cooked food for everyone in the house that was not working and get enough sleep to go to my second full-time job. But, if I had to work two jobs and cook for people that weren't working at all, what was the purpose of having those other people there, I thought? Yes, "I'm definitely being used," I confirmed along with the thought that Bertha faked the pregnancy just to keep using me. Now, I truly loved her kids and I didn't want them to see me leave so that they would have a complex about not having a father, but I was wondering am I hurting them more by being with their mother or not.

As I pondered on so many things, I began to think that the counsel that Bertha gave was twisted. I didn't think or rather I couldn't bring myself to believe that Bertha deliberately misconstrued and misunderstood the interpretation that she gave, but it was becoming very clear that she didn't know anything about what a good relationship was all about. In fact, I was starting to believe that she wasn't as spiritually experienced as she claimed. The more I saw how things played out convinced me that she didn't have any experience in a lot of subjects. This, combined with my ignorance, was causing both of us to go down a crazy road. So, she shouldn't have been giving any advice or counsel on what someone has to do to have a good relationship or anything.

Commonsense is what came to my mind and that's what I should have used. My parents told me this but somehow they didn't explain it correctly or I didn't get it correctly. It wasn't their fault, but I understood now that I should have looked at Bertha's credentials. Instead of listening to what she was saying, I should have looked at the fruit that she was bearing. If she was supposed to be so good and knowledgeable at what she did, she should have had some physical evidence to back up her claim. I should have listened to my parents, grandparents, aunts and uncles in regards to having a good relationship, because there is a low divorce rate in our family.

"I think I understand now," I told myself and that's when I really began to see that this whole situation was just a test to teach me something about my family.

As I thought about things, I was beginning to understand why Ms. B was telling me what some unscrupulous women would do to get men. I couldn't believe that Bertha would have done this to me but I wasn't sure. I know that she did claim that she was pregnant and she wasn't. I just wasn't sure. Whatever the case, the feeling of being used was beginning to settle in my head. It wasn't long that I became very suspicious of everything that she did and simply grew not to trust her.

There was no one I had to talk to during this

time, because I didn't know anyone except for the people I worked with. I really didn't have a lot of time to talk to people in the first place. Even if I did, Bertha would accuse me of trying to sleep with some woman. She did this on a daily basis since I worked with an office full of women. It was of course her own insecurities about herself that made her think that. Not understanding that out of common decency I wouldn't mess around on her, not to mention that I didn't have the time or the money to do so, but I couldn't get it through her head. In her eyes, I would eventually sleep around on her because I was a man and all men do it. She made sure to yell it at me every chance she got, especially in front of her daughter. When I was at work, she would call me and yell this same accusation from the other side of the telephone (as if to make it so that my co-workers could hear) that, "All men are dogs, because all men mess around!" I never hung up the phone on a woman, but usually, when she would do this, I would.

For a little bit I wondered, why all of a sudden was she just thinking that I was messing around on her? It didn't make sense because it seemed like it just happened out of the blue. I knew she didn't find any phone numbers, condoms or any other incriminating evidence in my pockets because I didn't have any. Where were all of these accusations coming from? I didn't know, then one time, without thinking, but tired of being accused of something I have never done and yelled at like I was an animal, I called her out-of-her name and when she screamed, "All men do it", I without thinking shot back at her, "Especially, when the woman ain't doing what she's supposed to do!"

I should have known better and I knew that my response was only going to make her scream at me some more, but I was tired of it and it was starting to click that this is not normal. This relationship simply was not right, no matter what she claimed about it being our destiny and we being soul mates. My parents, my grandparents and my aunts and uncles didn't use any special, spiritual stuff to have a good relationship with their spouses. All they had was love and it was through love they worked, played and did everything else for each other and their family. This was how I was raised. This is what I was doing. I wasn't coming home drunk, I wasn't spending my money on frivolous things and still I was going to be screamed at and treated like an animal. *I don't think so.*

Tired of working 17 hours a day and supporting people that didn't care, this whole thing about soul mates, I was beginning to see, was really garbage. It started dawning on me that if Bertha was like this with her last husband, it explained the reason why he divorced her, and why he left the house in shambles. But, still I wasn't absolutely sure. The "spiritual brainwashing" was very powerful and made me wonder, "What if we were destined to be together? " I just really didn't know and didn't have anyone to talk to about this. If I called my parents, I would get a lecture about how I shouldn't have got with that crazy woman in the first place, so calling them was out. I didn't need that right now. G was the only one who might listen.

G was the only one that somewhat understood what I was going through. When my 25th birthday rolled around, G understood how important it meant to beat the statistics as a young black male. He along with my immediate family called me. This so-called spiritual woman that I was with didn't even buy me a birthday card or wish me anything. That really hurt and further convinced me that she really didn't care. It wouldn't be long after, that G would fly down to Florida just to hang out during his vacation time and even give me money. He could see the torment that I was in but not knowing what to do he just listened and offered whatever advice he could. Celebrating my belated birthday, we would get a couple of drinks and just reminisce on all the things we had to go through to arrive where we were today.

A Brief Walk with a Cuban Saint

Figure 1: Ellegua - Orisha of the Crossroads

Nevertheless, I continued working, reading and studying my books. My experience with Ms. B gave me a new interest and made me look more closely at Afro-Diaspora religions. This helped me to get over the initial shock promoted by the media in movies like *Voodoo Dawn, The Believers, The Serpent and the Rainbow*, etc. that African derived practices and traditions are cannibalistic, spooky, demonic and evil.

By this time though, I had began feeling that learning about spiritual practices was a waste of time because I didn't feel that they were bringing me closer or helping me to learn about God. Then, that's when I met an old black Cuban man whom I came to call Papá Raúl.

Although Papá Raúl had not read or studied the Kamitic history and spiritual books as I had, he had a lot of insight and wisdom about traditional spirituality because he, like most Cubans, was Catholic. He also was a member of the Abakwa Society and he practiced Santeria, an Afro-Cuban religion originally from Nigeria similar but different to Haitian Vodu and a form of Spiritism. Papá Raúl understood but spoke very little English so his wife would usually do most of the translation for him. While Papá Raúl could not divulge any secrets to me about his spiritual background, he told me a number of stories about his life experience and historical events that I never learned in my history class, which I wrote in my *libro* —notebook. For instance, Papá Raúl told me about his childhood and how life was in Cuba before coming to the United States. He told me about his friendship he had with his older brother and the various things that his grandmother did to protect them both. Papá Raúl told me that the oldest city in the United States is St. Augustine, Florida, which was founded by Spanish settlers about 42 years before Jamestown, Virginia. He also told me that Florida use to be Spanish territory but a trade exchange between Britain and Spain led to Britain acquiring Florida and Spain having full control of Cuba.

It wasn't long after that, Papá Raúl and his wife began introducing Bertha and I to their cuisine and music. I learned about Beny Moré, Arsenio Rodríguez and Celia Cruz, that I soon began to appreciate and adore, because of these artists' love for their African heritage. Unlike in North America, where one could hear African retentions, many of the Cubans sung songs that openly talked about how a particular African divinity helped them to achieve some feat or a song of praise for a particular tradition, honoring their ancestors. It reminded me sort of like the blues without cultural interference and misinterpretation. It was like true expression. Even though I didn't understand what the artists were saying most of the time because they were speaking in Spanish or Spanish mixed with an African language. To make and sing a song in an African language with Afro-Latin rhythms and have it become a hit was not just ingenious but bold, stunning and a true expression of resistance against racism I thought.

It made sense to me why Papá Raúl told me that *salsa, Cuban son* and several other forms of Afro-Latin music should be also considered part of Black heritage, because it like the blues, R&B, hip-hop, reggae, soca and calypso has African roots and stems from the same beginnings. It was for this reason Papá Raúl said that he truly respected Bob Marley, because he was one artist that forced white people to accept him for who he was.

At first I didn't understand what Papá Raúl was telling me but when I thought about it I realized that he was right, people of African descent have made numerous contributions all over the world, but most people don't see this because they focus solely upon external differences. I began to see that I had been conditioned as a result of growing up in North America to believe that a person has to be "Black" based upon their skin complexion and the language that they spoke. Since one of my mother's good friends –Mrs. J, who was also one of my godmothers growing up– was very fair skinned with hazel eyes, along with other light skinned blacks that we knew that lived in Detroit and in Ontario, Canada, I got over identifying someone's *blackness* based upon his or her skin complexion a long time ago, but I never thought about language being a determining factor. I remembered that because my mother was an educator and her mother never got her high school diploma but they both stressed the importance of speaking proper

English so that "people (*whites*)" understood what we were saying and that was all. I never thought about other black people that spoke another language, how that would fit into the puzzle.

The more I continued to listen to the music and observe some of the foods that Papá Raúl and his family ate, the more I began to realize that there were a lot of things that we had in common. One day while talking to him he suggested that I should try to learn Spanish. Now, at first I thought that maybe he was suggesting it out of convenience. So, I didn't think too much about what he was saying because I knew a few phrases already. Then, I noticed that when I did speak a little Spanish people treated me different on both sides of the spectrum. A lot of Spanish speakers seeing that I was trying to speak Spanish respected me and would try to assist me, while some people would look at me suspiciously as if to wonder what was I doing or up to.

Then I remembered that Malcolm did meet with Fidel Castro before his death, because he was trying to internationalize the struggle of people of African decent. That's when I realize that Papá Raúl was encouraging me to learn Spanish because he understood, like Malcolm, that language was one of the factors that separates and unifies people.

Now, I remember Papá Raúl spoke about Malcolm X quite frequently. I remembered at first how surprised I was to hear Papá Raúl talk about Malcolm X and even about Marcus Garvey, because I never knew that their influence was so widespread throughout the diaspora. The other reason is when the media talks about Cubans they are usually portrayed as being white people. Again, I had to remind myself that I needed to think outside of the box and remember that *blackness* is not based solely upon skin complexion as it is viewed in the United States.

Then, Papá Raúl said something really interesting to me. He like some of the other Cubans I had met had a differing opinion about Fidel Castro whom he told me was the only white man that he respected because of what he had done for his people. This was confusing to me, until I learned from Papá Raúl that, even though he was sort of in-between on Fidel's politics, most of the Cubans that came to the United States after the Cuban Revolution (1959) are called white Cubans because their ancestry comes from Europe –particularly Spain. Before the Cuban Revolution, Cuba had laws that were similar to the Jim Crow laws of Southern United States. It was only after Fidel took power that these racist laws Papá Raúl said were eradicated.

What made this even more interesting was that I was trying to understand what Papá Raúl meant by calling Fidel white. He told me that even though there seems to be a lot of white Cubans, most of the Cubans on the island are either black or mulatto. He told me that, years ago white Cubans viewed everything that was African as being backwards, primitive and foolish. So a serious campaign was launched to rid Cuba of its African cultural heritage. He told me that the police would raid houses and arrest people in a serious effort to stomp out everything that was derived from Africa. But, black Cubans for the love of their ancestors and culture refused to stop practicing what made them who they were. A number of people Papá Raúl told me never forgot those days and hid their tradition from plain sight and practiced in secret, but most proudly continued despite the overwhelming odds against them, to show it wasn't backwards or evil. Papá Raúl told me that the Cuban government seriously tried to make black people ashamed to be black, but it didn't work for the most part. To remind him of that horrible time and to honor those that continued to fight back, he boldly displayed the little little cowry-eyed cement cone image that he called his Ellegua and his La Madama (a jet black mammy looking figure that Papá Raúl said was his Ellegua's wife) in his living room, while a huge iron pot, which he called his Ogun, sat in the corner standing guard, for all to see.

There were a couple of things I found interesting about Papá's La Madama. The first was that he referred to this figure as the wife of the little cone-head cowry-eyed image. I had read about Ellegua before in some books and I thought that the Brazilian Pomba Gira was supposed to be his wife. La Madama I thought was something else. I wasn't sure.

The other thing was that I had seen this iconic figure before, in some of the Puerto Rican households that I had visited, while in Philly with Ms. B. The figure looked to me like the stereotypical Aunt Jemima, mammy charicature that many African Americans despised because in the United States. The charicature portrayed older black women as being ugly, grotesque and happy-go-lucky slaves willing to give their own life for the slave masters' family and home. The truth, I was beginning to see based upon the fact that many Latinos in Afro-Caribbean spirituality seemed to believe in or possess La Madama, indicated to me that apparently older black women were viewed as strong matriarchs in the community and could see what others often missed. In other words, contrary to popular belief, they didn't work as house slaves as it is often portrayed.

I later learned from Papá that so many favored purchasing La Madama images depicted with jet-black skin as a sign of pride, indicating that she was from Africa and was not of mixed of heritage. It was becoming quite clear that there was a double meaning behind everything that occurred in this country. Practices and traditions that were done in other countries amongst people of color meant to empower, improve and uplift, in the United States were deliberately used by the white majority to disempower, curtail and degrade people of color.

Papá Raúl told me that the Spanish word "*negro*" (black) or "*negrito*" (little black) was just as offensive as saying the "N" word; that instead the more politically correct term is "*moreno*". While pointing to his skin he said he had been fighting for his people all of his life. Papá Raúl told me that racism in Cuba was bad and that blacks were once upon a time banned from certain establishments and had to go to the back door like blacks did during the Jim Crow segregation period in the United States. He said that all of that changed when Castro came into power because Castro outlawed these segregation laws. He said that he also remembered fighting in the Angolan War, which he personally interpreted as him fighting for the freedom of his heritage. This was the reason why even though he didn't agree with a lot of the things that Castro was doing presently, he respected him for what he had done.

Then Papá Raúl told me that racism in Cuba was nothing like the racism in the United States. He said that he never knew how bad Black Americans had it here until he came to the United States. When I asked what he meant by that, he told me that when he first came to the United States, that he and other

Cuban migrants were in a camp. Then one night, some men carrying torches and wearing white sheets rigind in horseback appeared. I remember Papá Raúl telling me that at first they thought that the men were there to welcome them until the men in sheets began attacking the people. Papá Raúl told me the Cuban refugees fought the Ku Klux Klan with everything that they had and drove them out of the camp, but it was that experience that made them unite together as a people. Papá Raúl told me that it was this little experience that gave him an idea of the overwhelming hardships that Black Americans had in this country.

He told me that they never had in Cuba people that wanted to kill them because of the color of their skin. Never did white people in Cuba organized like the KKK did in the United States to specifically terrorize black people by murdering and burning down churches. This, Papá Raúl told me, gave him a different perspective about the problems that black people have in the United States. It wasn't just about pulling up bootstraps and making things work, when you have people that terrorize you. At the same time he said it made him proud to see that the blacks had their own churches, banks, fraternities, clubs, colleges, etc. because it dispelled many of the stereotypes about black people that are spread throughout the Caribbean and Latin America. He said that it gave Afro-Latinos a sense of pride because blacks are running a race in which they are starting way behind white competitors.

Papá Raúl after telling me that story told me that just like here in the United States, Blacks in Cuba come in many colors and shades, while he was looking at his wife, who was making Bertha and I some ilekes[7], and two sons that had a very light complexion, that reminded me of my hazel eye, light-skinned godmother. After telling me this I began to interpret *blackness* from a completely different perspective. Instead of focusing on *blackness* from a limited North American perspective, I began to see it from a global viewpoint based upon one's cultural ways. At the time I didn't know that I would soon be called not being black because of seeing life from this perspective, but eventually it would happen, just like Malcolm was once criticized. It made me realize how silly this whole blackness concept was, just because one hasn't had the same racist experience as one has had in North America. The fact that one has experienced racism due to white supremacy based upon their culture and the color of their skin alone helped me to identify with them as being a sibling to the cause.

Interestingly, Papá Raúl pointed to a small painting of Saint Michael that he had. He told me that the saint is an archangel and protects against evil but that you have to get the right one. He said the wrong one has the angel trampling on the head of a dark skinned man. In Papá's eyes it was a racist image because others didn't depict the devil as such. Therefore, "Make sure you get the right image that empowers you", I remember him telling me.

The more I listened to Papá Raúl talk, the more I liked him, because he shattered my myth of what it truly meant to be spiritual. Spirituality to Papá Raúl wasn't about strict discipline and sacrifice as it is portrayed here in the United States. It wasn't about

---

[7] Hand beaded sacred necklaces that represent the orisahs/spirits.

not being able to do this, eat that or do whatever because if you did you were going to be condemned or go to hell. Spirituality to Papá Raúl had nothing to do with your attire, your knowledge of the metaphysical laws, etc. To Papá Raúl, spirituality was about having a personal relationship with God. If something were right or wrong in your life, you would know it. Not because some author wrote it and said that it was right or wrong based upon his or her theories. According to Papá Raúl you would know you're in the right or the wrong because God would tell you, if you just observed the signs. It was all about what you do and the life that you live. Spirituality was about living a righteous life based upon the principles established by our ancestors. These same principles according to Papá Raúl are the same moral principles that Jesus Christ taught, which is why he didn't see a difference from the core concepts of Christianity and African religion. Papá made sure that I understood what he meant by this, by emphasizing the "core" concepts of Christianity and not some "man's" personal agenda driven form of the religion.

    I got a different perspective on spirituality from observing Papá Raúl, which somewhat explained why religious syncretism occurred in Cuba. It was different and surprising especially when I learned that he was a high priest who worked as a mechanic and a handyman most of the time. You would have never had known that Papá Raúl was a priest unless he told you or you saw his sacred staff because he didn't go around boasting about his spiritual accomplishments. He like Ms. B didn't dress in expensive African garb nor did he follow any special dietary regimen, other than the taboo prescribed by his main spirit guide. Papá Raúl drank rum occasionally and smoked every now and then but none of this stopped him from living a righteous life. It was from looking at Papá Raúl and his humble dwelling that I began to see that this idea of spirituality that I was holding was truly a westernized conception based upon Eastern imagery. Papá Raúl showed me that spirituality should be exciting, intriguing, educational, but most importantly a personal relationship that you have with God.

I remembered Papá Raúl telling me a lot of things like about the spiritual frame or *cuadro espiritual* (personal power) that everyone has. Another thing he told me was that African religious tradition can help anyone and everyone but it is the birth right of all black people. This is why it upset him that some practitioners charged outrageous prices, swindled and cheated people. He said that so-called spiritual practitioners that cheat others don't understand that they give African derived traditions a bad reputation and contribute to religious maltreatment of legitimate practitioners. For this reason alone, Papá Raúl said that he was glad that the Abakwa society had a set of rules and standards in place, which prevented anyone and everyone from arbitrarily creating a spiritual lodge. As a result, Abakwa hasn't expanded as rapidly as other Afro-Cuban traditions have outside of Cuba.

With that being said, he told me that the skills or talents that we have are supposed to be used to help others but also to help us to make a living. He said if you're good at something you're supposed to use that to make a living with but you're not supposed to use the religion to make money. Papá Raúl said people that use the religion (any religion for that matter) to make money would eventually have to answer to God because that was not the purpose of religion. The purpose of religion was to help people connect to God and that is the responsibility of any true religious practitioner. The purpose of having talents is to make money, which is why he worked as a mechanic and handyman. When he learned that I could draw, paint and sculpt he told me to use my artistic skills to make things that will help people. He also encouraged me to go back to school and to get my degree.

There were a lot of other things that Papá Raúl taught me like not to lay with my feet pointed towards the door, because this was how the dead were carried out. I thought this was kind of odd hearing this because I had come across this in the Chinese feng shui practice. How did this black Cuban man know about this? Did he practice feng shui as well? I wasn't sure, but I continued to listen and write down what he told me in my *libro*. Papá told me about a lot of odd practices such as the way to absorb negativity, by placing a small glass of water with an uncracked egg under my bed. Of course, I didn't do this because I was too busy trying to figure out how and why this remedy was supposed to work.

Anyway, I admired him because he was a very proud man who reminded me of grandfather. The only difference was that Papá Raúl spoke Spanish and my grandfather spoke English. Like Ms. B, Papá Raúl used stories a lot of times to explain him self. Papá Raúl was a spiritual man that believed in the existence of spirits but he was not superstitious, meaning everything he did was not based upon some "taboo". From what I could tell, it was spiritual truths and wisdom taught to him by his grandmother, the spiritual matriarch of his family, that guided his actions. For instance, one day when I asked him if he believed in saying grace over his food, he told me that it was his experience that people would poison other people's food, so when the victim prayed over it they prayed over the poison as well. As a result, he gave thanks after he ate his food to God and the cooks.

I remember after telling me this he told me to always trust the Spirit when you are eating and drinking anything. He said that the Spirit would never lead you astray. He said when you are eating or drinking something to simply look at it and allow the Spirit to speak. He told me that if you get the sense not to eat or drink something, to follow the Spirit's instructions and don't do it because it will save your life.

There were other things that Papá Raúl taught me such as to always know where your shadow is when walking alone at night. Also, know the difference between your power hand and your receiving hand. Your power hand (usually your right hand) is used when you're giving something and your receiving hand (usually your left hand) is the hand you use to take care of sanitary matters. I had heard about this custom before from some practicing Muslims in school but I never knew that this practice extended beyond Islam. According to Papá Raúl this was a simple way of nullifying ill intent directed towards you. Besides it was bad manners to extend your left hand to shake someone else's hand and eat with your left hand.

Some of the more interesting stories that Papá Raúl told me about were the stories about his orishás from Yorubaland in Nigeria, Africa. During slavery it is believed that these ancient divinities traveled to the New World to be with their children and help them to overcome the oppressive conditions against them. There are a number of orishás that exist but only the most popular amongst the people taken to the Caribbean, Latin America and New Orleans survived:

Ellegua is the divine messenger and trickster
Obatala is the father of the white cloth and peace
Yemaya is the orishá of motherhood and the sea
Chango is the orishá of fire and thunder
Ochun is the orishá of sensuality and beauty
Oggun or Ogun is the orishá of war
Ochossi is the divine tracker and orishá of police
Babaluaiye is the orishá of smallpox and sickness
Oya is the orishá of the cemetery and tornados.

These spirits coincided with the ancient Kamitic divinities I had read about prior to meeting Bertha. The difference between the two was that the Kamitic divinities seemed distant, foreign and more like creation of fantasy, while the Yoruba divinities appeared to me to be more real and tangible having human faults and so on, as Papá Raúl expressed them to me. I tried to understand the rational reasoning why this was the case and the only thing I could find that made a little bit of sense was that the divinities seemed to be what Swiss psychiatrist Carl Gustav Jung theorizes as being archetypes, autonomous complexes that exist within the human personality, yet act independently and appear to be almost supernatural entities that exist in what he called the collective unconscious, which best I could understood was the closest thing in human terms that meant God. In other words, the archetypes or divinities appeared to be emanations from God or of the mind, but were they real?

According to Jung's theory each archetype controls a different aspect of the human endeavor and personality. This means that if one of these archetypes were allowed to overpower the entire human personality the results would be mentally catastrophic. Therefore, each archetype is needed in order for human beings to maintain a perfect state of mental balance. This still didn't explain if they were real beings or just figments of my imagination, so for now I just put the subject to the side.

Then I remembered *The Irritated Genie* on how the loa/orishá Oggun was the one responsible for inspiring the Haitian revolution, which led to Haiti winning its independence in 1804, shortly after the American Revolution. I remembered that when I first read it I wondered how a spirit could do this if spirits weren't real. Since I wasn't literally or officially taught about angels or spirits, I couldn't and didn't really believe in them, because they seemed imaginary. It was like praying to God: at some point in my life God didn't seem real, partly because we were taught to pray to some imaginary figure or some mystery Deity. In fact, when I read about the angels, spirits, orishás and God in other books, I viewed them as being nothing but figments of our imagination within our psyche. Then Papá Raúl told me something that made me see things a bit differently.

He said always be careful when going into bars and clubs because Ellegua (the trickster) likes to cause rackets at night by getting Oshun (the orishá of beauty/love) to dance which attracts Ogun (the hardworking orisha of iron/war), knowing that she only has eyes for Shango (the orishá of fire/thunder). Eventually Ogun and Shango are going to fight; knowing this, Ellegua goes and gets Ochossi (the tracker orishá and orishá of the police), thensits back and laughs at the whole situation. When I thought about some of the clubs and parties that I went to when I was attending school, I remembered that it was always, what we called "the knuckleheads" that would start the fights over some nonsense.

"Wow", I began to think, this story is so true!

After telling me this story, I remembered he told me that there are a lot of spirits and that everyone has spirits that walk with them, but people need to know which spirits are with them and which ones are not. To Papá Raúl, according to the way he was taught by hisgrandmother and family, the spirits were once human beings and they were all considered to be warriors so they sat on the floor as warriors did and not upon shelves hanging alongside walls as commonly depicted.

I was totally confused. I was feeling totally lost at what Papá Raúl was telling me. I wasn't sure if God and the spirits were real or not now. Could they actually exist? Could this be the reason why I have been having so many problems because I didn't believe that they exist and thought it was all me? Did I miss something? I wasn't sure. I was struggling with what I experienced versus what I had learned.

Now, I had a little ancestor shrine with a few pictures on it, but I only had it because I saw how Bertha and others I observed in Philly had one. Although it was my ancestor shrine I really didn't have a personal connection to it. The photos on the shrine were of people that are commonly acknowledged during Kwanza or Black History Month, but there was something that made me wonder. What if a part of these people still exists? I wasn't sure.

Anyway, the confusion, hesitation and mental distress I was feeling, made me see that my approach was not only being seriously challenged by a brush of spiritual reality but beginning to crumble. I don't know if Papá Raúl knew that this little story would shake me up like that or not but it did. Later, when he discovered that I was studying the Kamitic tradition and trying to implement it into my life, he scoffed at me for trying to put into practice the ancient Egyptian religion because he said it was foolish to try and replicate what was done a thousand years ago. The reason is because what ancient Egyptians faced was completely different from the issues we face today. He said that the Egyptian tradition focused upon addressing the issues of the Egyptian people. The Egyptian religion wasn't made to address the issues of people in the United States, Cuba or anywhere else. It was created to help the Egyptian people and the Egyptian people only. Once it served its purpose it ceased to exist because everything has to evolve, nothing stays the same.

    Papá Raúl told me that instead of focusing on trying to practice the Egyptian religion I should focus upon trying to understand the Kamitic concepts and principles, because these are the same concepts and principles that have empowered the traditional African way of life that exists today. Papá Raúl told me that African Americans have a rich ancestral legacy but the problem is that we haven't learned how to use it because we have been made to feel ashamed of it. He said that this is what made Lucumi (or Santeria) in Cuba uniquely different from the way it is practiced in Africa, which is how it survived. He said that in order for the religion to survive it has to adapt in order to serve the people. So, again he told me to learn the concepts and principles, because when that is done the ancestors will help one to adapt and modify everything else to be a tool of empowerment. This, Papá Raúl said, is way more important than trying to emulate what someone else did thousands of years ago.

The Candle Shop Visit

It wasn't too long after that I mysteriously lost contact with Papá Raúl, but what he had told me stayed with for a long time. As a result, I changed my focus and began honoring my ancestors more instead of trying to implement the Kamitic tradition into my life. I later met an elderly lady named Ms. Smith from Detroit who ran a candle shop. The only reason why I had visited her store was because I saw all of the different types of candles upon the wall, which reminded me of the candle shops I had seen back home. Now, I visited Ms. Smith's store several times and each time I visited her shop she was listening to a tape recorded sermon of a preacher, which I thought was weird because of what I was taught that people that engaged in spiritual practices were not godly. But, Ms. Smith just like Papá Raúl had made it clear that godliness has nothing to do with the cultural practices you engage in. It is how you are living and treat others that determine if you are living for God or not.

For example, Ms. Smith told me that one day there was a white lady that had come to her because her son had did something illegal and was locked up in jail. After doing a reading, she learned that lady's son had been warned before about doing a particular crime. Naturally the mother had wanted her son to be released, but Ms. Smith refused to do so. The reason was because the reading she had done indicated that the lady's son had been warned several times and he continued to engage in incorrect behavior, so he had to serve jail time and the spirits weren't going to help him this time. Ms. Smith said that she told the lady that there were things that could be done to protect him while he was there but that she was not going to go against God and try and do anything to get the lady's son released because it would be spiritually incorrect. She said that she warned the lady that there were some people out there that would claim that they could get her son released but that they were unscrupulous individuals that didn't care about doing what's right and wrong. Ms. Smith told me that she again warned the lady that if her son were released he would never learn from the consequences of his actions and commit the crime again with worse effects. Ms. Smith said that she knew that her advice fell upon deaf ears but that she was not going to lose her gift or her Holy Ghost just for a small material gain.

    This message basically coming from nowhere confirmed for me that there are some unscrupulous practitioners that exist and will do whatever they can for material gain. What Ms. Smith also told me made me understand that spiritual rewards and punishments do not just happen in the afterlife, such as a person being rewarded in heaven or punished in hell. No, spiritual rewards and punishments occur in one's present lifetime and continues through to afterlife, which are basically the consequences or effects of one's actions or causes. So, scrupulous practitioners act and behave in order to improve, strengthen and maintain their connection with God. This message from Ms. Smith also verified for me that I had been taken advantage of because of my ignorance and naiveté, but that now that I knew that something was wrong and the lesson was learned, a change was coming, which was kind of like what Harriet Tubman said after freeing close to 300 people that, "I could have saved thousands, if they had only knew that they were slaves". I wasn't a slave no more!

    Then Bertha, who had started receiving medical and financial benefits for her back injury, suddenly, out of the blue, told me one day, when I had come home from work, after talking to a girlfriend of hers, that I was using her and "getting the milk for free and not buying the cow", as she put it. *AHA! That's probably where she's getting her accusations that I was cheating on her from.*

Anyway, not seeing the signs and recognizing what was going on, I thought to myself *"What nerve! Me using her?"* It wasn't like I didn't want to marry her at first but we didn't have any money, and I wanted to have a decent marriage ceremony. I believed that she was using me. The other thing was that I was still confused about the God issue, which was another reason I didn't marry her, but I wasn't seeing the signs. I was just truly amazed that she was convinced that I was using her for sex. I mean I was really putting myself through all of this hell, working two full time jobs trying to provide for her kids and everything, for sex? Get real?

When I finally shut up and started to look at what was going on. Thought about how this happened right ater losing contact with Papá and receiving the message from Ms. Smith the candleshop owner. The sign was that I was being given an out. I didn't want to leave before because I didn't want Bertha to point out to her kids that men just run out and neglect their responsibilities when things get tough. I wanted them to see that I was leaving because she had asked me to do so. Afterall, I endured this spiritual hell long enough and now it was time for it to end, so without any contest. I gave her everything we had acquired together and took my books, music and the garbage bag of hand-me-downs clothes bought at the thrift stores. Then, I moved to Kansas where my family had relocated.

Part III:
Learning to Walk On My Own

The wisdom of the elderly
is like the sun; it illuminates the village
and the great river.

- Nilotic Proverb

In the Strange Land of Oz

One of my younger brothers had asked me to come live with him and his family in Michigan. As much as I wanted to, I decided instead to move into my parents' home because my brother and his wife were a young couple that hadn't been married too long. They didn't need my drama and I didn't need the drama that they were experiencing brought into my life. I needed time to reflect, refresh, figure out what went wrong and get back on my feet, so that's the reason why I chose to move to Kansas, where my parents had relocated.

This part of Kansas that we were living in was pretty weird. Many of the whites still called black people "Coloreds" as if we were truly living in a Civil Rights documentary, and a lot of the blacks in this area acted like they had never seen black people speak English without grabbing their body parts. It was so strange because I had never in my life heard white people ask what color are black babies when they are born. I remember the first time I heard that it took every ounce of strength within me, and the roots in the ground I stood on to keep from smacking the ignorant taste out of the individual's mouth.

I should have known something was up when some of the locals thought my parents (both working as educators now) were drug dealers, because they were one of the few blacks that purchased a house on the north side of town – that's where all the "rich people live", I was told. *Wow.*

As expected, I was called a "house nigger" by some of the local blacks. Funny how the table turns, I thought. I could have showed these people my KRS-1, Wu-Tang, Mos Def, Common (Sense), Dead Prez, Talib and other hip hop acquired collection, or maybe my jazz, blues, R&B collection. Or maybe my numerous African and African American history collection that I studied, but I don't think it would have mattered.

This whole idea of blackness, I was beginning to see, is really silly in the first place. Especially considering the fact that historically it has been our own people, from the early slave revolts of Denmark Vessey, Gabriel Prosser and Nat Turner to the assassination of Malcolm X, that have deterred (if not halted completely) our progress. I mean, I didn't' find it funny anymore when black comedians joked about former U.S. President Bill Clinton being the first "Black President" because he grew up in Arkansas poor, could play a saxophone, liked John Coltrane and slept around. In fact I found it to be quite insulting, especially considering the fact that during Clinton's presidency, there were not a lot of significant contributions made on his behalf to the African American community.

I understood the purpose of why the concept of blackness existed in the past, especially politically in western societies that placed great emphasis upon classification through skin complexion. But it seemed to me now that it would be more advantageous and beneficial that, if we need to classify and identify with others, we do so based upon cultural similarities. To do otherwise is to engage in the same racial game used by westerners (young and old), in which they will always win because it is their game and they can always change the rules to fit their purpose.

It can be debated until the cows come home the ethnicity of the Kamitic people, who, contrary to popular belief, depicted themselves as being a dark skinned race of people, similar to modern black people that exist all around the world in different shades. Anyone can perpetrate so-called "blackness" as well, but when it comes to culture, this is a completely different matter. People can't perpetrate when it comes to culture because culture, which means to cultivate, is about evolution. It is just like a wise man and a fool. A wise man knows what it is like to be a fool because he once was a fool, but a fool will never know what it is like to be a wise man because he was never wise.

Therefore, culturally speaking, I could find similarities between my own situation and others that didn't have anything to do with religion per se. Culturally speaking, the Kushites (Ancient Nubians) were kin to the Kamitic people, just like many throughout traditional Sub-Sahara Africa. It explains why, when the Africans were brought to the Americas, many were able to form alliances with the Amerindians, because they identified with each other based upon cultural similarities. For this reason alone, I think the tradition of the Mardi Gras Indians should be acknowledged, cherished and celebrated to preserve our ancestors' entire legacy in North America.

Anyway, back to this strange land, I was shocked and brought back to reality, when I tried to have a conversation with a young black woman who also attended a HBCU as I had. Expecting her to be exposed to some of the same concepts, ideas and philosophies I was exposed to, one day we got into a conversation about the people in the 21st century still calling black people "Colored". Then in the middle of the conversation after hearing me say African Americans, she boldly proclaimed that she was not an African American because she didn't know anything about Africa. I was floored and couldn't believe my ears that a person that recently attended a HBCU would even think like this still. I told her that the term "African American" has nothing to do with going or coming from Africa. It was a term of endearment chosen to replace the earlier labels placed upon us by whites and the ones that placed emphasis on color. It was Malcolm X whom I first heard coined the word Afro-American, which became Black-Americans and later African Americans. The term places more emphasis on heritage due to the Cultural Movements of the late 1960s and early 1970s. After telling her all that, I could see that I was wasting my time because she told me that she knew more about being a "nigger" and "niggerville" then about Africa.

"Ok, God bless you. Have a good day," was all that I could say because she was saying all of this publicly.

Of course, everyone that lived in Oz-ville wasn't like that, but a large number of the people (Blacks, Whites and the growing Hispanic community included) were just "IG-NANT[8] (ignorant)", that made quite a few people take notice. Especially my family, who along with a few of the other people helped to create and maintain a Black History group that organized various events to educate people about the contributions made by people of African descent, instead of idolizing black stereotypes. In Detroit I never saw the relevance of having such a group and even understood the argument rappers gave for using the infamous "N" word, but in an area where

---

[8] African American colloquialism meaning one is so ignorant they can't even afford the letter "o" in the spelling of the word.

ignorance is at an all-time high, where people believe that all blacks are thugs, gangsters, drug dealers, ghetto, stupid, shiftless, lazy people that have made no contribution to society, it was a challenge to ignore this stereotypical garbage because we had professionals that lived in our communities, but when you don't have this and not only do the children believe this but the adults as well? You either become part of the problem or solution, and I knew one day I would have to be a positive role model, so I needed to do what's right not just for myself but to help others as well.

Now, one of the good things about living in this strange land was that there were plenty of jobs and even though they taxed everything, the cost of living was relatively low. It didn't take me long to kick into gear and in a short time, I got a fairly decent job with an oil and gas company. Through this job I was able to eventually save up enough money to pay off the debt I had acquired while living with Bertha and use the money from investments to finally get my degree. Shortly after that I found a better job and eventually had enough money to live on my own, but I had no peace within me. I was still confused as to what I was supposed to do, so despite how much I had been taken advantage of, I continued to keep in touch with Bertha, even though every conversation that we had ended with an argument. Then one day after calling her, I remember we got into an argument that was so heated that I heard a voice ask,

"Why are you calling her? This is the reason why you left." That's right: this was the reason why I left, I thought, so why am I spending my money calling her to get into an argument? It was after asking that one question that made me stop calling and reflect upon the entire experience I had with Bertha.

The experience with Bertha, I found, had taught me a lot about myself. The relationship that I had with Bertha, rom the beginning to the end, was just something else that I couldn't at the time put into words. Easily I could point a finger at everything that she did to me but it was hard for me at first to understand my role in the whole matter. After recovering from the initial shock, I took a bath made of walnuts shells to permanently sever the relationship between us. While sitting in the bath it became clear to me that I should not put my faith in others and place them on a pedestal. I should instead put my faith in my own abilities and talents. In other circumstances I wouldn't have done it but it was because of my idealistic spiritual quest, spiritual ignorance and naiveté that led me to compromise my principles. A a result, I was taken advantage of... Lesson learned. Shortly after, the name Rau Khu came to me.

Help from a Lil' Cuban Saint

I got into this whole mess because of my pursuit for spiritual bliss, so I really didn't want to read, study or hear anything else about spirituality for a long time. Of course, I couldn't stay away for too long. Since I had lost connection with Papá Raúl, I tried to call Ms. B, but I was told that she was out of town. After several weeks of calling her and being told that she was still out of town, I began to believe for a second that she was avoiding me. I also wondered if Papá Raúl was a legitimate practitioner or not. I mean, I had never been to Cuba so I wouldn't know if what he was telling me was correct or not. It made me really think how vulnerable an individual is when they depend upon others, but really wonder how could you know what's right and wrong, what works and what doesn't. I guess the only way to find out is by applying it.

Then a week later, Ms. B called me. Apparently, she was unable to return to the country at the time because she had traveled to Cuba to make *asiento*, the traditional ritual crowning of the orishá, which can be received by all. Those that practice Palo Mayombe after being *scratched* –ritually cut, signifying initiation in the religion– commonly receive the ritual crowning of the orishá, I learned.

A couple of times, while talking to Ms. B, I asked her opinion on some of the things that Papá Raúl had taught me. She explained to me that each spiritual house is different and operates differently. That what might be practiced in one spiritual house differs in another because of the needs of the people at that particular spiritual house. This doesn't mean that one spiritual house is wrong and another is not, it only means that although there are similarities that exist throughout the religion, they are not always practiced exactly the same because the needs of the people are different.

Ms. B, after listening to some of the advice that Papá Raúl had given me, laughed and said that she was very thankful that the Cubans fought to preserve our way. She told me that although the Cubans were very poor, they were a very lovely, proud and strong people because of their culture. Ms. B helped me to understand some of the things that Papá Raúl had told me, by explaining to me that it is our family ethics and values that is in jeopardy because of the American capitalistic and materialistic way of life. This, in her opinion, is the reason why there was so much corruption on all levels. It was through her visit to

Cuba she said that she saw what it truly meant to have and belong to a family. She told me that one of the most beautiful things about the whole experience was feeling like she had a connection to our ancient ways reaching all the way back to Africa. This was truly an indescribable experience that she told me that she couldn't put into words, but through her practice she felt as if she was doing what her ancestors had done before her.

I didn't understand exactly what Ms. B was saying but I could comprehend the experience a little. This was because this was how I felt when I sat and listened to Papá Raúl and even my grandfather now that I think about it. It was an experience that was beyond rational thinking and couldn't be duplicated.

Ms. B also told me that what made the Afro-Cuban tradition so unique from the African tradition is that it adapted to address the issues that exist in the Western hemisphere. Ms. B told me that the Africans didn't have to deal with racism like we do over here in the Americas. It was because of this element that a new tradition was needed in order to empower people to face such adversity. This is why it was more important to focus upon the concepts and principles than upon doing what the Kamitic people did thousands of years ago.

Ms. B told me that Papá Raúl sounded like he was a legitimate *padrino* (godfather) and that I needed to follow his advice, because according to Ms. B., Papá Raúl saw something that was about to happen to me in my life and wanted to make sure I was on the right path. This was one of the reasons why he told me not to give away my luck and use what empowers me wisely.

Ms. B further encouraged me to stay strong and keep on going. Instead I tried to go on a hiatus from the spiritual subject and clear my head of all the dogmatic crap and misinformation that I was fed from Bertha. That's when I met my good friend Yazmin, a Cuban-American from New York who helped me to further understand what Papá Raúl was talking about by further introducing me to Afro-Latino culture.

Yazmin, or Z as I would call her, helped me to understand a lot. Besides expanding my interest in Afro-Cuban jazz by introducing me to the music of Cachao, Juan Formell y Los Van Van, Ibrahim Ferrer, Bebo Valdés, Chucho Valdés and the salsa timba group Bamboleo, she reminded me of the way my grandmother and great aunts use to cook with fresh vegetables and herbs by introducing me to the *sofrito*, a Caribbean and Latin American stir-fry sauce consisting primarily of garlic, onion, green bell peppers and tomatoes or tomato sauce.

It was through her that I learned how to cook with olive oil and the value of a freezer. At the same time, Z taught me from afar how to make better use of fresh vegetables and cook with them without totally diminishing their nutritional value. As a result, I learned and was inspired to cook picadillo, black beans and rice, plantains and Cuban-style tamales, which led me to eventually learning how to cooking Mississippi Delta style tamales. I also eventually began to include in my sofrito mixture celery and cilantro, borrowing from the Creole/Cajun trinity and Trini (Trinidad & Tobago culture) cuisine. Of course, Z didn't like my adaptations and substitutions because she was a hard nose Cuban purist, so she jokingly would call me the "Remix Chef". Whatever the case, I am thankful to Z for reintroducing fresh vegetables back into my diet.

There were other things about Latin America that Z taught me about, which aren't taught in history. Like, for instance, it was an ex-slave named Gasper Yanga that led a slave rebellion in Mexico, which led to the founding of Veracruz. Another thing that I didn't know was that Cuba's independence was due majorily because of the contributions of the legendary revolutionary Afro-Cuban leader Antonio Maceo (1848-1896). Maceo, along with the Mambises (the revolutionaries composed largely of blacks), fought against Spain to help Cuba win its independence. I remembered coming across this name before; then it hit me, it was one of the names that Marcus Garvey had on his Black Star Line ships: the SS Antonio Maceo.

Iya and the Calling

Another very interesting woman that I met was Iya (pronounce Ee-ya) a Yoruba priestess of Oshun. Iya (which means Mother in the Yoruba language) was unique in a number of ways. Iya was initiated into Santeria (Lucumi or Regla de Ocha) and later she was initated into the Ifa religion, by a Yoruba priest from Nigeria. It was this unique blend that allowed her to see things from a different perspective, such as seeing the Kamitic Osar as being the equivalent of Jesus Christ.

There were a lot of things that Iya told me that helped me to see things clearly. One of the things that Iya told me was that the name Rau Khu suited me well but it didn't mean what I thought it meant. She said I would be told what it meant in the future. Iya also told me that I definitely have a strong ancestral influence surrounding me. She also said that the Kamitic influence was quite strong but it was not the leading influence in my life but only acting as a mediator. Iya explained the reason why I was learning bits and pieces of everything were because it was my destiny to see the whole picture in order for me to fulfill my purpose of being here. She also explained that part of the problem I had in understanding things was due to me having a relationship with my teacher or Bertha. It was the relationship that changed the dynamics of things and made it difficult to truly understand and properly respect anything.

Then like a mother knowing what the future holds for their child, Iya told me in the sweetest way that she could to lick my wounds because my spiritual ordeal wasn't over yet. Iya said that I had been "Called" and when I told her that I had always wished that I was taught specifically by some elder or something like that, she told me that traditionally that's what should have been done for me, especially when they noted that I was breached at birth. She told me that it was because we live in a society that doesn't believe in spiritual culture that things aren't done like that anymore, because the way for most has been lost. She said the old ways were lost but not the paths. That's why the people that have been "Called" have been called: they are supposed to reestablish the ways, which is my calling.

Then when I told her about my childhood and all of the experiences I had when growing and being called a PK (preacher's kid), Iya told me that she understood because she too was a PK. She stated that she grew up in an Apostolic Pentecostal household like I had, where her father was a storefront preacher. The only members I believe she said they had were her family and a couple of other people totaling five. Iya understood the heartbreak, disgust and humiliation that went along with being a preacher kid firsthand but, she told me that "If you are 'Called' to do God's work you are 'Called' and can't run from it".

I told Iya that I didn't want to be a preacher because I had seen all the things that they went through. She said that she once thought the same thing because of her father's church membership. She then told me that being called doesn't mean I have to be a preacher. She said being called means that you are called to help people and do a particular job for God because it is your destiny. Iya said she learned this lesson the hard way and was able to help me to understand it because not only was she a PK herself but a seer, that is an individual that could psychically see things that others ordinarily couldn't because of the "gift of sight". She said that it was her gift, that she was "Called" to use it to help others. She explained that when we answer our "Calling" it comes natural and is almost like we are doing a hobby but we're helping people, which is doing God's work.

Everyone has a "Calling": some people are "Called" to be doctors, some teachers, some artists, some musicians, some are "Called" to be healers, etc., in which you can see that it comes natural and they are good at what they do but you have to accept it. She then told me that my calling was to be a shaman, (that is a go between, between humanity and God and the ancestors) by connecting the old with the new, the past to the present, and making sense of it all. Iya said that the reason I couldn't settle on any particular spiritual system was because I was called to be a shaman, and like most shamans had to know everything about how a particular system worked.

Shamans I was told have their own unique

system of beliefs and practices because they have gone through it, they have a personal experience with the system they believe in because they have seen it work. Some shamans know how to heal people from certain illness because they were afflicted with that same or similar illness. Shamans are like spiritual scientists, Iya said, not just relying upon some theory found in a book but applying and testing the theory out to see if it really works. She then told me that I was in exploration mode right now but that I would be discovering my way soon.

Now, when Iya told me that I was supposed to be a shaman, I was like "whatever" because I didn't really understand the work that shamans performed. All I knew was that in most of the movies that I saw, like the movies about Shaka Zulu and the Native American hero Tecumseh, whom I recently discovered was believed to be born on the same day that I was born, that shamans get hurt really bad because they go through a lot of spiritual crap. Afterwards however, they are some pretty bad (bad meaning good) people, so Iya hearing my apprehension recommended that I read James Hall's book *Sangoma: My Odyssey Into the Spirit World of Africa* to get a better understanding of shamanism and to help me find my way.

I took her advice and read the book but I never really gave what Iya told me any real serious thought, until I began to remember something that Papá Raúl had told me. It was that everything doesn't work for everybody. This is the reason you can never take anybody's word on face value in regards to something benefiting you or not. It is because we are all different, we have different experiences, different backgrounds and as a result different needs, and so what works for one person is not guaranteed to work for another. In order to see if something is going to be beneficial to you, you have to try it out for yourself and stop taking other peoples' word on face value and observe their energy. This coincided with what Iya had told me and confirmed that I was supposed to be a shaman. When I conducted more research about the subject, I discovered that one of the ways shamans enter into trance is by listening to music in a language that they don't literally understand, which was the childhood practice I learned how to do while in church to train my mind to focus. My déjà vu experiences, my longing to be alone when I was younger in the basement and garage, etc. were all signs that this was my path. The question now was how I was going to become a shaman. I had no idea and for a while I tried to look for ways for it to happen. Finally, I gave up and decided that if it was meant to be, it would happen, so after that I again went about my life.

My Friend, Best Friend, Girlfriend & Wife

There were a lot of other things the experience with Bertha made me question and wonder about. For one, I knew that I didn't want a spiritual woman ever again because when you ask for a spiritual woman there's no telling what type of spirit-energy they are going to have. Instead of asking for a spiritual woman or asking for anything remotely similar, I just wanted a good woman, so I stated, "I want a woman that loves me and is supportive". Months later, effortlessly I met my dear friend who became my best friend, girlfriend, fiancée and later my supporting wife.

Now before I married my wife, there were a few obstacles that we had to overcome. Her ex for instance, was very jealous, possessive and abusive. He was a tall and big man compared to me, but after the hell I had went through there was no way I was going to back down and not be respected. I was a different man, I could tell, because of my past experience. In the past, I would not have necessarily been a coward but I don't think I would have stood up to him the way I did. But I wanted to protect her when I was gone. Then, out of nowhere I got an idea to sprinkle a red pepper around the house to protect her and keep him away. I don't know where I got the idea to do this came from, it just popped in my head and I did it. Interestingly, I heard that he did drive by but he never stepped foot onto the property.

There were other issues that we faced as well. For one, I was a little leery on if my family was going to accept her or not because she was Latino. It wasn't that I thought my family was prejudiced against Latinos, because there were a number of Latinos that lived in Detroit. In fact, there were several Puerto Ricans that lived in our neighborhood that we were good friends with and never knew they were Latinos until we grew up and realized that they had a Spanish last name. It was just that no one in our family had married anyone that wasn't African American, so I was concerned to see how the reaction was going to be. Then again, I was concerned because they didn't accept Bertha, but when my late grandparents met my wife they welcomed her with open arms and in fact told me that this was what I was supposed to do the first time. That is, allow the elders and my family to meet the woman I am dealing with before running off with her, as was the case with Bertha.

Later my grandmother, mother and aunts took my fiancée into the kitchen, where they were preparing food and doing their woman *"thang"* (gossiping). I don't know why I was so worried about my family accepting her, but when she told me that her parents were also treated like dogs during the Civil Rights era and had to go to the back of the bus and give up their seats for whites, I realized that we had more in common than different. Later, when I learned that my wife's grandmother was a *curandera* (a Latin American traditional folk healer similar to the old hoodoo practitioners), I realized we were culturally linked. Another sign that my fiancée was culturally linked to me was when she told me that she saw the sun and moon as being the eyes of God. That's when it became clear to me since I didn't actively go out and chase her down, that we were definitely led to meet each other by some hidden force.

    This made me realize that the reason Bertha and I didn't get married was that, even though I couldn't logically explain it, my ancestors simply didn't approve, which is why we constantly argued with each other. Bertha was what Fela Kuti calls a *"Lady"*. My wife, on the other hand, was one that I could take *"A Long Walk"* with, as Jill Scott sings. My wife was someone who cared for me and was concerned about my well-being; as a result, we made compromises and did what we must to maintain the love and peace in our relationship, like not arguing and being adult enough to communicate with each other about how the other feels. Our compromising involved me sometimes watching chick-flicks but I did it in order for us to watch the horror/sci-fi flicks that I enjoyed.

    Having some understanding of God, our wedding ceremony consisted of blessed coins, the Jumping of the Broom ceremony and several other symbolic practices that we now perform yearly on our anniversary.

Trying to Understand this Quest

Since I was born and raised near water, born under a water sign, I was a water child but living in this part of Kansas I was in with no water was killing me. I stayed only because of my wife. Living in Kansas made me appreciate a lot of things that I took for granted. There was no one telling me what I should believe or think, no study groups, no communities, no one to talk to. Whatever you have or even imagine having it was not there in the part of the world I was living in. It wouldn't be long that I would soon lose contact with Z, my outside connection to the real world, and have to go at it alone. Although I had my wife who was easy to talk to she didn't quite understand my plight because she hadn't experienced all that I had, but she encouraged me and continued to stand by my side through it all.

It was truly a desert in Kansas, not a real desert because there was underbrush and enough trees to count on one hand, to go along with the dead birds that were tired of flying around looking for trees (smile). I considered this place to be a desert because besides no water, there just seemed to be no life here, period. Most of the people walked around like they were in a time warp because they were content with how things were no matter how bad they were. It was horrible. I hated it. In fact, I hated it so much that when people asked where I was at, I told them in a place where God even forgets (Laugh).

It took a lot of adjustment for me to accept and submit to change. It was only after looking at all of the farmland, seeing the clear sky at night, along with the moon, the stars, how the animals and livestock responded to the different weather patterns, the environmental changes, the time before, during and after a thunderstorm, dust storm and tornadoes, that it became clear to me that I was brought here for a reason. Besides meeting my wife, this desert was like Jesus' 40 days in the desert. It was an initial training ground where one prepares for something greater as the character Luke Skywalker did in the original *Star Wars* trilogy. It was Arrakis, the desert planet that Paul Atreides in the 1984 science fiction film *Dune,* based on the Frank Herbert novel of the same name, learned in order to avenge his father's death and become an irreconcilable force against evil.

It was by living in this "desert" I was given a chance to go within, which made me realize the ancient Kamitic people couldn't have had a pan-religion as so many believe. The people, like most traditionalist's ideas and beliefs, were influenced by their environment, which reflected their beliefs about God.

Though a little unnerved, I began to question everything, such as the whole aim and purpose of spirituality in my life, and why I had to have a spiritual problem or something. It came to me later something that I had read before, by John Mbiti, who stated in his book *African Religions & Philosophy*:

> "To be human is to belong to the whole community, and to do so involves participating in the beliefs, ceremonies, rituals and festivals of the community. A person cannot detach himself from the religion of his group, for to do so is to be severed from his roots, his foundation, his context of security, his kinships and the entire group of those who make him aware of his own existence. To be without one of these corporate elements is to be out of the whole picture. Therefore, to be without religion amounts to a self-excommunication

from the entire life of society, and African peoples do not know how to exist without religion."

I knew part of the reason why I was having so many problems was that I had no true spiritual connection to God, but I never thought about how the spiritual teachings from the church were basically my spiritual roots, no matter how much I tried to deny them. It came to me that a lot of our ancestors made numerous contributions to the church in order to make the religion as unique as it is. To further verify what Mbiti said, it came to me of how my family that attended church on a regular basis lived a pretty peaceful life, but those that didn't had a lot of problems and tragedy in their life. The church, I began to conclude, was more than just a religious institution. The church was also a corporate element, but like all institutions it had problems as well. I couldn't actually figure out what I didn't care for about the church but I knew it was something buried deep within causing this spiritual crisis.

    I knew that I liked certain things about the church and that there were certain things that I didn't like that led me to experiment with Eastern, Arabic and other forms of spirituality. I remember I left the church because I wanted the Holy Ghost in order to escape the ills that were plaguing my community. I remembered I wanted the Holy Ghost because the older people that I heard talk about this power testified of how it improved their life. It was because I wasn't able to retain my Holy Ghost that I went down this path of self-discovery, I remembered. One of the reasons I was so disgusted with the church was that the clergy only taught people to believe but didn't give any sense of reason behind it. For instance, you were taught to believe that you were born in sin, no matter if it made rational sense or not, just believe. The other thing was that the church always talked about being "saved" but they didn't teach people during those days how to use the power of God to live or be *"saved"*.

As a matter of fact, now that I think about it, when I was younger I was forced to do a lot of things in regards to church. We attended church, sung in the choir, participated in church functions and so forth because that is what we were told to do. We weren't given any explanation as to why we were supposed to do those things, we were just told to do it and accept what we were taught about the Bible without question.

I think now that if I were given an explanation as to why I should do something, versus just forcing me to do it, I would have been a little bit more receptive, because I would have had a better understanding of how to apply things in my life. For instance, if I were told that the Bible was not a world history book but a book that focuses upon the genealogy of Jesus from Adam, I don't think I ever would have questioned whom did Cain marry or even try to learn about how the ancient Jews and Christians borrowed concepts and ideas from the Kamitic tradition.

I think if I were told about spirits in the church and told that we all surrounded by two spiritual forces: a spiritual force that promotes good (angels, guides, guardians, etc.) and spiritual force that promotes evil on earth (demonic, etc.), I wouldn't have gone out looking and trying to learn about the various spirits that exist from other people, but I guess that is part of the quest. Some people have to struggle against poverty, some against substance abuse, some against bad relationships, etc. My quest, as I was beginning to understand it, was striving to live a better life with or without God. It is like I stood before God and God said, "Prove that you can make it with or without Me."

We are all meant to go through something. If we didn't have some thing that we had to struggle against, then I guess we wouldn't physically be here. So, I had to return back to the original purpose of why I embarked upon this quest, which was that I started studying the Kamitic tradition because the Kamitic people appeared to have known how to tap into the Power of God and use it to improve their lives. It was this theory that the Kamitic people apparently knew how to tap into "something" that led me to take this path, but I wondered why. Why was I on this path? Why was I looking so hard for some connection, I wondered? Then, I remembered my father, seeing the anguish in my face, one day told me that the old people use to say, "You have to go through something in order to get something." But what was the something I was trying to get? I didn't know what it was and I felt lost because I really didn't know what I was looking for anymore. Then, it came to me that I, like so many other people, was under the impression that I had lost my ancestral way.

That's when I began to remember that when I left the church at a young age and began venturing out learning about other faiths, many of the black Christians didn't seem to want to know about their history, their culture or anything that was African related. I recalled having many heated debates just talking about the Ancient Egyptians. All of this, along with some other things I didn't particularly like about the church, is what convinced me that the Christianity was the white man's religion.

Naturally, when I left the church and began studying African and African American history, it seemed to make sense why black Christians acted the way they did, when I learned that southern racist missionaries during slavery taught a version of Christianity to the slaves, in order to make them docile and accepting of their lowly fate as slaves, such as the introducing the curse of Noah on Ham, in order to justify slavery and claim that black people (and other people of color) were inferior to them. Again, it made sense why some black Christians didn't want to know about their history, culture, etc. This also made me wonder, how does one not know when they are following the true doctrine or the altered version that promotes docility. For that matter, how does one know if they are doing anything right for that matter if they don't have a connection to God?

All of these sentiments I remembered that I had weren't new, but had been held by black people (especially black men) for years before I was born. I learned that even my late grandfather, who became a minister later on in life, once held these same sentiments, as well as other males in my family. In my personal research and experience, I learned that it was these same sentiments that Christianity is a *"white man religion"* or a white washed version what inspired many African Americans during the 1950s through the 1970s to convert to the Nation of Islam and to Sunni Islam as well, so I knew I wasn't alone.

Then, from nowhere, I had a startling revelation. As I reflected back on my life and small events that took place, I could see that Bertha and I could not get along because there was a cultural difference. One's culture is a reflection of one's ancestors and this is why Bertha and I had problems.

Every family, I was starting to understand, has a set of cultural practices, rules and traditions that those in the family must follow. If one doesn't follow them, they will have troubles. This explained why my family didn't care for Bertha but accepted my wife. It was our cultural similarities.

This made me wonder if the problems that we have in our life are due to problems that our ancestors have had in their lifetime. Could spiritual problems from those that lived before us be passed to the next generation just like hereditary traits? I wasn't sure, but it sounded reasonable.

When I thought about it and did some further investigation into my family's history, I discovered that there were a number of men along my family lineage that had problems accepting Christianity and it was all for pretty much the same reason. It explained why, when I closed my eyes and called upon the name of Jesus, the image of a white blonde male with blue-eyes appeared to me, even though I know that Jesus, according to biblical records, was a person of color. This convinced me that there was something definitely going on in my spirit. It was contradicting what I wanted and what I knew. Then it hit me that if it is true that we are descendants of our ancestors and that we are the last link in a long ancestral chain, then the problems I had were most likely inherited or passed on to me by someone that is no longer physically here but who is here spiritually. Hopefully, the flip side would mean the spiritual prowess of our ancestors would also pass down. *Hopefully*.

Now, I didn't believe in reincarnation per se, but I did believe and had seen how generational curses work, especially in regards to family. Some things exist that just can't be explained. You just have to accept it and try to understand it later, I was beginning to surmise. Such as, why was I was born in the 1970s to an Apostolic-Pentecostal preacher and still have problems connecting with God. That's a true pickle, but when I started learning about reincarnation that made things a little bit more understandable.

Reincarnation, I learned, from an African perspective doesn't occur as it does in the Eastern philosophy, where one is reincarnated from a human being, to a dog, fish, beetle, human being, etc. In the African sense, reincarnation as I understood it is the evolution on one's soul, in which an individual tries to perfect him or herself by learning about God. The reason an individual has problems in life is that it is through these problems that they learn about God and about themselves. Theoretically this made sense but it sucked to some degree, because it meant that life is the teacher of hard knocks. It made perfect sense and explained that, if I had not looked at what I did in the relationship with Bertha, I would have made the same mistakes and picked another mate with similar if not worst problems. It was because I looked at my behavior in the relationship that I learned from my mistakes so that I wouldn't make the same mistakes again.

Clearly, if an individual never had problems and everything was good, they will never know what is bad. It is because we learn what is bad that we know how to be good. This is the reason why we have been born and it is only after we have perfected ourselves, learned our lesson, and fulfilled our destiny or whichever one comes first, that we are allowed to leave.

This understanding, however, made me wonder what was going on the years before I was conceived to bring me here. I mean, what were my parents thinking at that moment of conception? I wondered what was my mother thinking when she was carrying me in her womb and why did I decide to breech at that last moment, as if I was trying to renege on a contract. I knew that there were a lot of things happening during that time. For instance, Detroit was still recovering from a race riot that had occurred in the late 1960s as well as other parts of the country. Various cultural changes were occurring throughout the country, while the unpopular Vietnam War swung in the balance. I knew that there was no way I could get answers to some of these questions because it happened so long ago, "Go to those that know. Go to your *Ancestors,*" I heard.

Without rationalizing or thinking about what I was doing, before my simple ancestor altar, I let it all out. I explained to them as best I could what it was that I was trying to do. I told them that I meant no disrespect but that I was trying to reconnect spiritually back to God using our culture that was lost. I told them that I didn't believe that the Ancient Kamitic people were idol worshippers because it contradicted and went against everything that they stood for. I had a serious talk, and I am pretty sure that if anyone had seen me they would have thought I was crazy, but I did it because I got a vision that my ancestors were fighting amongst each other. That's how I felt, I felt like there was a tug of war going on in between my mind trying to accept some things and not accepting other things. I felt like I was trying to move ahead but something was keeping me back. Remembering that I am one of the last descendants in ancestral chain meant that I inherited all of their doubts, fears, worries and concerns, and they had to be addressed. *"It's them"*: even though I couldn't prove that they existed, I knew it was my ancestors.

My ancestors were Baptists, from the Church in God and Christ, Pentecostals, but there were other things that they (my ancestors) accepted that I was missing, which I concluded was one of the reason I was here. I needed to know the truth in order to end this spiritual dilemma that I was in. I needed to start at the very beginning to understand how this spiritual pickle began, because it was tearing me up inside.

After explaining to them all my intentions and just venting, I felt a lot better, because I felt as if a great burden had been lifted off my shoulders. I began to realize somewhat that God existed but proving that God exists is a silly and mute point because it can't be proven. You have to experience God. The same has to be done with our ancestors. You either believe or you don't based upon experience. When I put it all together, what this meant to me was that, since I was one of the last links along my ancestral chain, my problems are not my own, they are my ancestors' problems, which means by helping them I help myself and vice versa. That when I learn something, they learn something as well and vice versa, which means as I grow they grow as well because their deficiencies are a reflection of my owns. Maybe this is the reason why it's stated our problems are not our own. Whatever the case, this made a lot more sense but I didn't know how to make practical use of it as of yet. However, it was this understanding that opened the door for me to discover the hidden truths about African American spirituality.

The White Man's Religion Myth

The hidden truth I found was that an estimated ten million people were forcefully brought to the Americas from the West coast and Central regions of Africa over a period of four centuries, but unbeknownst to most is that these Africans that were forced to work in the various mines, households, sugar, tobacco and cotton plantations in the Americas, were ripped away from a vibrant familial, cultural and political system that organized every aspect of their life.

Slavery had existed before in other societies and had even been practiced throughout Africa as a form of indentured servitude, where slaves were not chattel, had rights to marry, own property, have offspring that were born free and could even purchase their freedom. What made the Transatlantic Slave Trade (or *Maafa*) so drastically different than any other slave system that existed in the world was that besides globalizing the system of slavery, slavery in the New World focused totally on the eradication of all aspects of African culture in order to create a *"perfect slave"* and prevent slaves from rebelling against their oppressors. Yet, the Africans brought to New World found ways to resist, rebel and overcome persecution in order to become the vibrant Afro-American cultures that exist today throughout the Americas.

There were many Africans that were brought to the Americas all with their own language and distinct cultural practices. The slave ships carted various African people like the Fons, Mandikas, Gambians, Bambaras, Senegalese, Fanti, Yoruba, Igbo, Wolofs and Angolans. There were even some Africans that were Muslim, like the Hausa, that were brought to the Americas but they weren't the first to be enslaved by the Europeans nor were they the first dark skinned people that the Europeans encountered.

Years before the Europeans entered into the trading of African slaves and the carving of the African continent into parts owned by Europeans, Portuguese merchants settled along the coast of Africa along the Zaire River estuary in 1483 to establish trade. Most believe that the Portuguese were attracted to Africa because of rumor of a very lucrative trade of gold, spices and slaves throughout trans-Saharan Africa between the various African nations (tribes) that produced the gold and the Muslims in North of Africa. In the beginning it is believed the Portuguese wanted to stamp out the Muslim influence as their forefathers had tried to do during the Crusades, so, after arriving in 1482 and establishing a trading post around 1491, the Portuguese were allowed into the interior and there they began introducing Christianity to the people of the Kongo-Angolan region.

The new faith spread amongst the Kongo-Angolan people so quickly and at such an alarming rate, that royal families, nobles and even the Mani-Kongo, the premier king of the Kongo Kingdom, readily converted to it. The Mani-Kongo, after converting to Christianity, changed his name to Afonso I and attempted to create a Christian state. After Afonso I ascended to the kingship, he began modeling his kingdom after the European Christian monarchies. Now, it is not known why the Kongo-Angolan people converted to Christianity so fast, but many believe that it was because of the numerous similarities that the Kongo-Angolan religion shared with their new faith.

Again, unbeknownst to most, prior to being

introduced to Christianity the Kongo-Angolan people believed in the existence of a Supreme Being whom they called Nzambi Mpungu. Nzambi Mpungu was the invisible source of seeds, rains, healing power and sacred medicines or magical charms. The Kongo-Angolan people also believed in the existence of lesser spirits whom they called **basimbi** (mysterious benevolent spirits like angels), **bakulu** (ancestral spirits that were honored by the chieftain, clan heads and smiths) and a set of malicious spirits called **bankuyu** (similar to trickster spirits like devils/demons) believed to be the spirits of people that practiced witchcraft (evil) in life and were refused entrance into the ancestors' realm after death (or heaven). However, the Kongo-Angolan people owed everything to Nzambi Mpungu – The Supreme Being.

Nzambi Mpungu was not given sacrifices but in times of difficulties and strife it was Nzambi that the people called upon for help. Nzambi Mpungu was the one that would deliver to them sacred medicines or magical charms called *minkisi* that would help the people to overcome their difficulties in life.

Other African nations, like the Yoruba, Dahomeans and Ibo, believed in a Supreme Being whom they called the great father, great Spirit, the great-grandfather, the supreme ancestor that all descended from. They also, however, believed in a host of smaller gods and goddesses as well, associated with the various forces of nature that were equivalent to the European angels and saints. The Africans that had this complex pantheon didn't address the Supreme Being with their problems because it was often believed that God was too busy managing the universe to deal with such petty issues. Instead, the people addressed their problems to God's emissaries, these smaller gods and goddesses, because they were like guardian angels, similar in role to the saints and angels in Roman Catholicism.

By the mid-sixteenth century, the dream of a Christian state that Afonso I and all of his successors tried to build fell through and never came to fruition, because the Portuguese had discovered the profitability of trading African captives to the newly discovered mines and plantations in the Americas. To increase the capture of slaves, the Portuguese encourage war between the various African tribes and nations. A century later, Christianity was banned by the Kongo monarchy as the Kingdom of Kongo declared war on the Portuguese. The lack of human and other resources resulted in the Kongo-Angolan region being dealt a deathblow by their enemy and succumbing fully under European rule.

The first Africans brought to the New World came by way of Spanish explorers and they weren't even slaves. Slavery wasn't even big business amongst the Europeans at first. It wasn't until a need for a workforce evolved to work the mines and clear lands in the New World that the Spanish involved themselves in the African slave trade, which came after failing to successfully enslave the indigenous population in the Americas and failing to maintain that system. The first slaves brought to the Americas, as well as the first slaves brought to Jamestown, Virginia, were of Kongo-Angolan descent.

Once the slave trade moved into full swing, it attracted the interests of other European nations that wanted to profit from the brutal chattel system. The continent of Africa was divided into parts amongst the European slave trading nations. The Portuguese came to rule Angola; the English dominated Gambia and Nigeria; the French seized control over the Cameroons, Dahomey, Senegal and parts of the Kongo. A great number of Ashanti were sent to the English Islands, while large concentrations of Yoruba people were sent to Brazil and Cuba. Haiti received a very significant number of Kongos and Dahomeans, while a number of Fons, Wolofs and Kongo people were shipped to North America.

Like most of the Africans shipped to the Americas, it was assumed by the Europeans that the Africans arriving on the shores of North America didn't have any culture or any concept of God. As a result, instruction was sent out from the Council of Foreign Plantations to Christianize the Indians and the Negroes in order to protect English interest (so that the colonies wouldn't be taken over by Spain and France), promote the Protestant Religion and to justify the enslavement of African people in 1660[9], but Christianizing the Africans wasn't as easy as it seemed. Many of the English slaveholders refused to give the Africans religious instructions because they feared that by baptizing them would lead many of them to believe that they were emancipated. Countless reports indicate that slaveholders prevented Protestant missionaries from baptizing the slaves for fear that the slaves would interpret it as them being free.

So, beginning in 1664, legislation was drawn up

---

[9] *Slave Religion: The "Invisible Institution" in the Antebellum South* by Albert J. Raboteau, pg. 97

in Maryland and soon followed by other English colonies that stated that slaves that were baptized were not emancipated from their bondage[10]. While the passing of legislation gave slaveholders legal rights to keep the Africans in eternal bondage, it is reported that religious instructions was still feared by many slaveholders because of cultural differences; racial distinctions that the Africans were inferior to whites; that Christianizing the slaves would make the slave proud, ungovernable and rebellious; and the belief that it would eventually contribute to an economic loss, since most plantations gave their slaves Sunday, the only day out of the week to rest and visit fellow slaves, dance and conduct other activities amongst themselves, which early missionaries saw as sacrilege on the Lord's day.

To placate the concerns of the slaveholder, the Anglican missionaries from the Society for the Propagation of the Gospel (S.P.G.) morphed the loving, just, peace, equal-rights teachings of Christ to justify slavery by introducing the Noah's curse on Ham[11]. The curse that Noah pronounced was equated with the dark skin of Africans, rationalizing that Canaan had turned black before settling in Africa. Thus all of the decedents of Canaan were black skinned, and centuries later dark skin was equated with Africa, slavery, evil, idolatry, beastlike, heathenism, etc.

To rid the slave of this curse they had to be given religious instruction, which not only saved their heathen soul but also made the slave more

---

[10] Ibid. pg. 99

[11] In truth the actual curse was on Ham's son Canaan.

manageable, docile and controllable. Slaves in the English colonies were taught the Lord's Prayer, the Creed and the Ten Commandments and strongly encouraged to obey their masters, which would result in them receiving their justly reward in heaven.

The catechism of slaves amongst the English colonies eventually backfired because the Africans were taught Christian prayers and rites but they weren't taught Christian beliefs. As a result, whites soon realized that they had a very limited control over their slaves. It is reported that in the late 1700s and early 1800 most of the enslaved African in North America had not converted to Christianity. This was in part because slaves felt very indifferent about Christianity. It has been found that many slaves upon discovering that baptism did not emancipate them became angry and plotted against the slave owners. Some planters claimed that their slaves had become lazy and had to be whipped in order for them to do their labor, while others spoke of slaves involved in secretly poisoning them as a means of doing bad in order to justify the good. There were other acts of insurrection that existed on the plantations as well.

It is not clearly known how many slaves accepted their new faith; what is known is that around the mid to late 1800s, after a widespread Protestant movement, enslaved and free African Americans readily converted to Christianity at Methodist and Baptist revivals. It became crystal clear to the whites that early African Americans clearly had used their cultural past to interpret Christianity when news of Denmark Vessey's rebellion of 1822 and Nat Turner's rebellion of 1831 came. Both enslaved religious African Americans used biblical passages to spark their revolt.

It was after these two major insurrections that overseers were appointed. Religious service had to be conducted in plain sight or police officers had to be present to make sure that slaves weren't plotting against their slaveholders. Records indicate that the number of African Americans outnumbered the number of Africans that were being imported into the country in the early 1800s. This meant that while there were cultural amongst the two groups (Africans and African Americans), the African Americans that had converted to Christianity were only briefly touched by the morphed and warped teachings of the racist missionaries. When these early African Americans began to convert to readily to Christianity, it was clearly because they interpreted baptism to include all sorts of freedom, as the revivals allowed them to praise God the way they desired.

During the Second Great Awakening of the late 18th and early 19th century, it is reported that an even larger numbers of early African Americans converted to Christianity because Baptist and Methodist ministers preached a plain-style message of hope and redemption, catered to the early African American styles of worship, including the call and response singing, dancing and spirit possession.

Vodu, Gris-Gris and the Louisiana Purchase

Prior to the Louisiana Territory becoming part of the union, it was a colony owned by the French and Spanish. Like most of the South, Louisiana's economy was based upon slave plantations that produced indigo, rice, cotton and sugar, but what made Louisiana unique was that it had a very prosperous city called New Orleans, which was a port town to the

Caribbean and a military patrol on the lower Mississippi River.

Slavery in Louisiana, particularly New Orleans, was uniquely different from that of the other colonies in North America because there were a number of urban slaves. The urban slaves were domesticated workers, blacksmiths, carpenters and masons that would lease themselves out in return for a portion of the earnings that they would give to their owners. The black society in Louisiana consisted of imported Africans, imported Afro-Caribbean-born slaves (particularly from St. Dominique and Cuba), Louisiana-born slaves and free people of color (*gens de coleur* –African & European mixed descendants that had rights to education and other privileges because of their European ancestry). This, along with the fact that the planters were predominantly Roman Catholic but engaged in a lot of folk-Catholicism as they bumped shoulders with local Native American cultures surrounding the Mississippi, made New Orleans fertile ground for magico-religious practices.

Unbeknownst to most, the Louisiana Purchase became possible because of a slave uprising in Saint Dominique believed to be sparked by a Vodu[12] priest named Dutty Boukman, whose last name came from his English nick name "Book man", meaning that he knew how to read. During the revolt, which later turned to a war for independence, the black general Touissant L'Ouveture was captured and sent to

---

[12] The word Vodu, which is from the Fon language ethnic group, literally means 'to serve God or the Spirit'. The word Vodu was purposely corrupted to the word Voodoo to mean black magic, curse, spell or witchcraft, in order to deter African descendants from using their religion against their slave owners.

France, but Napoleon's army was finally defeated by the guerilla war tactics of Jean-Jacques Dessalines, leading to the independence of Haiti in 1804.

Like the Anglican missionaries in the English territories, Roman Catholic missionaries sought ways of justifying slavery as well and eagerly tried to christianize Amerindians and the enslaved African descendants, while addressing the religious needs of Euro-Americans, refusing to give blacks total freedom and by not allowing them to serve or hold important positions in the church. Similar instructions were given to the enslaved, which led to several insurrections as well. The most devastating ones were the revolt of 1795 and 1811.

New Orleans is important in this study because many people believe that it is the birthplace or the source of African American magico-religious spiritual practices. The truth, according to records recovered from the colonial times, is that African descendants were involved in two distinct practices, which they labeled as voodoo and gris-gris.

Vodu, for those that don't know, is an organized religion that comes from the West Coast of Africa mainly the Ewe and Fon people. Like other major religions, Vodou has a set of organized rituals, a clergy, a theology, etc.

Gris-gris on the other hand is French for amulets, fetishes[13] and what African Americans call

---

[13] It should be noted that while Jews light candles and wear the Star of David, and Asians bow before the photos of their deceased loved ones and/or teachers. Christians eat and drink the symbolic body of Christ, wear crucifixes and have high regard for the Bible. Muslims proudly display and wear scriptures from the Koran on their homes and places of business for

mojos, luck balls, hands in the folk tradition known as hoodoo. While it is believed that all Africans had some form of folk tradition that they brought to the Americas, records indicate that the form that survived most likely came from West-Central Africa. In fact, the famed Vodou Priestess of New Orleans, who had a strong grip on the city between 1830 and 1880, distinguished herself from others by declaring herself as a priestess of an organized religion and not a mere conjure woman (a hoodoo practitioner).

The Influences of Spiritism and Spiritualism

The whole issue of slavery brought on a lot of ethical and moral questions that had to be addressed. The issue of slavery was already threatening to divide the nation through the America Civil War (1861-1865), as diseases like cholera and tropical diseases like malaria and yellow fever, which was carried and spread by mosquitoes brought unintentionally from Africa, claimed the lives of numerous people. All while scientific and technological advances were being made. With the constant thoughts of ethics, morality and science and the fear of death looming around, a new movement was born.

Hippolyte Leon Denizard Rivail, a French educator in astronomy, comparative anatomy, chemistry, mathematics, physics and physiology that wrote under the pen name Allan Kardec, inspired by three sisters (known as the Fox Sisters) and their

---

protection against the evil eye. It seems that only African derived traditions are distinctly ridiculed and considered paganistic for engaging in similar practices that others perform around the world.

experimentation with table rapping with the dead (a claim later on believed to be false), conducted various experiments about the afterlife and published his findings in his book called *The Spirits' Book*. To distinguish his scientific findings from the parlor tricks of magicians, simple table rappings done for mere entertainment and make it a refutable philosophy, Kardec called his new scientific/religious inspired philosophy Spiritism.

Now, I wondered why Kardec went through great lengths to distinguish his findings and philosophy from practices that appeared on the surface to be similar to his. So, I bought and tried to read Kardec's book, and what I found most interesting, which I didn't understand at first but understood later, was that Kardec himself was not a medium. In fact, he was quite skeptical, from what I read about the whole thing. So, Kardec asked various spiritualist mediums that were communicating with the dead or the other side questions about the afterlife. He composed a list of 1,019 questions, similarly to the way one would go about making a scientific investigation. It was based upon those answers that he published his book, which explains why he promoted Spiritism more like a scientific philosophy versus it being a religion. The answers to the Kardec's questions put a whole new twist on things, because when you know what's going to happen in the afterlife you have better idea on why and how to prepare for it, besides just following cookie cut version of religious instruction.

Types of Spirits per Allan Kardec

0. God
1. Pure Spirits
2. High Spirits
3. Wise Spirits

4. Learned Spirits
5. Caring Spirits
6. Boisterous Spirits
7. Neutral Spirits
8. Lying Spirits
9. Frivolous Spirits
10. Impure Spirits

Another interesting point worth mentioning was that Kardec learned through his work that there were ten classes of spirits that existed and they were all under God. These spirits were called pure, high, wise, learned, caring, boisterous, neutral, lying, frivolous and impure spirits. What made this even more interesting was that these ten spirit types seemed to overlap with the Supreme Mathematics, the esoteric Jewish Kabala system and the Paut Neteru as well.

Now, of course I could have taken a straight egotistical approach from here and just saw this as mere coincidence, but I instead took it as a sign that there definitely was a spirit involved in me, learning what I have learned. I seriously felt like I was led to find this information.

Spiritism, or Spiritualism as it became known in North America, took off mainly because it provided people with proof that the afterlife actually existed. It was popular amongst the elite and many intellectuals mainly because it was anti-clerical and against traditional Christianity with its beliefs that God was an Infinite Spirit.

Spiritualists, in an effort to promote science over the superstitions of religion, believed that natural law and science was key to attaining true knowledge, which could be attained by communicating with higher spirits via séances (as Kardec had done). In the interest of communicating with higher spirits for the purpose of scientific discovery, man not only became more knowledgeable about his and her human life but also a more ethical and moral human being. As a result, most spiritualists focus on more secular objectives (or the needs of an individual) versus doing something in order to go to heaven and not to hell.

Spiritism and Spiritualism spread rapidly throughout Europe and the Americas. They eventually became popular amongst the middle and lower classes as well because they seemed to verify folk beliefs. In the United States there were a number of clubs and societies dedicated to practicing spiritualism, which had contact with other societies in Europe and the Americas. It is not known how many North Americans actually participated in spiritual sessions. What is known is that the movement wasn't as successful as it could have been in Europe and Latin America because of poor planning on a national level.

So, by the time Spiritualism in North America moved to nationally organize, two other rising religious movements were already growing in popularity. This is important to note because, even though the Spiritualism movement didn't take firm root in North America, the Spiritualism beliefs and practices continued to exist in urban America and had an influence on the rising movements to come. I know this for a fact because I remember visiting a couple of Spiritist churches with my family as a child. Sometimes my mother would watch their programs on television Sunday afternoon before going back to church. I just didn't know that they were Spiritist churches. I knew that they were different because, even though they sung songs similar to the ones sung at my church, some of the things they did I found to be interestingly peculiar, like the use of altars and candles.

The Holiness and Pentecostalism Influences

Now, according to American religious history, Pentecostalism is an extension of a revival movement that first occurred around the mid to late 1700s. Many people after the Civil War were becoming more and more materialistic and less interested in their moral obligations instilled in them from organized religion. As a growing number of people throughout the country became more secular instead of spiritual, an interdenominational group called the National Camp Meeting Association for the Promotion of Holiness, consisting of people from various faiths and backgrounds, was organized in 1867 to return religious piousness back to America. This group believed that in order to return religious godliness back to America that one had to be:

1. Regenerated by grace through faith in order to achieve holiness.
2. Sanctification by grace in which one dedicates their life to God in order to be led by the Holy Spirit.

The Holiness movement appealed to both blacks and whites throughout North America, but due to the social pressures of American society, the movement, which began somewhat as an interdenominational interracial group, conformed and advocated segregation based upon race. As a result, African Americans associated with the Holiness movement left and eventually became part of another growing revivalist movement called the Pentecostal movement.

Now, growing up as a PK allowed me to see and hear a lot of things not privileged to most, because I saw how hard my father worked and could just imagine how hard the pastor of our church worked. I remember the good days of having my father around and the bad days of not having him around as well because he was spending so much time with the church. There were times the pastor and my father (as assistant pastor) would attend funerals, visit nursing homes, pick up people that didn't have transportation to church, pick up visiting ministers from the bus or train station, visit jails and prisons, visit other churches, start services at their own church, sometimes quell disputes amongst a husband and wife, and visit three or four hospitals in one day.

Unlike a lot of pastors of today that have not just one luxury car but several high price luxury cars, I could see why our pastor had a Cadillac, because it was a good road car, according to many mechanics. It was used specifically for traveling. My father didn't have a Cadillac; he and my mother had four growing boys, but he did have a good family car.

I once upon a time faulted his commitment to the church as being the reason why I left it, but I knew it wasn't, because he and my mother would make it up to my brothers and I by taking us all over the country and to Canada. To an outsider looking in and seeing all the things that they (the pastor and my father) did, all of this with no pay, it would have seemed crazy; it did convince me that I didn't want be a minister at all. This was the reason why I shrieked every time people would prophesize, "You're going to be a preacher," because in the back of my mind I was saying, "Not if I can help it".

Not understanding my father's commitment made me run from my destiny. I didn't see that my father was not committed to the church but committed to helping people, which was doing the work of God. This lack of understanding made me just shut up and observe, whenever preachers spoke amongst themselves.

One of the conversations that the preachers had all the time was about the origin of the Pentecostal Movement. When my father got around other ministers, being the assistant pastor, he would tell them what he was told by his pastor and had learned about the Holy Ghost on Azuza Street. All of the Pentecostal ministers that I have heard, seen, etc., all talked about Azuza Street. Even white ministers having no affiliation with black churches, I have seen them ask about the mysterious events that took place on Azuza Street, but strangely, growing up as child in a pastoral home, I knew nothing about that, because one of the biggest problems facing our community as a whole is passing things down to our descendants.

Again, I had to accept that I was being led to find and understand this information. So, in the 1900s, a former white Methodist minister named Charles Fox Parham established in Topeka, Kansas the Bethel Bible College and the Bible Training School in Houston, Texas in 1905. In 1906, William Joseph Seymour, a black student of Parham, inspired groups of people at an abandoned Methodist church they called the Azuza Street Mission. According to records, it was Easter season, and people from different racial groups and religious faiths were all, according to contemporary Pentecostals would call it, hit or struck with God's power, the Holy Ghost. It is said that for three days and three nights people "shouted" (danced) so much that the foundation of the old mission gave way.

The main difference between Holiness and Pentecostals, according to my research, was that the latter was inspired by the teachings of the Holiness minister Benjamin Hardin Irwin (which were initially rejected by Holiness ministers), who stated that there had to be assurance by sanctification that one has received the gift of the Holy Spirit by evidence of speaking in tongues. This was necessary in order to live a holy or Christ-like life. Other signs that one had received the gifts of the Holy Spirit or had been "baptized by fire", as it became called amongst many Pentecostals, were the abilities to heal, perform miracles, prophesize, teach and help others. Not to mention that by allowing the Holy Spirit to guide an individual they also acquired what is commonly called "fruit of the Spirit" which are patience, love, joy, peace, kindness, faithfulness, gentleness, longsuffering and self-control according to Galatians 5:22-23.

No wonder when Parham arrived at the Azuza Street revival later on in 1906, most of the black ministers and people I have heard talk about this event said that he was a racist. Others claimed that Parham simply didn't believe what was going on. According to Vinson Synan, author of *The Holiness-Pentecostal Movement in the United States*, Parham was more than just in disbelief. He was so alarmed by the event that in a sermon he denounced it as an event that apparently was taken over by 'hypnotists' and 'spiritualists'. In fact, according to Claude F. Jacobs and Andrew J. Kaslow, authors of *The Spiritual Churches of New Orleans: Origins, Beliefs and Rituals of an African-American Religion*, the Baltimore Catechism condemned spiritualism along with mesmerism or hypnotists, spirit mediums, and fortunetellers as:

"...persons who pretend to converse with the dead or with the spirits of the other world. They pretend also to give this power to others, that they may know what is going on in heaven, purgatory or hell... Another practice very dangerous to faith and morals is the use of mesmerism or hypnotism, because it is liable to sinful abuses for it deprives a person for a time of control of his reason and will and places his body and mind entirely in the power of another... Fortunetellers are imposters who, learning the past, or guessing at it, pretend to also know the future and to be able to reveal it to anyone who pays for this knowledge. They pretend also to know whatever concerns things lost or stolen, and the secret thoughts, actions or intentions of others... By believing in spells, charms, mediums, spiritists and fortunetellers we attribute to creatures the perfections of God because we expect these creatures to perform miracles, reveal hidden judgments of God, and make known His designs for the future with regard to His creatures, things that only God Himself may do".[14]

Whatever the case, William J. Seymour, according to most Pentecostals I met, especially African American and the growing number of Latin American Pentecostals, is considered the father of the Holiness-Pentecostal Movement.

The Holy Ghost or Holy Spirit to many Pentecostals is not considered to be a manifestation of

---

[14] *A Catechism of Christian Doctrine ... No. 3, Supplemented* by Rev. Thomas L. Kinkead. Benziger Brother, 1921 pg. 261-262

God but a distinct and unique personality of God according to "The Confessions of Faith of the Church of God in Christ." *The Encyclopedia of American Religions: Religious Creeds* by Melton J. Gordons. This explained to me how and why I as a teen (along with other teens) were strongly encouraged to tarry for the Holy Ghost to descend upon us, because it was believed that it would enter and change our mind and body. This also explained the reason why my parents (especially my mother) would make my brothers and I, when we were 'acting out' (bad) on Sunday afternoon, go and sit on the front pews in the church on Sunday night. I recall not only my brothers and I sitting there but occasionally also other children sitting there as well because of their behavior, and being teased for it. This was because, according to my parents and apparently others as well, there are various spirits, devils or demons that existed in us and it is through the Holy Ghost that they (the arguing devil, disrespectful devils, etc.) are going to be driven out of our body. The argumentative and quarrelsome spirit that entered my brothers and I on Sunday afternoon would soon be driven out later on in Sunday evening service when made to sit on the front pew. When people testified about overcoming illness, they were actually giving verbal testimony that the Holy Ghost had driven out of their mind and body a disease causing spirit, a cancer demon, and so on.

This was very important for me to know for several reasons. The first reason it was important for me to know was that it indicated that even though some Southern white missionaries tried to push a morphed version of Christianity to justify slavery, the core Afro-American spirituality, for the most part (before the acceptance of Islam, before the Cultural Movement of the late 1960s and early 1970s inspiring conversion to the Afro-Caribbean – mainly Haitian Vodun, Afro-Cuban Santeria, Palo Mayombe; and African religions Ife and Vodun), especially in regards to my own ancestry, was composed primarily of African mysticism and theology, consisting largely of Kongo-Angolan roots with small elements of the Vodu religion from West Africa, that through religious syncretism blended with Euro-American Protestant Christianity particularly – Methodist, Baptist, Spiritualism, Holiness and Pentecostalism – in order to become what John Thornton[15] calls it in his book *Africa and Africans in the Making of the Atlantic World*, 1400-1800 (Studies in Comparative World History) a "...new Afro-Atlantic religion".

W.J. Hollenweger says it best in *The Pentecostals: The Charismatic Movement in the Churches*, that:

"...the Pentecostal pastor, the baptism of the Spirit is indispensable equipment for the exercise of his calling. In terms of phenomenology of religion, a Pentecostal pastor might be described as a modern **'shaman'**. Through the baptism of the Spirit he learns to use levels of his soul and his body hitherto unknown to him, as sense organs with which to apprehend a psychological climate, a group dynamic situation." (Emphasis mine, because there was that word shaman again).

The second reason why this was important for me to know was that while I was away my mother had been diagnosed with having a cancerous tumor in her

---

[15] *Africa and Africans in the Making of the Atlantic World*, 1400-1800 by John Thorton (pg 235).

body. It wasn't until I moved to Kansas that I learned about her bout and how she defeated it through medication, diet but most importantly through prayer.

Religious Syncretism in North America

While it is often assumed and believed that African Americans, being the farthest removed from Africa, lost all of their African-ness and became docile, lost sheep in the belly of North America, this tidbit of history convinced me that the ancestors of African Americans fought and resisted slavery just like other Africans did throughout the Afro-Diaspora. Early African Americans resisted slavery every possible way they knew how, even by using the same Bible, which some racist whites tried to use against them, as a tool of empowerment.

African American spirituality is uniquely different from Euro-American spirituality because African Americans were unable to preserve more of their original culture as their kin had done in the Caribbean and Latin America. This was because according to Melville J. Herskovits, author of *The Myth of the Negro Past,* whites, generally speaking, outnumbered blacks in the American South. This, along with the fact that besides the Gullah Island, parts of Louisiana and a few other communities that existed in Florida, there weren't a lot of retreats where slaves could escape and develop a stable community without interference from whites. The only place where Africans and early African Americans could retreat, find refuge and eventually escape white interference was in the open fields and later the church, which thus became a tool of empowerment, which was jokingly recognized in one of my favorite musical comedies, John Landis' 1980 film *The Blues*

Brothers.

Given only the Apostles Creed, Ten Commandments, Lord's Prayer and baptism in order to justify and maintain slavery allowed for early African Americans to interpret this new Protestant religion per their cultural perspective. For te Africans whose religious beliefs consisted of a pantheon of divinities, similar to the martyrs and saints in Roman Catholicism, religious thought did not survive intact, but it didn't go away either. For those Africans that believed in the Oneness of God already, such as those from the Kongo-Angolan region, it did survive and the Kongo-Angolan Supreme Being, Nzambi Mpugu, became the African American God. This religious syncretism occurred in part because, according to Michael A. Gomez, author of *Exchanging Our Country Marks: The Transformation of African Identities in the Colonial and Antebellum South,* the largest percentage of Africans brought to the Americas[16] were from the Kongo-Angolan region. This, along with the fact that the Kongo-Angolan people were exposed to an untainted and unmolested form of Christianity (one that didn't try to justify slavery via the Hamitic curse) already or were at least familiar with Christianity prior to being brought to the Americas, not to mention that their traditional religious beliefs shared many similarities with Christianity in the first place, which is why they openly converted to the new faith prior to the Transatlantic Slave Trade, made fertile ground for African American spirituality to flourish and prosper.

---

[16] Gomez, Michael A. *Exchanging Our Country Marks: The Transformation of African Identities in the Colonial and Antebellum South* page 29. The University of North Carolina Press, 1998.

Proof that this religious syncretism or the Kongo-Angolan religious ideology occurred can be seen throughout the African American experience. When compared to early Euro-American beliefs about God, we see that God is the Supreme Being that created everything but rests in heaven. God, in the early Euro-American sense, although considered the cause of creation, which es acknowledged and mentioned in most of their important mottos, proceedings and other slogans such as *In God We Trust*, the *E Pluribus Unum* (from Many, One), etc., is a solemn Deity distant from His creation, so much so that to many early Euro-Americans it could not be fathomed that there was a mixing of races. God, to early Euro-Americans, was a segregationist and basically created what Charles Darwin would later define as his theory of evolution or survival of the fittest theory. Early Euro-Americans and Europeans alike were perplexed by their logic, which is why it was often thought that "God is Dead", a phrase later coined by the German philosopher Friedrich Nietzsche in *The Gay Science,* 1882. Simply because how would a just God create immoral things or allow immorality to run amuck? These same sentiments are still repeated by many so-called atheists, who will ask why would God allow slavery and other injustices to occur. The answer, to them, is that God simply does not exist.

This explains from a psycho-religious perspective why racist whites desperately tried to create a society that dominated the lives of others using religion[17]. It was because their concept of God influenced their social attitude and behavior into

---

[17] *Slave Religion: The Invisible Institution in the Antebellum South* by Albert Raboteau (Oxford University Press, 1978) pg 103

dominating others. Examples of this can be seen from their perversion of the Bible to justify slavery, to the racist Jim Crow codes of conduct and laws. Their whole purpose was to justify their authority and control using their concepts of their dominating God as a model. Historically, this concept of God has also led early Euro-Americans (and other Westerners) to engage in all sorts of inhumane treatment of other people including the Native Americans, African Americans, Pacific Islanders, Latin Americans, etc.

I remembered from reading Homer's *Illiad* and the *Odyssey*, this was the same relationship that the mortals had with the Greek gods. In Greek mythology the most important god was the lightning throwing Zeus. Zeus basically sat upon his throne in Mt. Olympus and threatened the other gods and human beings alike. He was constantly having sex with other gods and with mortals, which resulted in a lot of great epic adventures. In my opinion, it is this Hellenistic approach that many Westerners adhere to and even though they have changed the name of the Deity. This view of God as being a distant Being that threatens to strike one down with lightning if angered is the image most have.

The same, I was learning, cannot be said about the early African American concepts of God. An analysis of the African American concept of God is that God is the Supreme Being, the creator of the heavens and the earth with a distinct difference from the early Euro-American perspective of God, a humane and personal God. That is in the sense that the God of African Americans takes an active interest in all of their affairs, so much so that many African Americans believe that when they fail or have problems it is because they have turned their back on their loving and living God thus causing them to lose God's merciful grace like the biblical Israelites. Many of these concepts can be heard today in African American pulpits and gospel music. It is not uncommon to hear African American pray or sing for God not to pass them by or for God to lead, walk or stand by them during the turbulent times of life. Like their Kongo-Angolan ancestors, early African American men and women personified God in order for him and her to see the divinity within them so that they could overcome the various obstacles and troubles they faced in North America.

Unlike the European and early Euro-American viewpoint where it could be entertained that God does not exist because of something that cannot be logically understood, Africans and early African Americans when they cannot understand God simply put it off and accept that God is a mystery. Early African Americans and most African Americans today don't declare that God doesn't exist. They fault their logic or understanding as being incorrect about God and look for alternative ways of supporting their paradigm in an effort to understand God. This is why biblical stories, legends and testimonies are so important and relevant in many African American churches and spiritual experiences, because it attests to the mystery of God. This is why many early African Americans could identify with the biblical Children of Israel and with the biblical Moses on Mt. Sinai that to see God's hind parts is mesmerizing and mystical.

It was at that moment I recalled from my research and personal experience numerous examples of how God speaks, inspires or reveals some sort of message to create positive change in the lives of African Americans. Of course, as already mentioned, the various slave revolts that took place in this country were believed to be religiously or divinely inspired. There were other examples that came to mind of this unique concept of God as well.

For instance, I remember reading that various people were taught how to conjure by God. One informant who went by the name Seven Sisters, an Alabamian named Ida Carter[18], claimed that it was the spirit of God who taught her how to *conjure*[19] –that is, to magically create change, improve luck, etc. A former slave from Texas, William Adams, also claimed in an interview that God showed him how to use his powers through acts of revelation[20]. What made Adam's interview even more interesting, I remembered, was that he claimed that it was because "the confidence of southern whites in their own racial superiority blinded them to a sophisticated and spiritually empowered body of knowledge claimed by African Americans"[21].

This is very interesting to note because, as stated before, it is believed that conjure (hoodoo/rootwork) spread or was commercialized by Marie Levau or the Marie Levaus (her daughters assuming the same name). While the Leveaus may have had something to do with conjure, it was Vodou that she mainly practiced. This means that if she had

---

[18] *Conjure in African American Society* by Jeffrey E. Anderson pg. 36

[19] Ibid pg. 36

[20] *Working Cures: Healing, Health, and Power on Southern Slave Plantations* by Sharla M. Fett (University of North Carolina, 2002) pg. 52.

[21] Ibid pg. 52

a hand in spreading conjure it was able to take firm root because Kongo-Angolan syncretism was already firmly established throughout North America. This is why to this day many African Americans staunchly continue to practice an Afro-Protestant form of folk tradition that does not involve worshipping the saints, orishás, or loas of the Afro-Caribbean traditions.

Of course Dr. Martin L. King Jr. and his attempts to create a color-blind society with full equality with whites also appeared to be divinely inspired. Many of King's and other civil rights activists' speeches all seemed to be biblically inspired and reflect a personal relationship with God. Many of the Civil Rights leaders also appeared to take on the role of being a modern-day Moses for their people leading them out of an oppressed situation. This I saw by observing how many black preachers, when preparing to deliver a sermon, ask what is it that God wants to say. The Bible is turned into a tool of divination in order to perceive the Will of God, which is called bibliomancy. This is the reason why many African Americans hold it in a great regards and believe on passing older and used versions to their descendants, like other sacred objects are passed on to others amongst Kongo-Angolan practitioners[22] in the Afro-Diaspora. The Bible is held in such high regard that many will not allow it to touch the floor and even cover it up when not in use (just like I have observed charms in various Afro-Diaspora traditions covered up).

There were other examples of this unique

---

[22] In Palo Mayombe sacred charms are passed on to descendants or other people so that charm can continue to exist according to Ms. B.

concept of God that came to me as well. I began to remember that many African Americans churches used blessed olive oil for protection, healing and blessings because of the symbolism it held with the blood used to protect the first-born in Egypt. Some other African Americans congregations use blessed water. Now, from an outsider's perspective looking in, emphasis would be placed on the oil and the water as being the source of healing, blessing, etc. but this is grossly incorrect. I remember that when I asked my father about this practice he told me, "The blessing, healing and protection were not in the oil or water. The blessing, healing and protection came from God and the oil and water are basically tools"[23]. Some people he told me need visual aide to help them have faith in God. The symbolism is that the oil becomes the precious blood of the lamb used to save the firstborn; it, like blessed water, later becomes the blood of Jesus.

What made this practice and my father's explanation even more interesting was that it was very similar to the ancient Kongo-Angolan sacred medicine or *minkisi* tradition as well. In the Old Kongo-Angolan region the color white symbolizes the ancestors, purity, knowledge, etc., which was often times symbolized by various whites objects like white chickens. White chickens were therefore sacrificed in order to release its power from the "white realm"[24]. Kongo-Angolan descendants in African American churches apparently made the connection between the sacrificial blood of a white chicken and that of the

---

[23] This was similar to what my Afro-Cuban friend Raúl was struggling with.

[24] See *Flash of the Spirit: African & Afro-American Art & Philosophy* by Robert Farris Thompson, page 134-135.

sacrificial lamb, which was used according to Christian lore to spare the first born of ancient Hebrews, to the blessed olive oil. Blessed olive oil and blessed water became, based upon my understanding, the new blood of a white chicken. Blessed olive oil and blessed water are used, based upon the number of churches that I have visited (both black and white), mostly by African Americans to purify, heal, protect, exorcise evil, etc., in other words for its "whiteness".

All of these examples that were being brought to my attention helped me to realize that African American spirituality was uniquely an African American creation, developed to help early African Americans and their descendants to resist and survive slavery. This made me realize that my problem was not with the church per se but made me wonder why I really left the church.

Why I Left the Church

That's when it hit me what one of my problems was. I remembered that I liked certain things about the church but there were a lot of things that I didn't like that were going on. If the reader will recall, I attended one of the largest churches in Michigan and being a PK allowed me to see things not privileged to others. I remembered that I wanted the Holy Ghost to deal with the rising crack epidemic that had hit urban communities around the United States. I remembered that people left and right were either dying from use of crack cocaine or crack related deaths such as homicides, homelessness, and so on, not to mention the rising AIDS epidemic that had come on the scene. I remember times were horrible back then and many of the guys my age simply could not find any alternative. The pressure to use drugs was extremely high and the pressure to sell drugs was even higher during those hard times amidst a time where unemployment was on a rise.

I remembered that I tarried for the Holy Ghost to save me from the crack epidemic. I remembered, while trying to make sense of things in order to apply them to my young and impressionable life, I asked why it was a sin to dance, to drink alcohol, etc. when clearly people did it during biblical times. I went so far as to ask those that knew more than me what the definition of a sin was. This was important for me to know because, if there was no accurate guidelines or definition of what truly is a sin, then people could pick and choose per their likes and dislikes what they believe and considered to be a sin. I understood at an early age, to some extent, why there was so much confusion in the world of Christianity in regards to moral living. It was the same reason why I was led to find the 42 Declarations of Maa, which as stated before is believed to be the inspiration behind the Ten Commandments.

I am alive today because something saved me but was it the Holy Ghost, was it God's grace and mercy, was it God? That's all a mystery to me. I know what I had to do to survive but it is all a mystery, and I really don't know because I don't remember anyone teaching me what it was. What I do remember, it seems, is that, during the turn of events, it seemed like many of the larger churches were involved in a big religious cockfight of seeing whose doctrine was right or wrong. Was it Catholic, Methodist, Baptist, Pentecostal, Presbyterian, etc. doctrine that was the truth that will set us free? Was it the Holy Ghost, the Trinity, Jesus only, Jesus who is God, God who is Jesus or Jehovah, Jehovah who is God, God, El-

Shaddai, etc. that was right or wrong? I didn't know who was right or wrong, what I do know is that it seemed like the verification of whose doctrine was more right was not based upon vote but upon which denomination had the largest churches or the most membership and whose pastor had the best looking automobiles. That being said, I won't even speak about how many churches argued over the role women should play, which added another dimension to this big theological cockfight amongst men. As well as what was accepted and what was not expected as being a member of these churches.

During those times, I and a lot of guys my age, in order to escape the violent and horrific pressure put up on us daily by the news media, which reminded to us that many of us were going to die or be killed before we turned 18, 21 or 25, and in order to continue to do the right thing, had to learn from the first rappers of hip-hop, many of whom I later discovered were Five Percenters or in the Nation of Islam and/or some other smaller groups of similar interests. We turned to these rappers and these Afrocentric groups because they seemed to be the only ones that cared about what was going on in our community. At the time, it just really seemed like most churches abandoned us for personal gain.

Simply put, the social ills of the times weren't talked about or addressed in the pulpit as they were before (during the 1950s and early 1970s according to documentaries), because, I think, that would have deterred the membership. Instead, most of the preachers simply sermonized on being "saved" and never taught how to keep or stay "saved". The church, it seemed to me as a teen, simply moved from the business of saving souls to big business for souls.

Instead of being places of worship that helped the community, as it had done in the past through various hardships, many churches, it seemed, simply became tax-exempt Sunday businesses for entertainment[25].

It was becoming clear that the reason I left the church was that maybe I thought we lost our cultural practices. After being exposed to various spiritual traditions practiced throughout the Afro-Diaspora, I saw our cultural practices. They were the same or at least similar. They just had a different name. For instance, even though I couldn't explain it, I saw Shango doing the same thunderous, stomping dancing at church. The church people just didn't call him Shango. They simply said that it was the Spirit of God or the Holy Ghost. History revealed to me that we didn't lose our cultural practices either. This is what my ancestors wanted me to see!

What we lost was the context, theology and understanding of our cultural practices. As a result, with no clear purpose in mind, people were abandoning the cultural ways because they appeared as suppositious exercises in lieu of the dominant society. The loss of cultural traditions is what leads to deviant actions and deviant behaviors. This was the reason why I wasn't taught how to pray. This is why I kept asking and trying to get an accurate definition of what truly is a sin. It was the same reason why I believe a lot of the other church traditions weren't

---

[25] This explained why I liked the old gospel (and old school music), because many of the songwriters and singers were actually going through things and not just entertaining and performing, as many artists do today. The old gospel hymns and songs were meant to help people overcome struggle, whereas many of the songs of today are meant to make the artist money and make people feel good.

passed down and eventually many churches stopped focusing upon social ills and upon money.

I could see that the lack of cultural tradition is what led me to make dietary changes based upon incorrect beliefs and ideas. This also explained why I was attracted to Bertha. It was because of the whole romanticized idea of what I thought was "African". It was that warm casting "African glow" that made me fall in love with the form and idea of Africa but not understand the African concepts. Part of me understood that this was a problem, which was the reason why it didn't feel right wearing African garb, while at the same time becoming quite fond of Ms. B and Papá Raúl because of the life that they lived, which appeared to be authentic African even though it didn't fit the stereotype of what it meant to be an "African spiritual practitioner".

There was an even greater truth I was beginning to see as a result of not having a true understanding of our cultural practices and traditions. Since I didn't understand the concepts, everything that appeared to be "African" to me was looked upon as being something mysterious, powerful and magical. This meant that I expected, for some strange reason, that when I did something that was "African" it would miraculously fix whatever problem I had. For instance, the reason I changed my diet in the past was that it was believed that this is how it was done in Africa. It was almost as if I expected that if I did what was "African" that all my problems would go away. This explains why I wanted to get the Holy Ghost as a teenager. It was to make the crack epidemic magically disappear.

Clearly, there was a lot of confusion and

misunderstanding in my life (especially on my part). Fortunately, it took a series of hard knocks for me to learn that nothing happens magically or at least not without physical effort. For instance, in order to be a successful physician you have to follow the same steps that other physicians have taken. There's no magical pill, magical rite, spiritual power, etc. around it. The same can be said about if you want to be a millionaire. You need to map out a plan based upon what other millionaires have done and follow your plan.

It was this understanding that made me realize that I did map out a plan in regards to certain goals that I wanted to achieve and a way was made possible. I remember way back when, that the first time I crossed the finished line first it was because I imagined it and it happened. I remembered that I had no doubt in my mind that I would graduate from high school, I saw it and I did. I remembered in my first years of college, I refused to be a college drop out statistic so I followed a plan and did what I accomplished to do. I remembered after I put together a plan not to be a college dropout in the beginning how I got a medium high "B" grade point average, which I never had even when I was in high school.

Then I began to notice that, when things went down hill and became chaotic, ways opened up based upon the choices I made. Not only that: when Bertha and I broke up, I was given a way out, I noticed. At the same time, when I stated what I wanted in a woman, my wife suddenly appeared in my life. When I finished school and got my degree, a way was opened. I never thought about until now but they were all miracles.

There apparently was something definitely odd about this that I couldn't explain. Was it God? I didn't know because I didn't have the type of relationship that I heard people had with God. I wasn't sure if God was acting in my life still, even though I was uncertain in my beliefs. What I do know is that there were a number of miracles that definitely took place in my life. These miracles were proof that I stumbled upon something that made these miracles occur in my life. I didn't make these miracles occur. However, I could see that when my beliefs were combined with certain practices that triggered something or some force to make miracles in my life occur. This is what I should have been trying to understand and what was lost. It was the knowledge of how to connect to this force that was lost as a result of not having knowledge and understanding of our cultural traditions. *But why was Kamit so important?*

Why Ancient Kamit?

I knew that it was my beliefs about the Kamitic people that led me to read more about this ancient African culture, but it was a voice that inspired me to learn and study the Kamitic way. I knew that this voice that spoke to me and inspired me to take this course of action wasn't me but what or who it was, I wasn't sure. I had learned from my experience in salesmanship and from the car accident that I had, that what we believe and think affects our physical reality and also inspires our actions and behaviors, but this made me wonder why and how it related to this entire Kamitic experience. All of this prompted me to investigate and explore again the mysteries of the mind.

I had learned, based upon my experience in salesmanship, that the mind consisted of two parts, commonly called the conscious and the unconscious parts of our being. The conscious mind is the part of our being that we use to make choices and decisions. It corresponds to our rational thoughts and learns from direct experiences.

The unconscious part of our being is the storehouse of all of our learning experiences and it is composed of two parts, known as the subconscious mind and the unconscious mind. The difference between the two is that our subconscious mind corresponds to our personal beliefs and experiences. Everything that we have learned or memorized and experienced (the good, the bad and the ugly) from birth to the present is stored in our subconscious mind, which influences our actions and behaviors.

The unconscious mind, also called the super conscious or the collective unconscious, is what is commonly referred to as the Universal Mind or God, because it is the deeper part of our being that wisely controls all of the autonomous functions of our body that don't require our conscious input, such as the digestion of our food, the assimilation of blood cells, generating hormones, etc. Since this part of our being wisely controls our bodily functions without fail and it does the same with all of the other things that exist, it is believed to be very complex, which has led to it also being called the higher mind.

Most psychologists believed that when we don't engage in conscious thinking and, for instance, we fall asleep with a problem on our mind, the solution to that problem comes from our unconscious mind, which filters through to our subconscious that inspires our conscious actions and behaviors. I knew that part of this was true because I remember one time I firmly stated that I wanted around $3000 and several months later I was laid off from my job and received roughly

$3000 in severance pay. So, there was no denying to me that what I believe and think affects my physical reality, which also meant my words have to be cautiously chosen. I just didn't know how this all related to me studying the Kamitic mysteries. Then, it happened. One day, out of nowhere, I got deathly ill.

Now, I thought it was because I was stressed due to reading and studying spiritual matters, after putting in around 50 to 60 hours a week at my job, and having just about every other day clashes with my coworkers. Along with the fact that the seasons were changing in this dry-butt region that I was in, so I thought that it was just that I was having an allergy or sinus reaction. Then it became hard for me to walk and go up stairs, because my knee joints had hurt. Then I suddenly lost 50lbs. in a span of just a few months. When I went to the doctor, after several blood tests, they found that my thyroid was hyperactive and producing too much hormones. I was placed on medicine to see if it would regulate it, but I continued to get progressively worse.

When my wife took my temperature and saw that it was 104 degrees, she rushed me to the emergency, where they found that I had a very rare reaction to the medication that I was placed on, which caused me to have fluid in my lungs and around my heart and a viral infection. Apparently the fluid had been there for some time, at least long enough to almost shut down my left lung. It was discovered that I had pneumonia and an excessive amount of fluid around my heart and lungs, which if it weren't caught in time would have led to my death.

As I lay of the hospital gurney listening to the aches and moans of other patients throughout the night, contemplating on how I came very close to actually dying, I was tired of trying to figure out things. I had various thoughts and ideas come to me suggesting that I should just quit, give up and die. These thoughts were not my own. They were clearly negative ideas and thoughts that were coming to me because I was in the hospital. Just then I remembered that Papá Raúl had once told me that hospitals are full of bad luck. That's when I began to realize that a lot of the problems I had, I had because I was trying to figure out things that could not be fully explained.

As African American males growing up in North America in an Apostolic Pentecostal home, we weren't taught to believe in things like luck: we were encouraged to believe in things that we could physically see. But it was becoming quite clear that a lot of the things that my family did were to improve one's luck, such as cleaning on Saturday, anointing one and objects with blessed olive oil, etc. We, like many I imagined, practiced our cultural traditions on the down low away from prying, misunderstanding American eyes, because we didn't know the origin of certain practices. I knew this now, but it still didn't register for some reason. I felt that I was caught in the middle, because part of me couldn't accept and believe in these so-called spiritual things but another part of me accepted them as being true. The part that accepted these things as being real also was the part that pulled out of 'top hat' magical practices from nowhere, like the red pepper mixture to sprinkle around my wife's house for protection before we were married.

I was tired of fighting. I was tired of trying to figure things out. I was tired of trying to give a rational explanation to everything. I couldn't do it anymore, because this quest to prove that certain things exist was tearing me up. Lying on the gurney in the hospital listening to people cry out to Death to end their misery made me realize that some things I am not going to be able to fully comprehend. There just aren't enough words to accurately explain the experience. I realized that hospitals were bad luck because they were full of despair, depression, and thoughts of doom and gloom. It dawned on me that this is what Papá Raúl called negative spirits. They are forces or energies that move around us.

As the negative ideas, thoughts and images surrounded me, to block out this negative force, I turned on the television with the remote and flipped past the depressing news, the infomercials of impossible dreams fulfilled, the miracle pills with their 1,001 side effects, past the tale-evangelists, the thrillers and other violent prone programming, to the channels that would allow me my mind to think positive, hopeful, joyful and peaceful thoughts: the cooking shows, traveling shows and cartoons.

With my mind now in a somewhat peaceful state, I admitted that I was tired of reading and studying. I just wanted to know what I needed to do and move on with my life. I was tired of trying to figure things out. I was tired of fighting for something that seemed like it should've been given to me already. I was tired of putting up a good fight because I had gone as far as I could go. My external resources were completely exhausted. I had no choice but to surrender.

At that moment a voice spoke and asked, "How can you prove that I exist?" I briefly thought about the question and admitted it can't be done. "EXACTLY!" I heard. That's right, you can't prove that God exists because God is unimaginable, indescribable, unidentifiable, and it is hard to prove that some "thing" exists that you can't see, hear, smell, taste or touch.

"How do you know that I exist?"

Again, I thought about the question and admitted that I guess you just know. The Spirit spoke and said, "Experience. You have to experience Me and it is only through experience that you know that I exist."

That's when it suddenly dawned on me that it is all about having "FAITH". Faith, this Spirit showed me, is what gives one the ability to do the impossible but, as they say in the church, I was reminded, "we walk by faith, not by sight," meaning that I wasn't going to understand everything and that there is no rational explanation for everything that exists. That a lot of times we are not going to understand how things worked out. I was reminded of my experience in Pennsylvania and Florida, that even though it was hard times I am alive today. It was because God has the last say and God made a way for things to open up. The only way I could understand it was through experience, not by sight.

Then the Spirit told me that what I was trying to do was not to have blind faith. Blind faith is the strong belief that something is going take place even though there is no support or experience to back it up. It is blind faith that has led thousands of people to commit heinous acts all in the so-called name of God. It is blind faith that has led a number of people to even commit suicide, all in the belief of a second coming, and so on. Blind faith is what leads religious cults and it doesn't matter what an individual reads, if they have blind faith they can twist any holy book, which is the reason I (and a number of other people I knew) didn't trust the Bible, because it was blind faith that tried to justify slavery. Again, the Spirit told me that this is why I spent so much time reading, studying and trying to find a rational explanation behind everything. It was necessary for me to do that in the past, which is why I was inspired to meet Fred and learn about the Five Percent philosophy, but the time had come for me to learn how to trust my intuition now. The image of the right Eye of Ra came to mind, indicating that I learned what I needed to know and it was time for me to trust my intuition now. It was time for me to learn how to walk by faith.

In order to walk by faith, the Spirit told me that I need to first understand that it would never give us something that we aren't properly prepared for. God is not cruel. God wouldn't give a loaded weapon to a child. I had heard this before that God doesn't give you something that you can't bear, but it didn't make sense. Then, almost immediately after telling me this, the image of the Tree of Life and the whole story of Adam and Eve came to mind.

Could it be that the reason it was a sin for Adam and Eve to eat from the Tree of Life, is that they weren't ready?

Is it possible that Adam and Eve did jump the gun and tried to learn things their own way. Their sin was that they didn't trust that God would introduce it (the Tree of Life) to them slowly and surely[26]. In other words, Adam and Eve didn't believe that God would provide for them. I saw that it was like learning how to run before learning how to crawl or learning how to do advance calculus before learning how to do simple addition. God, I was shown, doesn't do things backwards like that and this is the premise of blind faith, which is out of alignment with God's plan.

I was shown that this is the real reason why God doesn't sanction the use of fortunetelling devices but allowed the ancient Hebrews to use divination devices. The difference between the two is that fortunetelling devices "foretell the future" but give no insight on how to prepare or make the necessary changes to improve one's life. This is the reason why I scoffed at prophecies that I was supposed to be a preacher, because, as the Spirit was revealing to me, the prophecy that was given was similar to having my fortune told. The individual was just seeing into my future (actually one possibility), but they weren't giving me a road map to follow to be a preacher. Just like when I was held up at gunpoint, the psychic reading "that a man is going to ask me to do something but, don't do it" didn't give me any detailed instructions on what man, who the man was, etc. The instructions were very vague, which could have cost me my life and life of others. Prophecies and psychic readings like this are like seeing one piece of the whole and not the whole picture. When one acts upon them, they can be disastrous.

---

[26] It was the devil as the serpent that inspired Adam and Eve to eat of the forbidden fruit, which is also an allusion about the emotional part of our being.

Divination devices, on the other hand, "give insight into God's will". By following a divination device, one's life is improved by the choices that they make, thus increasing one's faith in God and not in man and woman's abilities. Then it came to me that when preachers picked a verse to sermonize from they didn't just arbitrarily pick a subject. The subject came from the Spirit, because they learned how to use the Bible as a divination tool. This, I was told, was the reason why there was such high regard for the Bible in the old days. It is because those that understood how to use the Bible knew that the Bible was simply proof that what God has done for others, God can surely do you. This is what made the Bible a common divination tool amongst a number of African Americans.

It was becoming clear that there are two ways to accomplish an objective, the wrong way and the right way. The wrong way will always be fast, short and simple but in the end it will have a host of problems associated with it. The right way may be slow, long and arduous but in the end it will always pay off because it is done in a particular order. God does things the right way. Everything that God shows us is what we need in order to fulfill a task. Everything that we will experience, I was beginning to understand, is like a piece in a giant puzzle that only God knows and can see on the whole. This is why it is incorrect to judge others, because only God knows where that individual comes from, had to go through, is going through and experiencing, because God is omniscient – All Knowing. This revelation made me truly realize that me meeting Ms. B, Papá Raúl, Iya, Z and my wife was not by coincidence but all part of God's plan. The insight given to me from Iya was truly coming from God because she listed details about my past, present and future, which only God would have known.

Again, I was told that I would not have seen or learned about this without having faith in God, because faith in God is the belief that God will provide and make a way. Faith in God is not about having blind faith. I was beginning to understand that God doesn't put us in situations that we can't handle. God doesn't put us in predicaments that we aren't properly prepared for. God doesn't tell us to go work on a task knowing that we don't have any knowledge of it. God doesn't tell us to go and be a leader if we never learned how to follow. God doesn't tell us to do advanced calculus, if we don't know our numbers or how to do basic arithmetic. God doesn't put us in situations that we aren't comfortable with or lack confidence. God, I was assured, doesn't deal with blind faith.

When I thought about this, I almost became angry again at Bertha, because it was clear that she manipulated me for her own selfish purpose. Then it came to me: had I not undergone the experience, I would not have learned what I know now. In other words, she was just another piece in the puzzle that helped me to develop. It was revealed to me that she didn't know any better. She had learned how to do readings incorrectly and had definitely didn't learn the correct way to give counsel. I didn't know if she had glossed over a lot of the teachings and writings that she was given or not. What I was certain of was that what she had taught me didn't work. I couldn't fault her, evidently, because she was only teaching me what she had learned.

But it was clear that what I had learned about the Kamitic divinities and several other concepts was wrong. It was either because she most likely didn't understand the teacher that taught her, or I didn't understand her, or vice versa. It was a problem that often exists between teacher and student, I found, where concepts aren't properly explained and understood. It was because of this realization that I chose to forgive her, but it didn't change the situation. **I had to purge my entire system of incorrect and faulty teachings**, so I asked the Spirit, without knowledge of divination, how could one know when they are following God or some cult, incorrect teacher, etc. The Spirit showed me that before the Bible was written, the pious had another form of divination, which was intervention through the spirits.

I was shown that just like God cannot be understood because God is an Infinite Spirit that cannot be touched, smelled, tasted, seen or heard but has to be experienced, the same applies to the spirits or angels, which are also spiritual beings. The reason spirits exist, God revealed to me, is that they also help to provide us with insight into God's will. Spirits, when properly understood, are like part of a divination tool that helps us to prepare for events to come. This is the reason why all throughout the Bible, when the spirits and later angels spoke, they gave warnings and helped the biblical characters to make choices and decisions affecting their future. The instructions that these spiritual entities gave to biblical characters weren't based upon blind faith. Remembering that faith is the ability to do the impossible, when the spirits or angels gave the biblical characters instructions on how to do something, it was to accomplish a miraculous feat that produced physical results, thus increasing one's faith that God will provide.

I was reminded that from Abraham to Joseph and Mary, all the spirits or angels in the Bible gave spiritual instruction that was supported with physical proof, verifying that God is the source and controller of everything. For instance, when Joseph and Mary were told that they were going to give birth to Jesus, they were provided for by the wise men and shown that King Herod was going to come after them, so they needed to flee into Egypt. Now, I didn't focus on if the story was true or not; it was the spiritual truths of the story that were all of a sudden making sense to me. This, I understood, is how our leaders in the past (Gabriel Prosser, Nat Turner, Elijah Muhummad, Malcolm X, Martin L. King, Haile Selassie, etc.) were able to take the Bible and use it as a tool for liberation against oppression.

This clarification led me to make another important discovery, which is that it was the spirits of Martin L. King Jr. and Malcolm X that helped me when I was younger. I quickly came to the understanding that I didn't know what the heck I was thinking in the past. I wasn't sure what my thoughts of spirits were. I am not sure if I was influenced by all of the science fiction and horror movies I had watched or what. Whatever it was, I didn't see spirits as being actual energies that existed. Again, even though in theory I heard and knew that energy cannot be created or destroyed, in practice the dots were not connecting. When the dots began to connect, the understanding that spirits are energies that assist us by inspiring us made perfect sense.

Still, part of me wondered if the spirits were once real people or not. The legendary biblical Enoch was once, according to legend, a human before he became a divinity, according to Genesis 5:22-24. What was interesting about this chapter, I discovered, was that those that came before Enoch were said to have died but not Enoch, who instead was taken by God. There is nothing else mentioned about Enoch until the

New Testament: Hebrew 11:5 indicates that it was because of Enoch's faith that God took him up into heaven. I remembered reading how Enoch all of a sudden was said to have ascended to heaven a few times, until finally he was transformed into the fiery angel Metatron. The Ausar (Osiris), in the Kamitic tradition, is believed to be King Menes (or Narmer), the first ruler of Kamit, according to history, that united the kingdom, who was later deified. But the Spirit revealed to me that this was all irrelevant, because none of this was helping me to increase my faith in God.

I was taking the wrong approach or going about the doing things the wrong way, I was beginning to understand. The right way was for me to accept and have faith in God; through God I would find all the answers I needed. When I changed my perspective and started believing in God, suddenly I knew as I lay upon the gurney that I really was not going to die. I couldn't explain why I knew; I just knew that I was not going to die, which gave me a sense of inner peace.

As I relaxed into this unexplainable peace, I was reminded again of a conversation I had with Papá Raúl about various types of spirits that exist around us. I remember Papá Raúl said that he had ancestors, the orishás, and then there was the devil. Understanding that these were spirits or energies that inspire us led me to discover that the spirits surrounding me were my aakhu (ancestor spirits some which are known and others unknown), netcharu (guardian angels/spirits) and aapepu (malicious, misguided malevolent spirits). These spirits, I understood, didn't just appear to us before we die, but are always surrounding us and helping us, because it is their job. There was no book that was going to accurately define who these spirits were. The only way I could learn from them was by "trying the spirit". This is the only way to know if the spirit is of God and if the spirit is of God, it will not glorify man but God.

Next I was told that the reason why I was inspired to read and study the Kamitic tradition is that I had witnessed our families deteriorating due to social ills. I had seen the destruction due to social ills and wanted to do something about them, so I was brought here to help restore the old ways that had been lost. The old ways are not a system or religion but our cultural ways, because our ancestors never made a distinction between spiritual and secular living. This is what Iya was referring to as a shaman and what those in the church were calling a preacher. This cultural tradition, I was shown, originated in Kamit, which is why I was instructed to read, study and learn about Kamit.

**Aakhut: The Right Eye of RA
(Solar Eye)** [27]

Upon receipt of this information, I could see the pieces of the puzzle starting to come together. I understood that by having faith in God that all works

---

[27] The Aakhut or right Utchat (Eye of Ra) represents information controlled by the left hemisphere of the brain such as factual information, letters, numbers, words, aggressiveness, masculinity, the sun, the living, etc.

according to plan, so much so that when things come together you could sense that it was like it was meant to be. There was no need to force things to happen because all will work out. When we force things to happen, it is like saying that God doesn't know what God is doing, which was Adam and Eve's mistake! God knew that they were going to disobey the commandment, so that's a lame excuse that this is how sin came into being. True sin, I was beginning to understand, is any violation against the Spirit of God. It is when we doubt that God, who is omnipresent, omniscient and omnipotent, can and will make a way. It is failure to believe and have faith in God, because when you don't have faith in God that's when you take things into your own hands and screw things up.

This is how the devil tricked Adam and Eve. This is how I was tricked. This is why I sunk so low and found myself sleeping on the floors of peoples' houses. In theory, it was beginning to make sense that spirituality is not supposed to be difficult and hard, and if it is, something is not right. There was something that I wasn't doing right and something that I didn't learn correctly. Whose fault was it? At this point in time, I didn't really care. I just wanted it fixed. I need to stop depending upon people and start depending upon the Spirit of God. "I understand."

Then the Spirit said that the real reason why I was left the church was that I didn't want to be what I was called to be, a preacher. It was revealed to me that I hated everything about preaching, which is why I was led to meet Iya to help me to understand that preachers are shamans.

Lesson learned. Then, a scene from *The Matrix* came to mind, where Tank, the operator of the

Nebuchadnezzar, asks Neo, "Did you sleep?" and Neo states that he didn't. Tank then proceeds to load up various programs on his computer and tells Neo that he will now. It was all a sign from the Spirit to me that the real quest was about to begin because, of course, everything sounds good in theory, but it's applying it that makes it real.

Part IV:
Born Again

Men fall only in order to rise.

- African Proverb

Crossing Over to the Other Side

When I got out of the hospital a week later, unable to work because I couldn't stand for long periods of time and after draining about a half of pint of fluid out of one of my lungs. I still had a considerable amount of fluid surrounding my heart and lungs, which caused me to wheeze a bit still. Thinking about my experience in the hospital I understood that I had learned all that I needed to know from a rational perspective, which corresponded to my Aakhut. It was time for me to learn from another perspective, from within. So I tried my best to maintain at home the same peaceful, meditative state of mind that I had in the hospital, by watching similar television programs and even listening to religious music. I tried as best I could not to think about anything, even though I was somewhat concerned how the bills were going to get paid if I wasn't bringing in a paycheck.

As a result of my health, I was placed on medical disability because I was unable to work. Fortunately, I had a couple of checks coming from work that helped to pay the rent. Now, thanks to G, I had learned how to pay myself first from every paycheck, so I would take 15% out and place it in my savings. The money left over I used to pay bills. This allowed my wife and I to have a little bit of a nest egg for a rainy day. It was during this time my wife really showed that she cared about me and not too long after my release from the hospital took a part-time job, along with the full-time job she was already working, to help cover expenses.

Unable to work, I tried to help out as best I could by making sure since she was bringing home "the (turkey) bacon" – (smile) that she never came home to a dirty house, and that there was always a hot meal waiting for her.

The lack of money coming in made me think of a number of ways to bring money into the house. I went into panic mode but was reminded that I need to stop worrying. It was the worrying that led me to become stressed about things that weren't in my hands. Again, theory and application are two different things, so I tried getting unemployment, disability and social security benefits, which for the most part were all dead ends. I simply had to let things work out the best they could, but it didn't stop me from being creative and inventive and looking for new ways to make money. It was during this time I discovered that I really enjoyed cooking, so I cooked every type of bean, chicken, turkey and fish recipe that I could find. I also cooked every type of soup recipe I could find and even invented some.

Refusing to be idle, I began drawing, painting and writing while listening to inspirational and religious music. Trying my best not to think, I remembered I was told that the spirits that surrounded me when I was at the hospital were called netcharu, aakhu and aapepu.

Now, I had read and come across these terms before, so it wasn't the first time I heard of them when I was in the hospital. What made hearing about these terms different and unique this time around was that I was truly experiencing them. The experience I had in the hospital made me stop thinking and start seeing life from a different perspective. When I did this, it became apparent that these spirits had been in my life all along but I never called them spirits. It was because of these spirits that certain things took place in my life, and so on. I had to admit that it was confusing and that the best way to describe them was as Jung had defined them as archetypes, but it was clear that they were much more than just figments of my imagination. They were real, and when I accepted that they were real beings, I noticed that certain events that took place in nature corresponded to them.

When I began to recall my experience in Philly and in Jacksonville, it became clear that when I lived in Florida and began getting jobs, it was a hardworking, warrior spirit that kicked in and made that possible. When I decided not to go down the wrong path, it was a messenger spirit that came to me and encouraged me to go the other way. Not only that: I noticed that I didn't consciously or purposely set out to meet Ms. B, Papá Raúl, Iya or Z, I was led to meet them by some invisible force. The same happened with my wife: I didn't consciously set out to meet her; I put the request out there and was led to meet her.

I was noticing that there was a pattern going on, but I couldn't quite put a finger on it. What I discovered, though, through observation, was that, whenever I thought about things or tried to figure things out from a rational perspective, things would go awry. When I didn't worry about things, things seemed to always work out somehow, because some force would step in and assist at the right time. I experimented with this phenomenon for a little bit and noticed that whenever I would look for something that was lost, for instance, I would get frustrated, even though I just saw the thing that I was looking for. After a few more times of going through this, I remembered that Anpu, according to the Kamitic legend, helped Auset to find the body parts of Ausar.

So, without thinking, when I was looking for something, I called out to Anpu and, shortly after, I would find the thing that was lost. After doing this several times, I noticed that it would take longer and longer to find lost items, until I began remembering some of the lessons that Papá Raúl taught me about how he worked with his Ellegua. Following my intuition, I offered a little rum that I had left over from making mojitos to Anpu, because this is what I remembered Papá Raúl offered to his Ellegua. After that, whenever I was looking for something, I would instantly find it. This little experiment convinced me for sure: I couldn't deny it anymore. Not too long after that, I learned that Carl Jung worked with a spirit guide that he called Philemon. It appeared that even though Jung called these entities archetypes, he understood that it was best to approach or work with them as spirits that existed outside of our being.

When I stopped trying to put rhyme to reason, sort of speak, and just allow the Spirit to reveal things to me by surrendering my will, I began to see that interacting with my Spirit (and the spirits) simply required that one use what Jung called active imagination. When I began to interact with my Spirit, it felt weird in the beginning but at the same time like a long lost familiar practice that I hadn't done in a long time. This was how I was inspired to study the Kamitic way by the Spirit that spoke to me when I was a teen.

The more I practiced this meditative technique, the more I began to realize that my problem with engaging in the Spirit was due in part to the terminology. The reason I was having issues with the terminology, however, was my lust to rationally understand everything **and the refusal to trust my**

own intuition. It wasn't until I submitted and surrendered my will by ceasing to consciously think (rationalize) about events that I discovered that, when I did things effortlessly, they worked out. This was sort of hard to explain and put into words, but what it meant to me was that if I just "put out there" what I wanted and not think about how it was going to be done, that I would be shown how to make it physically manifest.

It was all beginning to make sense. That when I stopped thinking so much and trying to figure out how to make things work, the Spirit would show me how to make things work by giving me numerous signs. It was this understanding that led me to see that the Spirit communicated to me through various symbols, legends and myths. What I had to do was familiarize and reacquaint myself with my own personal symbols, because our personal symbols are powerful. Our personal symbols have great meaning to us and they outweigh anything else in terms of power. This means if an owl symbolizes "death" to one individual then that is what it means to them, but if to another individual it symbolizes something completely different like "wisdom", neither is wrong. It is just that many symbols have different meanings per our individual experience, but the importance of knowing about them is that they help us to better connect to God.

Once I began to trust in my own intuition and follow my gut feeling, I learned that when various symbols seem to pop into our awareness, especially when we are dreaming, they are messages sent to our conscious from the Spirit. It was through this discovery that I met the various spirits that existed under God surrounding me.

The Aakhu: Ancestral Spirits

The first group of spirits that I met was my aakhu. The aakhu, I was shown are our ancestral spirits, going back to when the first human beings walked the earth. They form a human chain going all the way back in time and we, the last of their descendants in this long chain, are the most recent living link. When we have children, our children become the last links in this human chain, but being the last descendant also meant I was the repository of my ancestors' experiences.

Also considered aakhu are the people that our ancestors knew in their lifetime. These spirits, although not blood relatives, are considered part of our spirit family because they were like the neighbors along the street that our ancestors befriended, to the point that they watched out for us, even when we didn't know who they were. It was because we were our parents', grandparents', great-grandparents', etc. child that these spirits kept an eye and ear out for us. I was shown that the reason why our parents and grandparents knew some of the things that we did and whom we hung around is because they had eyes and ears around the church, neighborhood, etc. Some of these people we might I have been introduced to as Uncle So-and-so or Auntie So-and-so when they were living, then again some of these people we may have never met at all, but they came up to us and ask, "You're So-and-so's boy (girl), ain't ya?" Whatever the case, these people that looked out for us did so because they knew our grandparents and parents, but they also understood the importance of unity, hence community. They knew that if people watched each other's children and worked together they would have a protected, prosperous and safe community. From beyond the grave, these individuals, when they passed into the spiritual realm, continued to fulfill these same duties for our biological ancestors.

The aakhu, I learned, can appear as or alongside historical figures, elders, teachers and ordinary people. They can even cross cultural boundaries to include Native American, European and people of Asian descent as well, because there's no telling whom our ancestors knew in their lifetime. The only thing that is for certain is that it is because of our ancestors and the people that they knew, that we are who we are today. *The apple doesn't fall too far from the tree.*

It is from this perspective, I was shown, that the aakhu function in our life as spirit guides and spirit helpers. Like all good parents, they know that they cannot live our lives for us, but they can give us all sorts of wise advice and insight so that we do not make similar mistakes to those they made in their lifetime. The aakhu help us to learn about our past so that we can make better decisions about the future.

It was difficult for me at first to understand how the aakhu appear to us because, again, I wasn't taught about our cultural traditions. I had to learn by trial and error. This is what caused me at times to think so much about things, but the Spirit revealed to me that our aakhu appear to us through images of our mind's eye. They don't appear like ghosts and things like that but as flashbacks, memories, thoughts and ideas. You might, for instanc,e have all a sudden a flashback of seeing their photo or remember them doing something when they were alive. They may appear to us when we are awake or they may appear in our dreams. Since many of our aakhu have been long gone before we knew them, they may appear as a familiar face that we have a particular fondness for but have no memory of who they are. You know that feeling like we have met before but you can't place where. It's the aakhu providing us with proof that they are still alive spiritually and that they continue to exist as spirits in the heavenly realms.

The Ancestors Speak

It was through my aakhu I learned about the other spirits that exist under God that surround me. Although I have no physical proof to support this, nor do I know of any author that has written about this or will validate it, this is simply what my aakhu revealed to me to help me to make sense of something that cannot be physically experienced. That millions of years ago people knew their ancestors before they passed away because people had knowledge of how their ancestors did things before they died. It wasn't that people didn't believe in God; quite to the contrary, people believed in God but God was too abstract and complex for early man and woman to even fathom, just like God is in these contemporary times. The ancestors, on the other hand, weren't difficult to understand because they were once people that worked, hunted, fished, gathered food, etc. right alongside others. It was through these people that all of the high ideals, ethics, morals and standards that one exhibited were equated with God. It was through these high ideals that early man and woman came to understand God. As a result, a man with great hunting skills was understood to have these skills because they were attributes and blessings from God. A woman with great nurturing skills were said to possess these skills because God or the Goddess (the female aspect of God since God is androgynous[28]) gave them to her.

By observing nature, early man and woman eventually began to equate natural phenomenons with these early ancestral spirits. It wasn't long after that, for instance, that the memories of a hardworking ancestor spirit that used various animal parts as tools and weapons would eventually inspire the living to forge metals to be used for a similar purpose. The nurturing ancestress remembered for administering herbal remedies during pregnancy would eventually inspire midwifery and other nurturing practices. In time, specific ancestors were deified and said to be closer to God than others, while others were said to be further away, which led to the creation of a spiritual hierarchy. These entities later became known as spirits, angels, cherubims, cupids, gods, goddesses, demons, devils, etc. but in the Kamitic tradition they were known as netcharu and aapepu.

The netcharu and aapepu, according to my aakhu, were spirits that once upon a time walked the earth but had died years ago. These ancient men and women, I was shown, were once leaders of actual tribal clans that had acquired reputation while alive of possessing extraordinary skills and talents that they acquired from God. Initially, these people (or clan heads) I was instructed to call were: Osar, Oset, HruUr (Hruaakhuti), Nebhet and Set (called the

---

[28] Dialogue on the gender of God is truly foolish because God being incomprehensible and beyond man and woman's ability to describe is for the most part genderless and could be properly defined more as an "It" or "No Thing".

Children of Nut and Geb or the Children of Heaven and Earth). The other five people (or clans) were Djahuti, Sokār, Maat, Npu (Anpu) and later Hru (the Child of Osar and Oset). Together, these ten individuals, before their death, were called brothers and sisters, because they were dedicated and devoted to a common cause, which was the unification of Kamit against foreign invaders. But when Set, fueled by his jealousy, rage and lust for power, murdered Osar and usurped the throne, when the thrown was finally recovered, the remaining nine[29] individuals became nine ancestral spirits and later deified ancestral spirits known as the netcharu. Set, on the other hand, because of his behavior, was cast out and forced to roam with the invaders he had sided with. He was later immortalized as an evil, wild and outcast spirit that later became known as an aapepu.

As eternal spirits, the netcharu and aapepu settled into nature and can be found at the crossroads, hospitals, banks, trees, cemeteries, parks, rivers, mountains, hilltops, the night sky, alleyways, walking along railroad tracks, etc. inspiring people in various ways. Similar to other Afro-Diaspora spirits, the netcharu act as guardian angels[30] with extraordinary

---

[29] I was shown that this is the reason why the number nine is a sacred number in the Kamitic (and other Afro-Diaspora) tradtions and the number ten is an unlucky number.

[30] From my understanding when an ancestor has no living descendants to honor them. The ancestral spirit in order to continue to exist gets energy from natural environment. Depending on the type of life the individual lived determines if the spirit will either be giving this energy willingly by working with a higher spirit or if it will have to scavenge for it like negative spirits do in bars, alleyways and other unfortunate places.

powers, similar to Catholic saints, that have a particular color, number, food, drink and fondness of certain animals. The netcharu also have the ability to appear in dreams, influence cooperation from complete strangers and assist one in achieving their goals. At the same time their polar opposites, the aapepu, also have similar abilities to do the same things, but their intentions and purposes are usually destructive. This, I was shown, is the reason why the number nine was a sacred number in the ancient Kamitic tradition and continues to be a sacred number in Afro-Diaspora traditions today.

Ancestral Healing

After receiving a better understanding of the spirits that existed around me, I rearranged my ancestral shrine to properly honor my ancestors and their assistance in my spiritual development.

Before proceeding, it should be understood that there are many ways to honor those that have come before us. It is a common practice in North America to simply have a moment of silence. I once attended a professional development program and, in honor of the war veterans, an empty plate was placed on a white cloth table, with an inverted glass symbolizing the dead's inability to partake in food and drink. But Afro-Diaspora practices celebrate the life of those that came before us and even though the dead are not physically with us, it is believed that they continue to exist as spiritual beings.

Now, I must admit that before, my ancestor altar took on the appearance of similar Caribbean Spiritist altars that I had seen in the various Afro-Latino houses that I had seen in Pennsylvania and Florida. These altars were gorgeous, mystifying, but I had no real connection to them because I didn't understand the purpose of a lot of the objects used on them. I simply built a similar altar because it was what I saw that others had done. When I asked someone to comment as to why a certain number of objects were used, I usually got mixed opinions and views as for the reasoning behind certain practices, because I didn't understand that one's ancestor altar or bóveda (as it is called in Caribbean Spiritism) can be constructed based upon one's particular taste. There are only two rules when it comes to having a bóveda, which are never allow it to decay and become untidy, and never place a living person's photo on it.

So, led by the Spirit, after cleansing my space and borrowing from the Caribbean Spiritist tradition, I quickly rearranged my ancestral altar to reflect what I now knew and understood about God and the spirits that I wanted to surround me. Following my intuition and the inspiration given to me, I imagined what my spiritual court or Hall of Maa would look like, because it is the Final Judgment that matters. In other words, all of my actions, words and deeds are going to be read at this place before God. When I stand before God, God is not going to ask what did these people do and what did these other people do in this situation. God is going to hold me responsible for my actions, words and deeds, and is going to ask what I did in this situation. "Did you do what you know was right?" is what God is going to ask, no if, ands or buts. It is in this great hall that I will be renewed or born again.

Since life is a reflection of death, just like my loved ones would come and support me in life at court, pending I gave them no reason to abandon me because of my behavior. in death, my deceased loved ones would come to support me and hear of the deeds that I had done when on the other side, as well. They would stand under the protection of the great ram of renewal.

Based upon this Divine inspiration, I placed upon the table a white cloth to symbolize knowledge, wisdom and purity. Upon the table I placed eight goblets of the same size along with a larger glass, totaling nine, to represent the first netcharu, nine divine principles, the nine clans that united the kingdom and the nine primary ancestral spirits that assist and guide my being. The largest goblet I dedicated to my spirits of Osar. The number ten instantly signified Set (kabalistically 10 is the number of the earth) and the aapepu, so it became a taboo number, symbolizing division and a separation from the whole, the number one "1" from the "0" cipher (whole).

The left side of the altar, since everything must have a cause, an action, a Shu —the Kamitic Yang principle—, is dedicated to the masculine ancestors, so a small statue of an old black elder sits overlooking photos of my grandfathers and other deceased men of influence that have been influential in my life.

The right side of the altar I dedicated to the feminine ancestors that walked with me, since everything has an effect, reaction, a Tefnut –the Kamitic Yin principle–, so a small statue of an old black female elder sits overlooking photos of my grandmothers and other deceased women of influence in my life.

The two elder statues symbolized my earliest ancestors that established the cultural tradition. They are the ancestral patriarchs and matriarchs that tie me, my parents, my siblings, my grandparents, etc. to our ancestral lineage. They are the ones that tie me to the Kamitic theme and the whole idea of cultural unity, because they symbolize the Eyes (Right & Left) of RA.

Since the bóveda is a multi-purpose altar that goes by how you feel, you place candles, candies, flowers, rum, whiskey or whatever you feel that the aakhu want or need in order for you to help them and them to help you. If something doesn't seem right you simply take it off the altar or add something to it to make it feel right. To overlook the altar and all of its inhabitants, I anointed a white painted rooster and placed it on the altar to eat the worms and fight the aapepu.

Every Saturday, I wash my glasses, refill them with fresh water and place them back on my bóveda while listening sometimes to the hymn *Hold to God's Unchanging Hand,* Sister Rosetta Tharpe's *Precious Memories,* Aretha Franklin's *Wholy Holy,* Nina Simone's *If You Pray Right (Heaven Belongs to You),* Anita Baker's *Angel,* Giberto Gil's *Oju-Oba,* Beny Moré's *Mata Siguaraya,* Celina González's *Santa Barbara,* Chucho Valdés' *Briyumba Palo Congo,* King

Sunny Ade's *Ja Funmi,* Bob Marley's *Rastaman Chant* or whatever inspirational music I can find at the time. Sometimes or on special occasions (like Thanksgiving, etc.) I play these songs because the ancestors want to vibe on them.

Anyway, led by the Spirit and following my intuition[31], I arrange my glasses according to how I feel. Sometimes my glasses are placed in parallel lines, horizontal lines, and then other times in a diamond formation. I also have an ancestral staff that is decorated with the colors of the netcharu, tiny bells and other items.

After praying and thanking God for my aakhu and netcharu, I call unto my ancestors while tapping my decorated ancestral staff[32]. During this time, I ask God to bless and strengthen them with knowledge and wisdom, so that they can in turn assist me. I offer my aakhu strong black coffee, a shot of rum, a cigar, perfume and incense. When they really come through for me, I offer them fruit, sweet breads or some other food that they favored (without salt) that they enjoyed before they passed.

---

[31] Keeping in mind that it is always best to have an understanding of the inspirational idea before acting upon it.

[32] The ancestral staff can take on many forms and, depending upon the owner, can have numerous purposes. My ancestral staff is used to represent the mysteries of KAMTA. It is used to signify to the KAMTA residence that I have come to speak with them and serves as a mental trigger: when I pick up my staff, my mind realizes it is time to focus and get into a receptive mind state. The staff also serves as an instrument by driving away negative spirits with its bells.

Now, when my body became ill, my wife was always by my side, but my family, especially my father, was also. The relationship between my father and I was always rocky and strained because of his busy schedule when I was younger. My father and I never talked a whole lot during my childhood, and when I became older we didn't talk a lot either. I loved my father and I knew that he loved me because he made numerous sacrifices for my brother and I, but that was as far as it went. It was after doing this little rite and rebuilding my aakhu altar that things began to change between us.

One of the aakhu I honored on my bóveda was my father's father, because I remembered him being a tall reddish man believed to be half African American and Creek Indian. He was a strong man that I remembered as being very reserved in speech. I didn't know much about him, until one day my father opened up and started telling me about his childhood. According to my father, my grandfather had a good job working at a factory in Chicago, but lost his job because he got into a fight with a white man who accused him of drinking coffee like a "sissy", a certain characteristic (or bourgie trait) I noticed my brothers and I demonstrate sometimes when we drink, by putting our pinky in the air. As a result, my grandfather had to struggle to make ends meet. My father and his sister grew up very poor and never went anywhere. So my father, determined to do better, made sure that he had a good job so that we could experience the world.

Along with that, my grandfather, I learned, was very hard on my father. He never supported my father in a lot of the things that he did because he was too busy working. He never told my father that he loved him or showed him that he cared because, back then, men just didn't do that. I learned that when my father was a teenager my grandfather kicked him out of the house because he felt that he was challenging his authority. The same thing, I noticed, happened to my brother and me, indicating that curses (ills) are generational.

There were a lot of things that my father just all of a sudden just decided to tell me, which helped me to understand why he did the things that he did. My father told me about some of the infidelity and commitment issues that grandfather apparently struggled with that deeply affected my father. It was through these stories that I got a better understanding of why my father was so devoted to the church. I learned that, because of my father's childhood, he too had contemplated committing suicide. Thanks to his now deceased aunt (whose picture rests in my father's office facing the west[33]) and deceased uncle, his life was saved through the church.

At the time, I didn't know what possessed my father to tell me this tidbit of information but, again, I was beginning to see a lot of trends play out in my life and my brother's as well. It was interesting to learn that, like my father, I once contemplated suicide for similar reasons. I like my grandfather struggled with commitment, just like my brother and several of my cousins on my father's side.

---

[33] This was interesting to me because I have noticed that a number of my family members not familiar with Afro-Diaspora traditions subconsciously place photos of their deceased loved ones in the western direction, just like the ancient Kamites did thousands of years ago.

When my father told me more about his childhood, he eventually came to understanding that his father didn't know any better, which brought healing to him. As I saw my father's attitude change, grow and transform, I could sense my grandfather on the other side grow and feeling better about his situation. I simply began to get *flashes* of him smiling at me and feeling more at peace.

Not too long after that, the relationship between my father and I greatly improved. I found myself talking to him about what I had experienced and had learned. Even though my father didn't agree with a lot of my beliefs, it was a real blessing to be able to talk to him about my experiences still.

Eventually, as time moved on, I began to learn a lot of other things from my grandfather that helped me in my life. For one, it became obvious to me that part of the reason why I had problems fulfilling certain tasks was that I didn't have any positive reinforcement. Had I had someone in my corner reminding me to keep doing what works for me, I may have never questioned or second guessed myself. Therefore, I came to understand that one of the reasons for being a father is to be a foundation or support for one's children. Loving support is not a sign of weakness, but a sign of strength, so we should always support each other and congratulate one another for our accomplishments, no matter how insignificant they may seem.

Some of the other lessons that my grandfather taught me from beyond the grave, to break this generational cycle, were to explain to my brothers, nephews, nieces and other kinfolks the purpose of certain practices. I have learned as a result never to bark an order to another person, but to always try to explain why certain actions should be done.

My grandfather (my father's father) also encouraged me, before I make a decision, to think about the consequences it will have upon my family and those whom I love. He inspired me to encourage my brothers to do the same, so that they don't just do something that they are going to regret in the long run. Another important lesson that my grandfather through my father helped me to understand and tell others in regards to relationships is that, *if an individual is not worthy to marry, they are not worthy to have sex with*. Now, just to show you how the honored dead work, shortly after I was told this, I had several cousins on my father's side that had not married the women that they were with all of sudden decide it would seem to get married. Coincidence, I think not.

It is through ancestor veneration that I have learned a great deal about my ancestral past, which has helped me to become a better man, by understanding that we are connected to God through our ancestral lineage, which means that karmic reward and debt stretches along our ancestral line as well.

I wasn't sure where this was coming from, but it became clear to me at that moment that, in an attempt to enlighten people about this concept, the original sin principle was mostly created to inform people that the sins of the father (and mother) are passed on to the children, so it is important for one to strive for righteousness in this lifetime.

Luck, Growth and Healing from the Dead

Now, this experience taught me about 1st John 4:1, which states, "Beloved, believe not every spirit, but try the spirits whether they are of God..." meaning test to see if what the spirit says is true or not. It was because the relationship between my father and I was healed that I know that my grandfather truly is an aakhu and of God. I understood, after working with my aakhu, that our spirits communicate to us all the time and when one learns how to listen they will discover that this is the way that their spirits will normally communicate to them. For instance, my spirits will appear to me as flashes of insight, but this is one of the ways they come to me. For others, they may appear only through their dreams. Whichever way they communicate to us it is important to familiarize oneself with their signs (numbers, colors, animals, etc.) because it will help us to understand what God is trying to tell us.

It was also through this experience with my grandfather's spirit and my father that I became convinced that African and African American spirituality is real, and that people don't die. Their soul simply continues to exist or live on in a spiritual form. It helped me to understand that real spiritual evolution or spiritual growth is about moving forward and not backwards. All good parents want their child to do better than them, I learned by talking to my father and communing with my grandfather's spirit, even if they don't know how to do it. This meant to me that reincarnation doesn't occur in the general sense that one becomes an animal and so forth. True reincarnation is the evolution of the soul –conscious that evolves from a lower understanding to a higher one. Just like in grade school, after one learns a lesson, they move to the next level of education, our soul does the same thing. The only difference is that our conscious moves a lower state of conscious or awareness to a higher level of conscious or awareness. The lowest conscious is that of an animal and the highest conscious is the Divine. When we see people acting and behaving beast-like it is because these individuals are solely controlled and influenced by their instinctive behaviors. Whereas an individual that acts from the opposite is ruled by the higher and divine qualities within.

Another thing I noticed was that as one's conscious or awareness evolves their characteristics, personality, etc. also evolve as well. It can be said that we all have animal-like behaviors and instincts but through spiritual evolution we learn to master these emotions so that we can control them and not let our emotions control us.

The shocking thing about this is that most of us are not going to complete our task in one lifetime. Just looking at the situation between my grandfather, father and I, made me realize that it took at least three generations (that I know of) for us to get this one lesson right, in order for me to instruct my brothers on how to break that particular ill occurring along our ancestral lineage. We still have other issues to work on as well. For instance, my brothers and I have had temper problems, like many male children, which means that these temper problems aren't our own creation but a problem that an ancestor had as well. So, this is something that we have to work on, which will help our ancestor and ourselves spiritually evolve.

Now, this may sound like disappointing news at first –that we are not going to complete this spiritual evolution in one life time. But it is a relief, because it verifies that we are not required by God to be perfect before we physically die. We are, however, required to do our best and do the best we can. Hence the purpose of wanting to be an honorable ancestor, which my aakhu understood was the same as being Christ-like. Life, from this perspective, means that we, the last of our ancestral lineage, were born to fix certain problems that occurred along our ancestral line. All of our problems in life are basically spiritual tests—*pruebas* designed to teach us about self and help us to understand that we can only depend upon God. This is our true destiny.

It was this epiphany that led me to also see that spirits can only inspire us but they can't make us do anything. I remembered that when I was in the hospital there was definitely a negative influence present that encouraged me to just give up, throw in the towel and die, but I chose not to. I chose to surround myself as best I could with a different type of energy. This experience made me try and understand how I was able to escape the negative influences that were surrounding me. So, when I began to think about it, it became clear that there was bad luck that was surrounding me and I tried to surround myself with as much good luck as I possibly could. Bad luck, I was seeing, was definitely associated with the aapepu, while good luck was associated with netcharu and aakhu.

Luck, I was beginning to understand, is when you do everything right and everything goes according to plan (then you have good luck), or when you do all that you know to do and things go awry (then you have bad luck). When people pray for spiritual solutions to their problems, it is because they have exhausted all of their physical resources and are trying to acquire good luck in their endeavors, or what some would call a miracle. Luck or a miracle has no rational or scientific explanation; like divine grace and blessings, they are part of a force.

When I thought about how in the hospital I was trying to surround myself with positive energies, and how these energies correspond to netcharu and aakhu, I began to see that luck has a lot to do with the way we feel. If we are at our low point then we feel pretty unlucky, but if we're at a high point we will feel pretty lucky, blessed or as if God has personally smiled upon us. Obviously it is best that we try and keep this peaceful state of mind, but realistically speaking, there are a lot of things that occur in our life that will try to keep this from happening. Again, I noticed that when I was in the hospital it took more than just thinking positive to stay positive. I had to do several things to stay focused and keep my mind at a certain level of peace. It was the things that I had to do to keep from being overwhelmed by the negative forces that were surrounding me in the hospital that made me realize that what I was trying to do was keep my peace. When we lose our peace, that's when the negative forces are able to strongly influence us to make foolish and unwise decisions, thus affecting our luck. It's all about the "vibes".

So, to maintain our peace, we have to surround ourselves with things that will help us keep our peace, which also will improve our luck. It was this understanding that made me realize that my recovery from this illness would not come from just taking medication alone. My full recovery could come from anything that would improve my wellbeing or basically help me to keep my peace. This meant that whatever makes me happy and keeps me in this peaceful mind state would help heal my body and also improve my luck. This was the reason why watching cooking shows, traveling shows, cartoons and comedies helped me to get into a peaceful mind state. Besides affecting my mind it was also affecting how I felt, which had a positive reaction on my body. This meant to me that when we accept and live our destiny, things seem to fall into place or we experience good luck. This doesn't mean that everything is going to be miraculously easy and simple. Things will just work out.

My recovery from this illness, I understood, was nothing more than a *prueba,* for sure created to help my ancestral lineage. Again, proof that I was on the right track could be seen that if I had not had this experience, I would not have learned what I had to learn and the relationship between my father and I would not have been healed. This meant that, in order for me to fully recover from this illness, it was going to require a combination of physical and spiritual efforts. Medication alone was not going to heal my body. There were things I understood and didn't understand that were going to assist in healing my body. My healing was going to come from eating delicious meals, enjoying a comedy, laughing, crying, shouting, enjoying a movie, getting a message, meditating, praying, painting, drawing, talking to a long lost friend, speaking with my spirits, drumming, dancing, exercising, reading a book, etc. Since I read and studied books already, which caused me to overanalyze things, I saw that whatever I did had to be done in moderation. If it were done excessively it would cause problems, so whatever I did would help me to recover so long as it was ethical, right and done in moderation. All of these activities, I understood, would increase my luck, improve my wellbeing and heal me overall, because they addressed both my spiritual and physical needs. It was this understanding that inspired me to read the *Story of RA and Oset*.

The Story of RA and Oset

Now, I had read and studied just about every Kamitic story there was, but the difference from now and the past was that I was allowing the Spirit to lead me. I was simply following the Spirit and the inspiration given to me to read. When I did that, certain things were revealed to me that I had overlooked in the past.

According to legend, Oset was a woman that possessed words of power but wanted to know the secret name of RA, so that she could become a divinity (goddess) that was cherished in the heavens and the earth. So she devised of a plan to get the great RA to share his secret name with her.

Every day, RA entered and established himself upon the throne of the two horizons, Oset noticed that he had grown old: he dribbled at the mouth, his spit fell upon the earth, and his slobbering dropped upon the ground. On one particular day when this happened, Oset took the slobber of RA and kneaded it with the earth in her hand, and made a serpent in the form of spear. She set the serpent upright before her face, but allowed it to lie upon the ground on the path so that when RA passes by it during his journey through his kingdom, it would afflict him.

As before, RA arose and set forth upon his daily journey and, when he came across the serpent lying on the path, it bit him, causing the sacred fire of life to depart from him. RA opened his mouth and cried out, "What has happened?" and all that was with him exclaimed, "What is it?", but RA could not answer because his members quaked and his mouth trembled, because the poison of the serpent had swiftly spread throughout his body.

RA stated to all those who had accompanied him on his journey to tell KhepeRA that a dire calamity had fallen upon him, thereby preventing him from continuing his journey. He exclaimed that he didn't see what ailed him or what caused the great pain and agony that he was in, nor did he know who had did it to him. All that he knew was that he had never felt pain like the pain that he was in. RA, in total disbelief that someone would dare harm him, cried out that he was a prince, the son of a prince, a sacred essence that came from God. RA cried out further that he was the son of a great one whose name was planned and as a result, he had a multitude of names and a multitude of forms, and he existed in everything.

RA further proclaimed that all heralds his coming as his father and mother utter his name, that was secret and hidden within him by the one that begat him, which he would not divulge to anyone for fear that they would have dominion over him. RA recounted his journey by stating that he came forth to survey all that he created and it was while passing through the world that something mysteriously stung him. What was it, RA wondered. Was it fire that made him hotter than fire or water that made him feel so cold? He wondered what made his heart feel like it was on fire, his body tremble and his flesh to shake with sweat.

Furious, RA called upon all of his children to come before him and to assist him in destroying the illness, but none could heal RA and he wept heavily.

When Oset appeared before the trembling king, she asked RA what had happened to him, and if it was a serpent that rose against him and bit him. She told RA that with his power and her words she could drive the illness away.

RA told Oset that he was passing along in his daily journey, and was going through the two regions of his lands according to his heart's desire, in order to see that which he had created, when suddenly, out of nowhere, a serpent bit him, which he did not see. RA asked, was it fire or was it water?, because he was colder than water and hotter than fire. RA said that his flesh sweat, quaked, and his eyes had no strength. He told Oset that he could not even see the sky and that sweat rushed to his face as if he was in the summer.

Oset told the great RA that she would drive the poison of the serpent away only if he would tell her his secret name, because whosoever shall be delivered by his secret name would live.

RA responded telling Oset: *"I have made the heavens and the earth, I have ordered the mountains, I have created all that is above them, I have made the water, I have made to come into being the great and wide sea, I have made the 'Bull of his mother,' from whom spring the delights of love. I have made the heavens, I have stretched out the two horizons like a curtain, and I have placed the soul of the gods within them. I am he who, if he openeth his eyes, doth make the light, and, if he closeth them, darkness cometh into being. At his command the Nile riseth, and the gods know not his name. I have made the hours, I have created the days, I bring forward the festivals of the year, I create the Nile-flood. I make the fire of life, and I provide food in the houses. I am KhepeRA in the morning, I am RA at noon, and I am Tmu at evening."*

The poison burned through RA's body and prevented the great one from walking. Oset, noticing that RA's condition was getting worse, told him that what he has said was not his hidden name and it was not driving the poison away. Again she asked that RA reveal his secret name to her as the poison burned deeper and hotter in RA's body. Finally, RA consented and hid himself from the company before him, and when the two could not be seen the name of RA passed from his body into her. And when the heart of RA came forth, Oset called her son Hru to come forth saying, "RA hath bound himself by an oath to deliver up his two eyes" (i.e., the sun and moon). After Oset took the name of RA, she drove the poison out of RA's body and commanded the Eye of Hru to go forth and shine outside of RA's mouth. She enchanted, "May RA live and the poison die and the poison die and RA live". And, that is how the great RA, who suffered the frailty and weakness of a man, almost perished, but was healed.

The Kamitic Holy Ghost

It took me a long time to really be able to understand what this story was all about, because when interpreting another's religious spiritual perspective you can't have a narrow mind, and you have to try as hard as you can not to interpret it based upon your limited experience. What made interpreting this story even more challenging were the numerous metaphors, analogies and puns that the ancient Kamitic writers used. But, when I approached this with an open mind and allowed the Spirit to lead me, the question that came to me was what was it that RA gave Oset so that she could give to her son, which was a metaphor for all humankind so that we may all live a full life. In short, what was it that God gives man and woman in order for us to live? The answer that came to me was that it was the ancient Kamitic version of the Holy Ghost. I was then shown that one of the reasons I was encouraged to study the ancient Kamitic history was to see proof that the ancient Kamites had the Holy Ghost, by evidence of the "fruit" that they produce.

Nowhere in the history of the ancient Kamitic people can it be cited that the rulers and leaders acted, behaved and/or performed heinous acts like the vicious, tyrannical, sex-crazed, psychopathic, sociopaths leaders of other civilizations. Clearly the Ancient Kamites (3150 BC – 31 BC when it became a province of Roman)[34] were doing something right that allowed their civilization to exist and prosper relatively in peace for thousands of years and continue to be an inspiration as well as a mystery to numerous generations after.

Since one of the gifts of the Holy Ghost is that it enters the mind and body and gives direction, this made me realize that I did have the Holy Ghost or that it visited me, but years ago it manifested itself in my life differently from most believers. It took me in a totally different direction where I experienced a lot of ups and downs, and was led to learn about various faiths. Why, I wondered? The answer that came to me was that it was so that I could learn truly who and what God was in my life. Identifying with Oset led me

---

[34] Some scholars place the decline of Kamit much earlier after the Kushite rulers tried to restore Kamit to glory again but were driven out of the country before accomplishing their goal.

to see that I was trying to learn God's name, which can't be verbally spoken nor can it be properly understood because it is impossible to understand in human language some 'thing' that is so abstract, complex, incomprehensible. One simply has to accept, understand and learn about God through direct physical experience.

Now, the *Story of RA and Oset* makes it clear that RA is not God, the sun God, nor is he the sun, which was called Aten in the Kamitic language. Who then is God? God is, as the Spiritualist defined, an Infinite Spirit, which means that God is a Spirit that has the ability to become an infinite number of things. God is the unknown and the known, the hidden and the seen, the knowable and the unknowable. God is the beginning and the end, the Alpha and the Omega and everything in between. God is the Father, the Mother, and the Son. God, according to old gospel singers, is a Healer, Comforter, a Peacemaker; whatever you want and need, God is, because God, simply put, is EVERYTHING. I understood, but I still wasn't seeing the whole picture.

One of the problems I was beginning to see as to the reason why there is so much confusion, so many denominations, religious affiliations, associations, etc. arguing with each other is that human beings are trying to define a "thing" (for lack of a better word) that cannot be accurately or properly defined. How can you measure a thing that you cannot physically see? Describe a thing that you cannot physically taste? Define a thing that you cannot physically touch or feel? Explain a thing that you cannot physically hear? Or enjoy a thing that you cannot physically smell? Yet you know that this thing, for a lack of a better word, is real? It is impossible to do, as I soon learned. This is why earlier I couldn't prove that God existed.

This meant that the reason I was filled with the Power of God and inspired to go a completely different route when I was younger was to learn that there is only One Supreme God. This is not everyone's task. Some people may have been born to see how far they can get without direct interaction with God. Others may have been to discover how far they could go with God's power. We all have a destiny and I was beginning to see mine. The confusion, I was beginning to see, stems from the fact that Afro-American spirituality like their ancient African ancestors along the Nile River is truly a monotheistic religion that expresses itself in a totally polytheistic way. This is why I needed proof that God was who God claimed that He/She is and the only way to get that proof was to experience it by living it.

Again it cannot be overstated that the reason we have problems in our life or bad experiences is that without these problems or bad experiences we would not be able to appreciate or know the good. How do you know what cleanliness is, if you have never been filthy? How do you know what sweet is if you have never tasted the sourness of life? How do you know what hot is if you have never experienced the cold? And so on. How do you know that God is a healer if you have never been ill? Again, how can you define God if you have never physically seen, heard, taste, touched or smelled – simply experienced God? The only way is through experience. It is through our hardships, problems, trials and tribulations that we discover the wondrous and mysterious power of God. It is through the power of God that one becomes a vessel for God as they learn about him or herselves.

Discovering more Hidden Hands

That's when it happened. While following the Spirit and allowing it to guide me, one day out of the blue I was led to look at my late grandmother's obituary that had passed a year after meeting my wife.

My grandmother, my mother's mother, the one that approved of my wife, was a strong and loving woman that was married to my grandfather for over 60 years, who passed away a year before her. My grandmother loved children and between her and my grandfather the two of them they had nine children, two adopted children and not to mention the children that would come to the house from their church or the neighborhood to play with their own. People loved my grandparents because they were God-fearing, hardworking people that established a standard based upon the old ways. It was because of this standard they were both looked upon and treated in our family as royalty. To give you an example, unless they were participating in a conversation, when they spoke everyone literally was quiet. This is how all the elders in our family were treated. Another thing that I noticed about my family because of my grandparents is that we didn't have a large number of divorces and infidelity issues, because there was something that my grandparents instilled within their children and grandchildren that for the most part curtailed that behavior.

Now, there were a lot of traditions that my family practiced and were passed down to succeeding generations, which I later learned were not created by them. Some of these traditions were created or at least given to my grandparents from my great-grandparents, whom I had the pleasure of meeting before they passed. But there were a lot of other cultural traditions that were in practiced before them and clearly came from someone else I had never known.

Both of my grandparents lived good full lives. Then, my grandfather passed away, and a year later my grandmother followed. Both my grandparents were well loved and when she passed away people from all over the state of Michigan (and country) came to pay their respect. Unlike most funerals that I attended (especially where the deceased dies at a young age), my grandmother's funeral was not a somber event full of gloom, but a jovial event. The choir tried to sing somber and soothing gospel songs to comfort the family and guests, but the tempo would always change and it would turn into a spiritual party. This explains the reason why it wasn't even called a funeral but a "home going celebration".

As I looked at the photo of her on the obituary and began thinking about some of the experiences I shared with her, I noticed that beneath my grandmother's photo it read 'Sunrise: (Her birth date) and Sunset: (The day of her death)'.

Now, I had looked at this obituary several times before, but I never noticed that it said that. That's when a familiar voice that I hadn't heard for years spoke to me and revealed that if a person outside of our culture saw this obituary they would jump to the conclusion that we **black folks were worshipping the sun**.

I am not sure if my grandmother's spirit was the one that showed me this or not, but the fact that I had a fond memory of her and was directed to her obituary continued to verify for me the old African belief that our loved ones are not dead but continue to exist as spirits. As spirits or ancestral spirits, they still take an interest in the lives of their descendants that they left behind. I imagined my grandmother smiling and looking at me over my shoulders, which verified to me that my grandmother was definitely an aakhu (ancestral spirit guide) that was watching over me.

At that moment, things began to instantly clear up, because I began to see the common misconception held and publicized by Egyptologists, archeologists and all other authors that claimed that the ancient Kamitic people worshipped the sun. Simply put, these western scholars just didn't know how to interpret what our people did because it was and still is a foreign concept to most of them.

The equating of one's life to the sun was not something that the people in the church my grandparents attended created. It was created thousands of years ago. The concept that most Afro-Americans are familiar with, I learned, came from the Kongo-Angolan region during slavery, and was called the Yowa Cross.

The Yowa Cross, also called the Dikenga, Tendwa Nza Kongo and the Kongo Cross, according to Robert Farris Thompson, author of *Flash of the Spirit: African and Afro-American Art and Philosophy,* was a simple diagram predating Christianity that showed the evolution of the soul. The horizontal line of the cross is believed to be the dividing line between the mountain of the living (above) and their polar opposite the mountain of the dead (below).

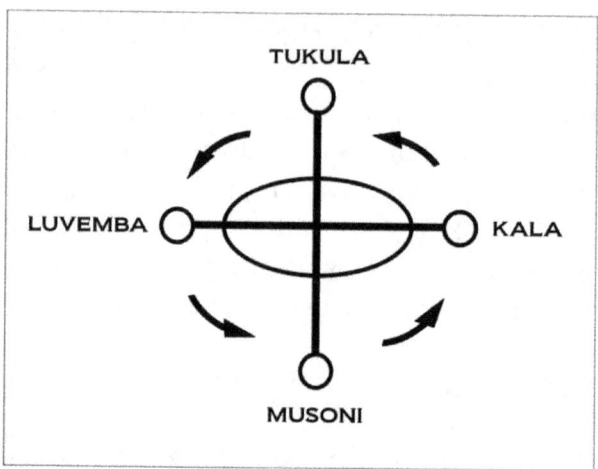

Figure 2: The Kongo Yowa Cross or Tendwa Kia nza-n' Kongo

The mountain of the living is called *ntoto* (earth) and the mountain of the dead is called *mpemba* (white clay), which is believed to be resting under the body of water symbolized as the horizontal line called *kalunga*. In fact, in some interpretations the whole bottom half of the cosmogram is referred to as kalunga to signify that the land of the dead is complete, whole, in regards to understanding the both sides in the cycle of life.

The discs surrounding the Kongo cosmogram (from right to left) are the sunrise, midday, sunset and midnight (when the sun is believed to be shining on the other side) and the four stages of life —birth, growth, death and rebirth, thus indicating the Kongo belief that the righteous will never truly die but will be reborn like the sun, either in the body or name of their descendant or as an everlasting spirit of nature called a *simbi*, which I learned from Papá Raúl is the equivalent to a Christian saint.

Then I began to remember that in the *Story of RA and Oset*, when RA was asked what his true name is, he responded by saying,"*I have a <u>multitude of names</u> and a <u>multitude of forms</u>*". In this response, I noticed that the ancient Kamitic people used the word "RA" as a prefix and suffix to create words, names and places like Auf RA, RA-Ptah, KhafRA, MenkauRA, Asr RA, Khnemu-RA, similarly to the way the ancient Hebrews used the word "el" to create words, names and places like EL-Shaddai, EL-ohim, EL-Olam, ang-EL, Rapha-EL, Micha-EL, Gabri-EL, and Isra-EL (Israel).

When I looked up the word/name "el", I found that it roughly translates to mean "might, strength, action, work and power" and was used to signify the true God of Israel. Exactly like the ancient Kamitic word "RA", which means "To do, act, action, power, the act of working, etc." and was made into a pronoun to become RA. When I found that the Ancient Semitic name EL-Ro'I or El Rohi (The God of Seeing –meaning we rely upon God to help us to humble ourselves by allowing us to see our faults and weaknesses because God is our shepherd) was phonetically and etymologically simlilar to RA, that's when I realized that the ancient Hebrews borrowed this concept and practice of using El as a prefix and suffix from the ancient Kamitic people, because the latter were older and had a far longer history of using this exercise. This meant that the Hebrew El was the Kamitic version of RA.

That's when it became crystal clear that, if I was able to see this connection, I am sure that archeologists, Egyptologists and other Western scholars, including theologians, could have found this as well, and either they chose to ignore it, or totally disregarded it in order to continue to perpetuate the myth that the ancient Kamitic people (and all people of color) worshipped deities, idols, animals and other things like the sun.

Then I remembered the various testimonies that were given at the church of my youth. The people that testified made claims of how they were able to accomplish miraculous things because of the power of the Holy Ghost that they had within them. The Holy Ghost, which they claimed is **"like fire shut up in their bones"**, gave them, according to Galatians 5:22-23, "…joy, peace, patience, kindness, goodness, faithfulness, gentleness and self-control". Other gifts of the Holy Spirit I remember were generosity, modesty, and chastity. As well as the ability to exorcise evil spirits, see angels/demons, perform miracles and speak in tongues.

Now, in one part of the *Story of RA and Oset*, RA states that he is "<u>KhepeRA in the morning</u>, <u>RA at noon</u> and <u>Tmu (RA Atum) in the evening</u>", but he still hadn't told Oset his name. When RA finally reveals his hidden name to Oset he steps out and allows this name to pass from him to her, which causes the dying RA to be renewed. The hidden name of RA was cleverly weaved into the story to mean **Amun RA – The Hidden RA**. That's when I began to see the complexity in using RA as a symbol. RA was symbolized as the sun to symbolize that God's Consciousness is eternal and cannot be created nor destroyed. Yet at the same time RA was understood to be a powerful force. A similar problem existed in the church, which is why there are so many a denominations arguing over whose doctrine is right or wrong. Was it Jesus Only, Jesus and the Trinity, the Trinity, the Father, Son and Holy Ghost…? No one knows, I was shown, because God is an Infinite Spirit and it is difficult to define and describe something (for a lack of better words) that you cannot physically see. This is the same problem the Kamau had. They couldn't properly define and describe God because they understood the human perception of things was extremely limited. The Kamau understood, it seems, that the only way to define and describe God is based upon inesperience, which is why they used so many stories with allusion and puns, in order to get the listener or reader to delve deeper within.

When I thought about how God cannot be physically seen and compared this to my personal experiences, it made sense why the Kamau had so many different names for God. These names of God weren't labels but words meant to describe and somewhat define who God is. The reason there were so many names is because no one can properly define who and what God is. No one can put God in a box. It just cannot be done. It is like trying to put the ocean in a box. So, to clarify matters, God, the Supreme Being, was called in the Kamitic language Nebertcher, which means *Lord of Everything*.

It's understood that it is the Spirit of God that has the ability to change an individual's life, because the Spirit of God is an awesome Power. This is why Oset wanted to know the name of God: so that she could be changed from a mere mortal to a divine being. It is the same reason why people in the church seek the Holy Ghost, so that they can overcome their earthly problems through spiritual means. It is the same reason why I sought the Holy Ghost when I was a teen. This all led me to see that there were two RAs that existed in the story. There were the RA talking to Oset that journeyed through the two regions, and the RA that exists at midday, according to the *Story of RA and Oset*. This explained why RA was described as being strong, mighty and powerful at noonday, yet feeble and old like an old man that could be tricked. If God is omnipotent, omniscient and omnipresent, clearly God cannot be tricked because this would contradict who and what God really is. Not to mention the fact that God already knew that someone was trying to trick him. Clearly RA is not Nebertcher. It is an aspect and attribute of God.

The RA talking to Oset, it came to me, corresponded to the Consciousness of God. According to Kamitic thought, in the beginning God didn't exist but had to self-create Itself[35] because the earth (and everything that existed) was without form, because there was a great void (Genesis 1:2). When RA states to Oset that he is KhepeRA, RA and Tmu (or RA Atum), it is understood that the hidden name is Amun RA. It became clear to me that these were all allusions to the fact that God is always Aware, Alert and Conscious, because God's Consciousness is always coming into being and transforming like the sun. This meant to me that:

Figure 3: KHEPERA - The Coming Into Existence RA

---

[35] God is androgynous in African thought consisting of both the active masculine energies and receptive feminine energies.

KHEPERA is the "Coming into existence (RA)" and is associated with the scarab beetle. Since the scarab beetles lay their eggs in dung balls (a symbol of

nothing or no-form) and roll them into holes where they were buried, after which the larvae would be born, this was seen by the Kamitians as a sign of birth, resurrection and renewal outof nothing. *KHEPERA* symbolizes the creative powers and consciousness of the God. It is associated with the rising sun, lower life, plants and newborns.

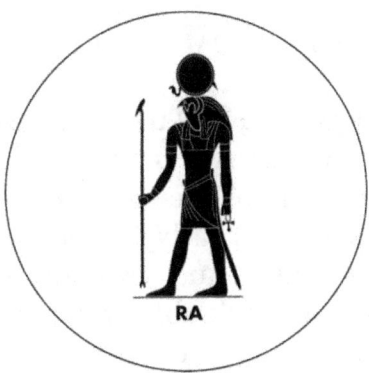

Figure 4: RA

RA is the one that was often portrayed as a youthful man with a falcon head. Living in the country allowed me to see that many falcons and hawks usually hunt their prey from high perches or while hovering in the air, and, most of the time, at dawn or dusk, when prey is mostactive. The Kamitians apparently saw RA as one that sees everything from beginning to end, so they sometimes called him RA- HruKhuti –RA the Hru of the Horizon.The word "RA" also means "ruler". RA, therefore, symbolizes the

aggressive aspects of the God's Power and consciousness that is used to stand upright and fight the enemy, associated with the midday sun, seen as young adulthood to adulthood/maturity, also an individual of authority.

Figure 5: RA ATUM - The Complete RA

RA ATUM (also called ***RA* Tum** or **Atum *RA***) means "The Complete RA." RA Atum symbolizes the transformative powers of the God's Power to make one stronger and wiser spiritually (especially after a tests, trials and tribulations), thus RA Atum is portrayed as an old man wearing the double crown of Kamit indicating the beginning of the end. As such he is symbolized as the setting sun.

Figure 6: AMUN RA - The Hidden RA

AMUN RA means "The Hidden RA" and is portrayed as a victorious man wearing a crown of plumes, ususally either sitting or standing. In Kush (Ancient Nubia) Amun RA was often portrayed as a mountainous ram. This is because the spiraling of the ram's horn[36] indicates that Amun RA symbolizes the rejuvenating, renewal, purifying, rebirthing, reviving, reforming miraculous and prophetic aspects of the God's Power, that are a complete mystery to humankind. Amun RA is the most profound mystery in the universe, associated with the hidden moon and the mysteries of rebirth. This is why the Kamitians credited Amun RA with their victory in the expulsion of the Hyksos.

The RA that could be tricked and manipulated is the Power or Spirit of God because it is an indescribable force. This force could not only be tricked but the forces of evil often attacked RA, according to Kamitic legend, as well. This clearly indicates that the Kamau were speaking metaphorically when talking about RA and that he is not God nor is he the sun. Again, when I compared this to my life, I remembered when hanging out with the Rastas when I was attending school, they would drum and get a spiritual feeling called "irie". This "irie" feeling is what people in the church called the "annoininting". When a singer in the church sung with the annoininting, like when the great Mahalia Jackson sung *How I Got Over* (live), she touched the hearts of all people. This is because the Power or Spirit of God can be manipulated through singing, music, drumming, dancing, breathing, etc. It

---

[36] Early Christians borrowed this concept and changed the precious blood of the ram to the precious blood of the lamb.

is what the Chinese called Chi energy because it exists throughout the universe, but I am reminded through my experience that it could be lost. Funny, I remember my parents saying when they became angry with us boys that "You almost made me say something." Meaning, there was something within that helped them to refrain from saying, acting and behaving like "saved" people or saints. On other occasions I have heard other people's parents say, "You 'bout to make me lose my Holy Ghost." I could never understand how or what would make them lose their Holy Ghost because I didn't understand really how they got it in the first place, but it was all starting to make a lot more sense now, through studying the Kamitic tradition.

For this reason I was instructed to spell the RA that could be tricked with a "u" at the end, to distinguish between these two RAs. RA ending with a 'u' pluralizes RA to spell Rau, to indicate that it is a force or is the Power and Spirit of God. This form of RA, symbolized as the encircling serpent by the Kamau, corresponded to the radiant, fiery energy that is said to be like fire in one's bones according to Christian lore. This is another reference made in the story that RA's body trembled and quaked. I could see now how some equated RA with the Yoruba orishá Aganyu –the spirit of volcanoes, but the Spirit informed me that I still wasn't seeing the whole picture.

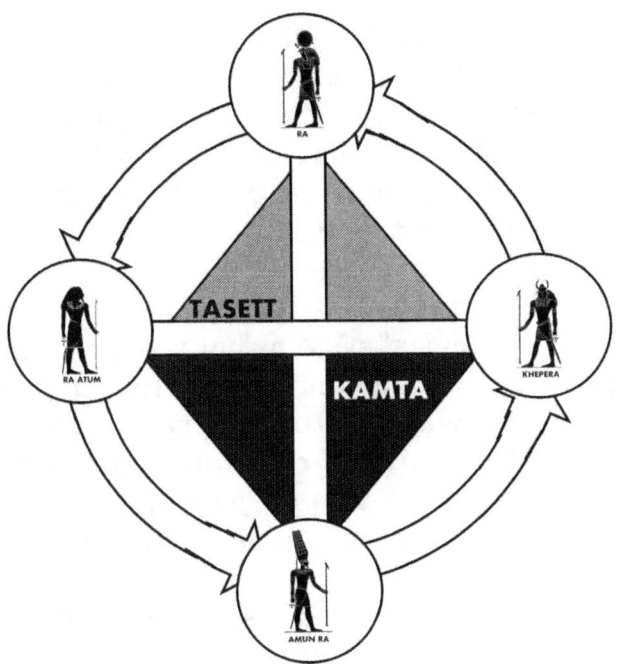

Figure 7: Maa Aankh Cosmogram

So, I was inspired to put the four forms of RA together based upon their association with the sun, along with the ancient Kamitic theory of the universe, and compare it with the Yowa Cross. After doing so, I discovered the following cosmogram, which I was told is called the Maa Aankh.

The Maa Aankh

Immediately, when the word the maa aankh came to me, I looked up in my *An Egyptian Hieroglyphic Dictionary Vol. I and II* and found that it was not a Kamitic word, but a word coined using the Kamitic language. The word maa aankh was composed of the ancient Kamitic word **"maa"**, which means to be true, to be upright, truthful, real, actual and veritable, and the word **"aankh"**, that means eternal life, to live and to swear an oath. Literally it meant to balance an oath, swear to live truth, to live by law/order, which roughly means, *"To swear an oath to live upright, truthful and veritable."* I was later told that one that followed this path was called a **sa (t)' maa aankh, which means son (or daughter) of the one that swears to live truth.**

The maa aankh, I was told, simply put, is the name of a cosmological system that was given to me by the Spirit of God and my ancestors. **The purpose of the maa aankh was not to resurrect, recreate or reconstruct the Kamitic religion of old for contemporary times.** The purpose of the maa aankh, simply put, was to help me to see God in the universe, others, and most importantly see God in me, because it was explained to me that what **separates us from God is what we believe and see**. The maa aankh, I could see, was inspired and similar to the Kongo Cross, but I was shown that it was different, because it is based upon the Kamitic concepts and principles expressed in the Story of RA and Oset.

I was shown that, even though no diagram has been found indicating that the Kamitic people lived their life based upon such a system, there are all sorts of clues that reveal that their life was influenced by something closely similar. I was shown that the maa aankh was created based upon the understanding that ancient Kamit (Ancient Egypt) became a very powerful, peaceful and prosperous nation in ancient times because the people united and worked together to take advantage of the north-flowing Nile River, which flooded annually, providing near the southern section very fertile soil. This allowed the Kamitic people to cultivate crops and grains from the very fertile soil, thus giving rise to agriculture, trade and a very stable economy. With no **concerns or worries** about their survival, because their immediate needs were provided for through the annual inundation of the Nile, surrounded by a sea of desert on all sides making their lands for the most part difficult (not impossible) for foreign invasion, the ancient Kamites turned their sights inwards and began to ponder about the mysteries of the universe and how it related to human kind.

Through their self-exploration they made numerous discoveries that led to them unraveling the mysteries of life. This also allowed them to put into practice numerous customs and laws that appeared to be very bizarre and strange to ancient foreigners during that time, such as allowing people from lower social classes to advance to higher social status based upon morals and ethics, giving women rights similar to that of men such as the right to own land, get a divorce and even enter into the priesthood, a feat contemporary religious organizations are still struggling with to this day. This is how their society functioned for hundreds of years undisturbed[37], until foreign invaders from the north finally stalled and halted their progress.

The ancient Kamitic way of life began one day after noticing that the sun seemed to rise in the east, peak at midday, set in the evening and was mysteriously reborn to start a new day. It was during these times that it appeared to the ancient dwellers along the Nile that the energy of everything around

---

[37] This is similar to the experience of Africans brought to the New World that escaped slavery and set up societies away from their enslavers.

seemed to correspond with the different movements of the sun as well. At sunrise it appeared that everything came alive or awake. Then, at midday, everything (plants, animals and human beings) was all bustling with life. When the sun began to set, it appeared to them that all of the creatures on the earth –human beings included– slowed and winded down as the stillness of the night set in. Then everything would start all over again the next day and so on.

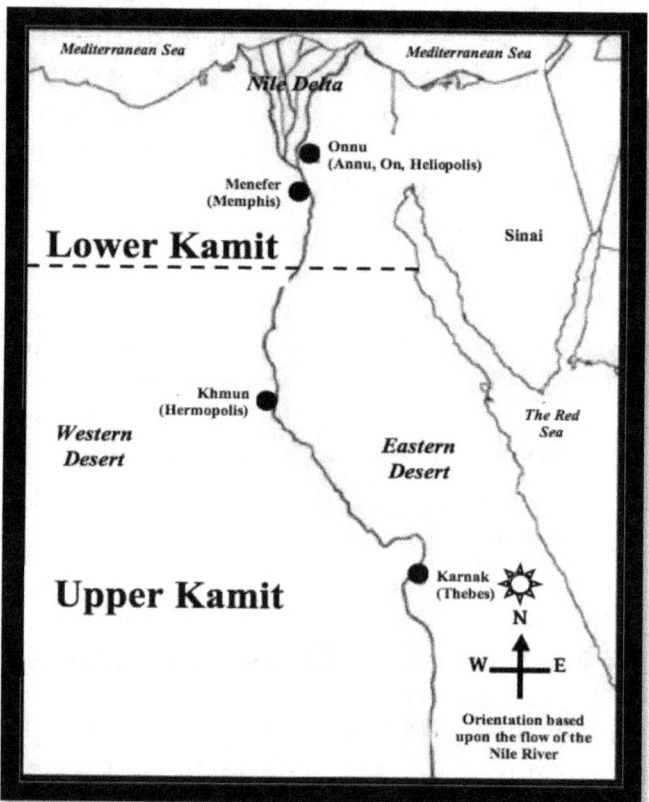

Map of Upper and Lower Kamit

This observation inspired them to associate sunrise with the emerging scarab beetle that comes out of the dark hole and called it KhepeRA. Since at midday everything seemed to be aware, alert and conscientious, they saw it as being like a bird of prey and called this moment RA. As they approached the end of the day and life seemed to slow down or come to a halt, they saw this as being like a human being aging and called it RA Atum.

They didn't understand how it was done but they knew that somehow things were reborn and renewed through a mysterious process that they associated with the stillness of the night, and so they called this particular moment Amun RA. As their understanding of life expanded so did their view of the universe around them. Until eventually KhepeRA (sunrise) meant Birth/Beginning, RA (midday) meant Life, RA Atum (sunset) was associated with the Death and Amun RA (midnight) indicated Rebirth. Together these four forms governed their country that was divided into two great lands, known as TASETT and KAMTA.

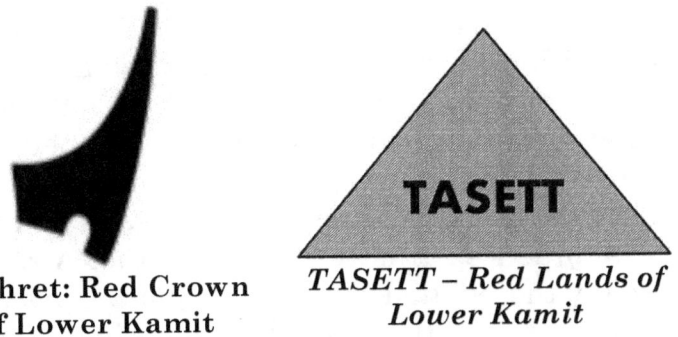

Deshret: Red Crown of Lower Kamit   *TASETT – Red Lands of Lower Kamit*

Figure 8: Crown of the Red Lands

TASETT, which means The Red Lands, is the northern section of the country, where the Nile flowed through the desert until finally branching out to the Mediterranean, which was also known as Lower Egypt and was represented by the red crown called the Deshret.

Hedjet: White Crown of Upper Kamit

KAMTA – The Black Lands of Upper Kamit

Figure 9: Crown of the Black Lands

KAMTA, which means The Black Lands, is the southern section of the country, where the Nile flowed and produced rich, fertile and black soil. It was a white crown called the Hedjet that represented this region, also known as Upper Egypt or Upper Kamit.

Now, in my research I noticed that most scholars don't comment as to why the Kamitic visionaries chose to symbolize TASETT (the Red Lands) with a red crown and KAMTA (the Black Lands) with a white crown instead of a black crown, because many are still in denial that the ancient Kamitic people were black and brown skinned Africans. When it is accepted that the ancient Kamitic people were black and brown Africans and had similar cultural practices, traditions, etc. as other Africans especially those found throughout Sub-Sahara Africa, it can be assumed that according to ancient African color symbolism the color red symbolizes fire, anger, life, mediation, etc. The color black symbolizes mystery, the unknown, the hidden, etc. and the color white symbolizes knowledge, wisdom, purity, death, peace and the honorable dead or ancestors.

This means from a metaphorical perspective TASETT, the Red Lands, symbolizes the land of the living, the physical realm, and exemplifies how the physical realm is truly barren and lifeless, like a desert full of mirages and illusions of grandeur at high noon. TASETT is a dangerous land. It is where most of the foreign invaders resided and brought chaos. It is the realm of storms, the land of harsh winds, the valley, the realm, according to occultists, where Satanel (Satan) established his kingdom and where the tree of good and evil resides. In other words, it is the physical hell, and for this reason Set[38] was said to be the ruler of this land.

KAMTA, the Black Lands, on the other hand, symbolized the land of the spirits, the spiritual realm, and exemplifies the fertile and mysterious phenomenon of rebirth at midnight. KAMTA was the relatively safe land that provided peace, security, shelter and stability, the further inland one ventured. The further south the ancient Kamites traveled led them to discover their ancestral roots that dwelled beyond their borders in ancient Ethiopia. KAMTA thereby became the home of the greatest Kamitic ancestor Osar[39] and thus the origin of their beginning. It is here in the south, where the tree of life and

---

[38] Keeping in mind what was stated about Set earlier, as being a wild foreigner that settled alongside the Nile that was later outcast, makes this revelation given to me even more interesting because, at one point of time, hell was believed to be in the north. It is in the north where Nicholas the Sinister, who later became Sinter Clause and eventually later Santa Clause, resided. To appease the northern spirit, food, wine and sweets were left, to keep Old Nick (short for Nicholas) jolly.

[39] It is interesting to note that hundreds of years later early Christians would identify Osar with Jesus Christ. Then, thousands of years afterwards, early African Americans would identify Jesus Christ as being the great ancestor. Now, hundreds of years later, Osar has returned, indicating that there is clearly nothing new under the sun.

everything associated with purity resides[40]. It is the allusion of heaven, which is the land governed mysteriously by a cosmic order.

Clearly it was the Nile River that separated Upper Kamit from Lower Kamit and made these two lands distinct, unique polar opposites of one another. It was therefore imagined that these two lands, symbolized by two opposing crowns (the red and white crown) and ruled by two opposing brothers, had to have come from the same source. So, the horizontal dividing line I was shown on the maa aankh symbolizes the Nile River but metaphorically is called **Nyun** (Nu, Nun), the sacred, primeval waters of beginning, the sacred lake, pool, the cosmic slop, the great void, that mirrors that which is above below. Just like the Kongo-Angolan cross, from some viewpoints the whole bottom half of the maa aankh can be interpreted as **Nyun**, to indicate that the entire bottom half of the maa aankh is a pure, sacred, hidden and a mysterious sea of nothingness. From this perspective it becomes easy to see that the amniotic fluid of the female womb[41] can be said to be a physical manifestation[42] of Nyu. We therefore all come from the sea of great beginning.

---

[40] Those familiar with Christian lore will also note that the biblical Cain, associated with evil, corresponds to the north, while Abel, associated with good and purity, corresponds to the south.

[41] It was this understanding that women are birth givers and that their womb is sacred what led to women rights and matriarchal societies in traditional Africa.

[42] This is one of the reasons why women were sacred and respected in African societies.

The vertical line on the maa aankh represents the first principle that was created by Nebertcher, the **Maa,** which brings the two great lands together and unites Amun RA below with its polar opposite RA above. It connects the land of the living with the land of the dead making it possible for one to bridge the gap of the great divide. **Maa** therefore, allows one to see the whole picture by connecting the Right Eye of RA with the Left Eye of RA proving as the saying goes, *"Two eyes see better than one"* [43]. The **Maa** is what provides the balance, law and order or foundation for Shu and Tefnut.

Shu and Tefnut are called in the ancient Kamitic writings the first divine siblings and/or the first divine couple to come into existence after the **Maa.** This is because that **Maa** ensures everything its time in the sun, so that for every cause there's an effect. Everything that rise will eventually fall, etc. Shu therefore is the Kamitic Yang —responsible for heat, fire, light, cause, rational, positive, action, etc. He is interdependent upon his polar opposite sister-wife Tefnut who is the Kamitic Yin —responsible for coolness, water, darkness, effect, intuitive, negative, reaction, etc.

It is important to understand that failure to recognize that Shu and Tefnut symbolize the dual

---

[43] The right Eye of Rã symbolizes the Sun (Solar), representing factual, rational information, material mundane/secular thought and the "male perspective" controlled by the left-hemisphere of the brain, while the left Eye of Rã symbolizes the Moon (Lunar), representing abstract and esoteric information, spiritual thought, feelings, intuition, the "female perspective" dominated by the right hemisphere of the brain. Together, these eyes give a whole or holistic perspective.

aspects in nature has led to the chauvinistic attitude that women are the weaker of the sexes and in many western religions the source of evil. On the flip side, in response to male chauvinistic attitudes, feminists have tried to portray the feminine principle as being more dominant and powerful than its polar opposite. Both concepts are incorrect according to ancient African thinking. Neither is stronger, better or weaker than the other. Both are dependent upon the other and reason we label things this way is to try and understand the nature of God.

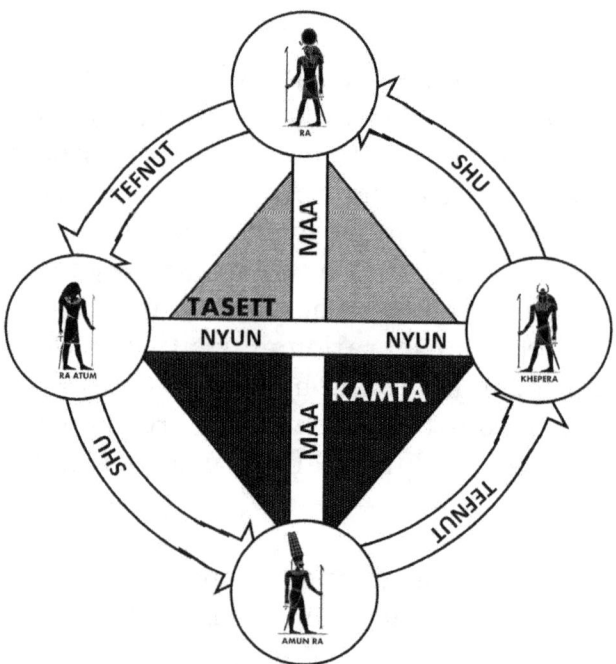

Figure 10: KAMTA & TASETT

In reality, when it is understood that both symbolize the dual aspect of nature and that both are dependent upon the other for its survival, it should become clear that without one the other would cease to exist and vice versa. For instance, without the female species being able to carry the egg, the male species would not have an egg to fertilize. This was the logic and wisdom of the ancient Africans that led to women having similar rights as men in traditional African society. This is the reason the ancient Kamitic philosophers indicated that first Shu and then Tefnut emerged after the *Maa* –balance, reciprocity, etc. In some of the legends it is believed that Shu and Tefnut were so close together that they were emitted as twins. Still one has to come after the other. There has to be a cause, in order to be an effect.

That being said, the African queen was not just arbitrarily given the title queen mother and wined and dined, as we see in fairytales and storybooks. She was considered the mother of a nation because of her duties and responsibilities to the people. An analysis of the great African civilizations reveals that many of these societies were based upon matrilineality, where the women hold very important roles in the community. This is not the same as feminism, and does not mean that men do not hold important roles in such a society. What it means as Papá Raúl once explained to me is that greater emphasis is placed upon the maternal line versus the paternal line. Papá Raúl told me that some spiritual societies in Cuba still function this way, which is why my aakhu introduced Oset to me as being a queen mother that gives birth to revolutionary change.

Returning back to our subject at hand, I was assured that even though no such diagram as the maa aankh has been discovered amongst the tombs of Kamit, a thorough analysis reveals that many of the ancient Kamitic people lived their life according to the maa aankh. This is the reason why deceased rulers were commonly buried in the west and further down south[44] and why life-bringing activities were conducted in the eastern region of the country. Praise songs and hymns were sung to Amun RA because this is the aspect of God that the priesthood of Karnak found renews our being, and so on. There are all sorts of examples that can be found supporting the theory that the Kamau lived their lives according to maa aankh, I was shown. To state them all would simply take us beyond the scope of this work. The best documentation that the Kamau left for their descendants was the *Story of Osar*.

The Story of Osar

Now, as stated before, I had read most of the Kamitic stories numerous times. I had read the *Story of Osar* a number of times as well and each time I arrived at the same conclusion, which was that the power of right defeats the power of might. It was only after studying the maa aankh and allowing the Spirit to have some input that I arrived at a different, new and unique

---

[44] For more information see *Nile Valley Contributions to Civilization*, by Anthony H. Browder, pg. 85.

conclusion that would forever change my life. This is because the maa aankh helped me to see how God manifests Himself[45] throughout the universe and how I am connected to my Creator. It helped me to understand that nothing happens by coincidence. Everything that exists in the universe follows the same cyclic procedure, the same order, and the same divine plan, which I could see is just perfect. For the first time in my life I could see the beauty of God because I could see God, which led me to interpret the *Story of Osar* differently.

There are many versions of the story that exist because the story appeared to change with time and change with each new ruler in support of the spiritual system that ruler followed. Briefly, the story is about two brothers, one-named Osar and his younger brother Set. According to legend, Osar became king in a very horrific time, when his people were warring against each other. Wanting to bring peace to his land, it is said in some versions that Osar went and spoke with Djahuti, and in another version, which I am more in favor of accepting based upon my new understanding, it is said that Osar spoke with RA, who pronounced him heir of the throne[46], after which Osar proceeded to

---

[45] God, in all reality, is both masculine and feminine, meaning there is a part of God that initiates change and a part that manifests change, similar to how the sperm of a man initiates life within a woman, but it is the gestation within that woman's womb that brings that new life into being/existence.

[46] Rã, according to the maã ãankh, is the controller and governor of life at midday that corresponds to our waking awareness, since the word for ruler is rã.

govern and teach his people correctly by introducing a body of laws for them to govern themselves with[47].

Later, Osar taught his people agriculture, a trade he learned from his wife Oset. In a relatively short while the teachings of Osar had spread all throughout the land. All loved Osar and cherished their beloved ruler except for his younger brother, who had become very jealous of Osar's success and fame.

Osar, seeing that everything was good, decided to spread his teachings throughout the world to help others. In his absence, he decided to leave Oset in charge, but, unbeknownst to them both, Set was devising of a plan with several conspirators to murder his brother upon return.

When Osar returned back from his voyage, Set welcomed his unsuspecting brother and all the dignataries of the kingdom with a great celebration. When all was full and merry with ale, Set presented a beautifully decorated chest and promised to give it to whoever fit perfectly inside. One by one, each of the guests tried to fit inside the chest, but no one could. Set knowing all along that Osar would fit inside of the chest, after much coaxing[48] Osar laid down in the chest and before he was able to regain his stance, Set and his conspirators nailed and poured molten lead on the

---

[47] The studious reader will note that this is the same path that Jesus took once he returned from his hiatus and began to teach the people the new way.

[48] This is an allusion to the fact that we ultimately have the power to choose to do whatever we will. Just because you have the Rāu doesn't mean life is going to be a piece of cake, that you aren't going to go through some struggles or have adversaries. You still have to use commonsense.

chest, thereby suffocating and killing Osar. They then threw the chest into the Nile. No one stood against Set as he usurped the throne because he could have easily killed him or her as well. It is said that even RA turned his head aside and wept of the news of Osar's death, for not even he could stand against Set.

When news of Osar's death reached Oset she cut a lock of her hair, put on her mourning clothes and went in search for her king. She secretly searched high and low, because she was now a fugitive in her own land and abroad. Unable to find the chest, RA having pity upon her sent forth Npu to assist her. With Npu's help, Oset was guided to a distant land where she found that a tree that was cut down and made into a pillar for the ruler of the foreign land had engulfed the chest. After pleading with the king to return the chest to her, through magical means it is said in one version that Oset caused the weary member of Osar to impregnate her, so that she could give Osar an heir. In another version it is said that Oset sung songs of mourning and transformed her self into a magnificent swallow and while flying and encircling the body she sung for Osar to impregnate her with an heir.

Secretly, the pregnant Oset traveled back to her land to give birth to Osar's heir. Before doing so, she secretly hid the chest containing the body of Osar in the marsh. While away preparing to give birth, Set, during a hunting expedition, found the chest and, in a rage of anger, hacked up the body into pieces. It was after Oset gave birth to Osar's heir Hru, that she returned and found what Set had done. Again Oset searched for the body of her beloved king with Npu, but this time she was accompanied by her younger sister Nebhet, believed at once to be the former wife of Set. Together they searched everywhere for the pieces of Osar's body, and everywhere where they found a piece of Osar's body they created a shrine reminding the people that it was a sacred place where a part of Osar's body was found. It wasn't long that all of the body parts of Osar were recovered except for his genitals, which were swallowed by a fish.

Now, Oset was still very saddened by the lost of her husband and she mourned heavily over Osar's lifeless body. Wishing that he returned, she asked Djahuti if he could bring Osar back to life. Djahuti, knowing that Osar's spirit had departed from his body a long time ago, knew that it would be difficult, because Osar's spirit may not recognize the deformed body now. After searching for a way, Djahuti instructed that Osar's body be wrapped in linen and be given a proper burial ceremony, so that Osar's body could finally be allowed to rest in peace and exist forever as the first honorable ancestor.

Now, many attempts were made on the young Hru's life, and when he became of age, he was inspired in a dream to avenge his father's wrongful death. Hru followed suit and challenged his uncle to battle. Set, however, being older and more knowledgeable of war would lose some battles but win most of the battles against Hru. In one battle Hru lost his eye and he retreated to vizier of his father, Dajhuti, who repaired his eye. When Hru met Set on the battlefield again, he quickly and swiftly defeated his uncle by cutting Set at the seat of his pants and making Set a eunuch. Hru then dragged Set, wounded and defeated, to be judged.

Unknowingly, Set's sway swept through the whole land and as a result a tribunal was called to meet by Neith, who was a warrior but wise, in order to bring balance and justice to the land. When the tribunal met and tried to deliver justice, which could have brought an end to the Great War, they failed miserably by bickering and fighting amongst each other, because some of the members sided with Set as the ruler of the land, and some sided with Hru as the heir of Osar. As a result, the tribunal was divided and could not reach a final just decision.

Then it was suggested that Osar, as Tum, speak from beyond the grave. When Osar (Tum) spoke, he expressed his disappointment in the members for not being able to reach a fair decision. He reminded the tribunal that he was the one that taught and civilized the people of their wicked ways. That the barley that they grew and the cattle that they had they owed to him, for he taught them all how to become prosperous. In other words, Osar knew right from wrong, knew what worked and didn't work, because he was right alongside them practicing what he preached. Osar didn't say one thing and do another because he was not a hypocrite. Everything that he said, he knew because he did it as well, based upon his knowledge of the Spirit.

Osar, it is said, gave thanks to God for establishing the Halls of Justice in the Underworld[49], but due to the fact that Maa had been cast down by Set, making physical living unfair, Osar, because of his ethical and moral accomplishments in the living world, would reestablish the Maa in the Underworld, thus becoming the first Lord of the Land of the Living as well as the First Lord in the Land of the Dead or

---

[49] This is a metaphor for the unconscious, the spiritual realm and spirit world.

Underworld[50]. Osar told the tribunal that as Lord of the Underworld, he had at his disposal messengers[51] that could fetch the heart of anyone.

Therefore, if the tribunal didn't reach a fair decision, it would be all right, but the judges had to remember that a just and fair decision would be delivered upon each one of them when they met him in the Underworld, because death does not play favorites.

Based upon the words of Osar, the tribunal ruled in Hru's favor out of fear, so that upon their death they would receive a favorable ruling in the Last Judgment. This is like what some people do today: they do what is right not because it is the right thing to do, but because they don't want to go to hell and be punished.

Anyway, Hru was declared the victor because he was found to be *maakhru (maaxeru)*, "true of voice". Set was punished as a donkey to carry the very thing that could save him and bring him eternal life (the teachings of Osar), while Hru on the other hand was

---

[50] Balance, truth, order, justice and the law would be reestablished in the Underworld, so that what we do in the physical realm will have its corresponding effect in the spiritual world and vice versa.

[51] The messengers being spoken of are the forces and spirits that influence and inspire physical manifestation. One of these spirits is called the devourer in the Christian tradition that makes it so that no matter how hard a person works they are not able to keep any money or have anything at all. This is the reason why some individuals that win the lottery soon after lose all of their money and are in a worst condition then when they started. The same can be said about entertainers that are physically rich but not happy or people that are rich but not wealthy and so on. Osar is telling the tribunal that if they don't do right he has at his disposal the ability to make anyone tremble in fear especially one's conscience.

rewarded the white Hedjet crown, thus forming the double Pschent crown.

Figure 11: Pschent (White & Red Crown)

Hru restored Maa throughout the land, rebuilt his ancestors' temples that were destroyed by Set, and built new temples commemorating his victory over his uncle.

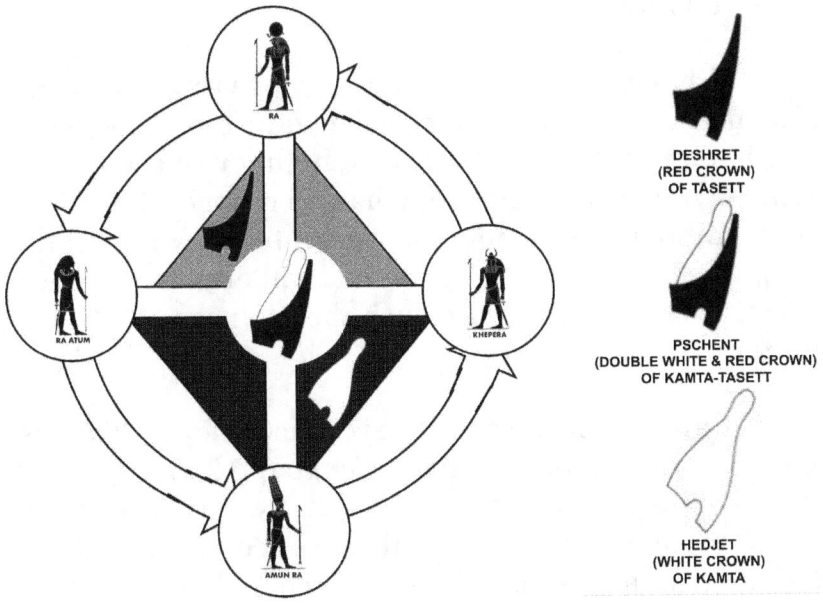

Figure 12: Maa Aankh & Kamitic Crowns

The Power of Whiteness

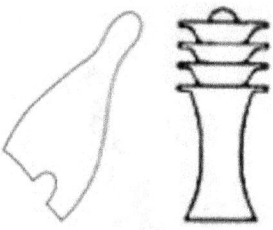

Figure 13: Hedjet Crown & Djet Pillar

Now, after reading the *Story of Osar* I would have normally drawn the same conclusion. I didn't this time, because I was shown that Hru would not have defeated Set and won the war if Osar had not interceded on his behalf. It was because Osar interceded on Hru's behalf that Hru was awarded the red and white crown.

What made this even more interesting was that I learned shortly after that in the Old Kongo, people that had grey or white hair were highly respected because it was said that they had a crown of fire. This, in my mind, corresponded to the double crown, because it signified that, like Hru, one had undergone a great ordeal to temper one's fire with the coolness of whiteness.

I also found that in Wyatt MacGaffey's *Customs and Government in the Lower Congo* (pg 256) says that in the Old Kongo when there was a lawsuit between two or more parties a tribunal convened to settle the dispute (I imagine under a great tree[52]). Each involved

---

[52] Trees (especially very large and old ones) are symbolic of the maa aankh.

in the lawsuit discussed and explained their point and even those that had nothing to do with the parties involved had the right to speak during the law trial. The trial was often a lengthy trial because of this, but the whole purpose of this kind of trial was to observe the effects that a particular action or behavior had upon the community and cure the guilty of the negative behavior.

When the tribunal chose a winner of the lawsuit, the winner would basically dance and cry tears of joy[53] because they had been found to be innocent[54]. The winner, for a short time, was said to have been reborn from the humiliating and suffering experience (a little like spiritual death) brought on by the lawsuit in the first place. The winner temporarily became the king of the court, because they spiritually died and were spiritually brought back by the awarding decision that purified them of their abominations brought on by the lawsuit. In some villages, the winner was anointed with strips of white cloth. I imagine that in other villages the winner was anointed with white clay or chalk.

What this meant to me in regards to the *Story of Osar* is that when I began to see Hru as the sun on the maa aankh, it revealed that Hru defeated Set and won the war because Osar interceded on Hru's behalf from beyond the grave in KAMTA. Therefore, the red and white double crown meant more than just the

---

[53] This gives us a new interpretation of the biblical David dancing out of his clothes, as well.

[54] Those familiar with the Kamitic teachings will now see why Hru is identified with winning, dancing, triumph, victory and justice.

unifying of the two lands. It also indicated, since the red crown symbolizes the physical realm, physical problems, trials, the known, tribulations, mediation, danger, concerns, the living, etc., while the white Hedjet crown stands for the spiritual realm, clarity, peace, knowledge, wisdom, security, stability, the ancestors, etc., that Hru was successful because he had allowed coolness to temper his fire, knowledge and wisdom to guide his actions, his ancestors to direct his path, and most importantly the Spirit to guide his will.

What Cha Goin' to Do?

It was sheer poetry, but I still didn't see the whole picture that was being revealed to me because, although I had made some changes in my life, I knew within that it wasn't enough. I still wasn't content. I was still stressed and somewhat worrisome about how events were going to unfold. The good thing was that I did manage to get a part time job teaching and tutoring, but things seemed to spiral out of control again.

I wasn't sure if it was because I wasn't sleeping, eating or taking care of myself like I knew I should. All I know is that somehow I took my eyes off the Spirit and after several months of taking cough suppressants, antibiotics, steroids for chest and breathing problems and hypertension medication, and avoiding going downstairs, taking out the garbage and driving, along with missing work and having to be totally humble and dependant upon others, my temperature shot up again and was around 103 degrees for several days. Again, I was rushed to the hospital. The physician in the emergency room, noting that my body was having trouble breathing, had a history of hyperthyroidism, periconditis, chest pains, etc., had no choice but to rush me to the nearest major hospital, which again was three to fours hours away. Assuming that I could have had a heart attack any minute, they instead chose to fly me on an airplane, to cut down on time.

For a second time, I lay up in a hospital with tubes in my nose and arm for a week, as numerous nurses came into my room and poked with me needles. Several times, because my body was so dehydrated, it would take 30 to 45 minutes just for them to draw several vials of blood. I mean, my arms had so many bandages from the "best people" that could find a vein that my body looked like a little mummy (smile – exaggerating). Seriously, my arms were pricked several times, to the point that I don't even have a fear of needles. All of this went on, while the physicians speculated as to what could be causing my body to have the problems it was having.

Again, as I laid up on the gurney, I remembered what I did the first time I was emitted to the hospital. To keep upbeat, to get my mind back on the Spirit, I turned the television on some shows that would allow my mind to think and dream of peace, wonder, joy and excitement and encourage my change of attitude. When I finally had arrived back to my enjoyable peaceful state of mind, I again opened up dialogue with the Spirit. I discovered that had I just chanted positive thoughts, that I would have lost my mind, because those thoughts would have conflicted with my present reality. Thankfully, I simply relied upon the Spirit.

Shortly after the doctors gave up and recommended that I see a specialist. After several extensive long blood tests, they told me that they thought I had sickle cell anemia. Naturally I didn't believe them, because no one in my family had a sickle cell trait. The doctors couldn't answer that question, so they recommended I see another specialist, who told me that the reason my body was so ill was because it had systemic lupus erythematosus (SLE). This made me realize that I had to make a life change through the maa aankh.

Of course, hearing the news that my body was diagnosed with having lupus was not what I wanted to hear. Naturally, I wondered how this could have happened, especially after eating and trying to be as healthy as I possibly could. I didn't eat certain foods and took dietary supplements and still I got deathly ill. "What is the purpose?" was one of the thoughts that came to mind.

Then, on the other side, I was glad to receive the news, only because now I knew what I was dealing with, but it still wasn't what I wanted to hear. Especially after hearing that one of my favorite DJ/producers, fellow born and raised Detroiter, James Dewitt Yancey a.k.a. J Dilla (*rest in peace*), a former member of the Detroit based group Slum Village who also produced for Janet Jackson, Tribe, De La Soul, Q-Tip, Common and host of others, it is believed possibly died from SLE complications according to the *Detroit Free Press, February 23, 2006* a few years earlier.

For a few fleeting moments thoughts of despair, resentment and anger entered my awareness, but, before I could ask the question, "Why me?", I quickly changed my thinking. I refused to go down that road of self-pity and why me. I refused to go down that road of being depressed, having thoughts of jealousy, suicide, worry and despair. Not this time, because I knew that everything happens for a reason and that it was one more way to learn about God. That's what I had just learned. Instead, it all made me wonder what I was doing wrong. Again, instead of trying to figure things out, I devoted myself to allowing the Spirit to lead me.

Up until this point, everything that I had learned was a theory. It sounded right, it checked out according to the books that I had read, but the only way I could really know if it was real was by living it. I knew what I had to do. I had to make a serious commitment to live truth. I had to make maa aankh. I remember not too long afterwards one of my brothers telling me that it was all about faith at this point, and he was right, that's what it was all about. I had to either put up or shut up. Refusing to die, not like this, I made maa aankh.

When I made maa aankh, I submitted and surrendered to God and the aakhu, committing that I would live upright, be ethical and balanced and strive for perfection in exchange for the blessings, grace and power of God. This pledge I made was truly powerful, because after doing so, I felt a surge of awesomeness fill my debilitating body. I could seriously sense a change beginning to occur. I didn't start speaking in tongues but I did seriously feel full with the power of love, gratitude, peace and an unexplainable joy. It was simply because I knew that everything was going to be all right. I mean, I seriously knew that I was going to get better and that this was all a *prueba* for real. I didn't know how it was going to happen, I just knew that it was going to happen and this made me smile deep from the inside out. It was truly an unexplainable happiness and inner peace that had me glowing.

I mean, when people saw me after hearing what had happened, they would apologize for me being stricken with an illness at such a young age. They had a grave look upon their face, as if I was dying, but I was smiling and was seriously "cool" about it all. This was truly the Rau that was transforming me.

Part V:
Becoming a Vessel for God

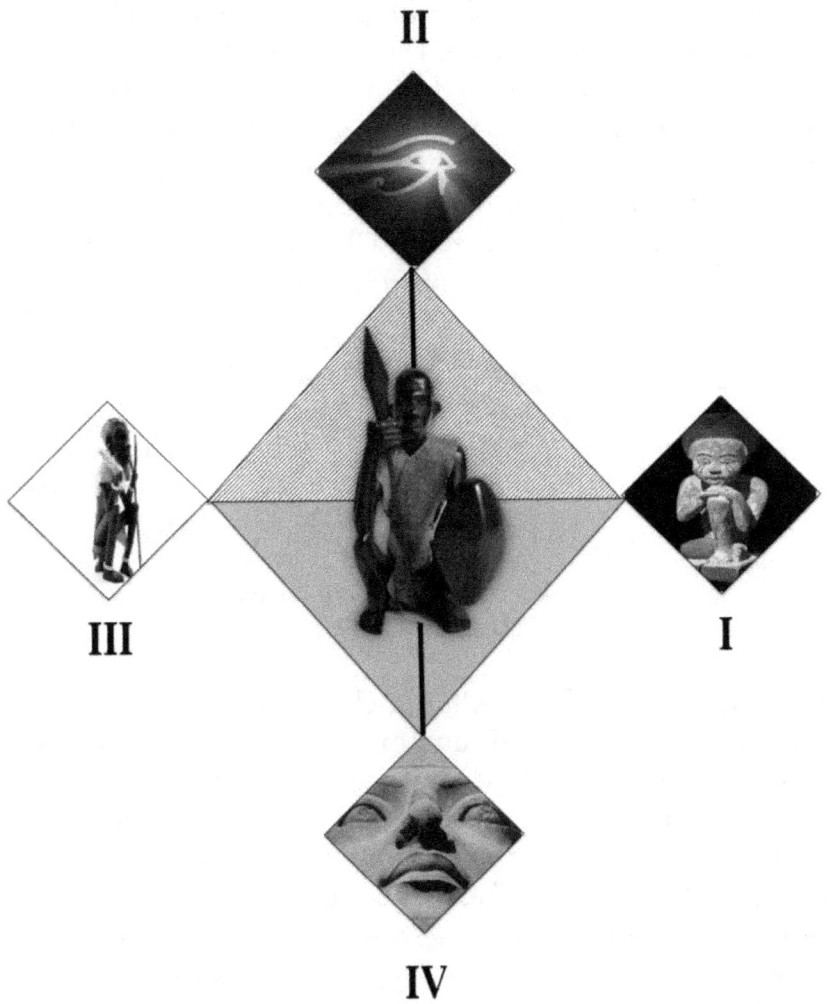

One is not born a warrior,
you become one.

–Arab Proverb

Accepting That He Will Work It Out

Did I mention that I didn't see the whole picture when I put two and two together about the red and white crown; I mean, correction, the white and red crown? Well, I wasn't even close, but after taking the oath – maa aankh–, boy were my eyes opened. I was hesitant at first to giving my life to God I was shown because when I was a youngster. I identified spiritual living with the Shaolin monk, Kwai Chang Caine from the American television series *Kung Fu*.

Aabit: The Left Eye of RA (Lunar Eye) [55]

I loved watching Kwai Chang Caine because he could kick butt and his blind master was even *sweeter* –good. What I didn't like about Caine was that he was spiritual and all but straight up bummed out walking around with no shoes, carrying a flute and hobo sack (laugh). What was so funny about this was that the Spirit showed me that this was how I used to live, as a person not concerned about my physical well being.

---

[55] The Aabit or left Utchat (Eye of Ra) represents information processed by the right hemisphere of the brain such as abstract ideas, dreams, esoteric thinking, feelings, intuitive thoughts, receptivity, femininity, the moon, ancestors (or spirits), etc.

Shortly after being told this, the image of St. Lazarus (*Lázaro*), the Catholic Sokār, came to my awareness. It was the same reason, I was shown, why I fought being a preacher: because I didn't see any balance between the spiritual and the physical. Then, interestingly, the Spirit revealed to me that I imitated Caine somewhat through my quest. Like Caine, I lived in a homeless state, went without having clothes and food to eat and carried a hobo sack too (laugh).

I laugh now because it was a humbling experience, but it was these misinformed beliefs and ideas, due to not having a serious understanding of our cultural tradition, that led me to live this way. I was shown that I changed my diet based upon these so-called spiritual theories several times for the same reason. Like so many others, I was so confused about the foods I should and shouldn't eat because every dietary author claimed that their diet was the best, to the point that I didn't know what was right or wrong anymore. Spiritually and physically, I was a mess, and this is why I felt so confused, unhappy and why I was unhealthy even though I thought I was eating the right foods, taking my vitamin supplements and now medication.

The Spirit showed me that I was living "un-holistically" because I didn't include my spirit. I was making a lot of physical or cosmetic changes, but none of this was changing what was going on within me. As a result, I was living for tomorrow instead of living for today. In other words, I was living and basing my life on what "might" happen; such as I might get cancer if I eat certain foods, so I didn't do it. I might have this problem, if I do things a certain way. This thinking that something might happen prevented me from doing certain things. It made me live for tomorrow and not focus on what was going on in my present. The constant worrying, wandering, pondering, etc. were all stemming from fear: the fear of the unknown and the fear of not being in control.

Not too long after being shown this truth, a very popular gospel song called *Jesus Will Work It Out,* by Reverend Charles Hayes and the Cosmopolitan Choir, came to mind. I remember the song from my childhood because, besides being a fast tempo song, the soloist sung about real issues of how God worked miracles in her life. In a typical call and response fashion the choir respectively sings, "Jesus will work it out", while the soloist responds by singing, "If you let him". Then the song gets real bluesy when the soloist begins asking the audience how are they going to pay their rent, put food on the table, pay bills, and take care of family needs without any money. In other words, how can you accomplish physical objectives when all of your material resources have been exhausted? The only way to do it, according to the soloist, was by turning it over to the Lord[56], so he can work it out.

This song was a sign given to me informing me that this is what I had to do. I had to allow the Spirit to lead and the only way to do this was to surrender my will, which required me having faith in God. It is only with faith that I will be able to tap into the power of God. That's when I began to see the whole picture, which is that the Power of God or the Holy Ghost, in

---

[56] The Lord, of course, is symbolized by Osar in the Kamitic tradition and Jesus in the Christian tradition, because God, remember, is too abstract and complex for the human mind to conceive. The human mind needs something to focus upon, so the highest ideals associated with one's greatest ancestor represents and symbolizes the true Son of God.

the Kamitic tradition, I was reminded, was called Rau.

It was the Rau that gave them the ability to rule their country relatively in peace as well as accomplish extraordinary feats. Like the ancient biblical writers would soon discover, the ancient Kamites believed that the Rau or Spirit of God hovered over everything and was the power that gave life to or animated everything. But the ancient Kamitic people also knew, like early Christians discovered hundreds of years later, that the Power of God has the ability to change a man and woman's mind, body and soul whenever God willed Its[57] Spirit to enter into a human being. If the Power of God were not within an individual than that individual would not act or behave as such.

Esoteric Understanding of Ancient Kamit

You see, unlike the early Christians, the ancient Kamitic people believed that the Power of God was within every man and woman, but part of it was in a dormant state. In other words, every man and woman, from the ancient Kamitic perspective, has God's divine potential within them, which means everyone regardless of their race, affiliation, background, etc. had the ability to achieve great things. One simply had to choose to tap into this power by implementing divine laws and principles into their life. The difference between a sage and a criminal, from the ancient Kamitic perspective, was simply the choices that the individual made. It was because the wise man and woman chose to be a sage they were able to

---

[57] Don't forget God is essentially although viewed as masculine is in reality androgynous.

awaken or gain access to the Power of God that had the ability to change an individual's mind, body and soul. Whereas a criminal chose not to be a sage so they continued to receive the basic blessings of life from God but had no miracles as such. *This is what Osar and Set symbolize.*

Understand that the Rau is the Power and Spirit of God that animates our being, takes care of all our needs, as well as enlightens the mind of every human being. Psychologically speaking, it is what westerners refer to as the unconscious mind (also called the collective unconscious or super-conscious), which is the part of our being that works like a computer, stores our habits (both good and bad), inspires, guides, reveals information to us intuitively, stores our memories, houses our experiences, never sleeps, helps us to create new thoughts and ideas, controls all of the autonomous functions of our being perfectly (such as our digestion, assimilation of hormones, carrying of oxygen through our bloodstream, etc.), not to mention plays host to all of the spiritual beings (surviving characteristics and personalities) that exist within our being.

To distinguish between the lower parts or the basic blessings of the Rau that everyone is privileged to, that animates our being, stores our memories, etc. from the higher parts of the Rau, that has an infinite amount of wisdom, has the power to change an individual's mind, body and soul, the ancient Kamites decided to explore and study the Spirit of God. Upon doing so, they discovered that the Spirit of God or the Rau had nine divisions (some believe were seven). These nine divisions of the Spirit, from lowest to highest, are:

Divisions of the Spirit

9. The **Khab** division governs the physical body.
8. The **Khabit** division, also called the shadow, governs our emotions, senses and instinctive nature of our being.
7. The **Sahu** division, also called the spiritual vehicle, stores our personal memories, ideas, and beliefs. It is our personal source of inspiration and motivation that corresponds to our subconscious.
6. The **Ka** division corresponds to man and woman's personal power *or espiritual cuadro*.
5. **The Ab division, called the spiritual heart, allows man and woman to exercise his or her freedom.**
4. The **Ren** division, called the name, corresponds to the man and woman's destiny and their racial memories (ancestors). There is a story connected to our name, even if our parents made the name up because of the way it sounds[58]. Our ren reflects how we act, our destiny and energy. If our ren is negative in any way it should be changed.
3. The **Shekhem** division gives man and woman the ability to perform miracles in their life. It corresponds to the all-powerful aspect of the unconscious.
2. The **Khu** division allows man and woman to learn the Will of God. It corresponds to the all-knowing aspect of the unconscious.
1. The **Ba** division, called the divine spark, is

---

[58] This is important for us to understand because in recent years we have been made to believe that the names are "ghetto" and not authentic because our parents made the names up. When it is understood why our parents created the name or the story behind the chosen name we were given, we can hopefully find pride and dignity in wearing it.

responsible for uniting man and woman with all of the living things in the universe. It corresponds to the omnipresent aspect of the unconscious and gives human beings the ability to know everything.

I found it quite interesting that this seemed to correspond with the Supreme Mathematics, the Paut Neteru, the Kabala and Kardec's Types of Spirits listing. The difference being that I was beginning to see how this corresponded to the radiant, fiery and encircling serpent on the head of RA. It appeared to be more like a rippling effect, beginning with the innermost sphere and expanding outward. Thus, indicating that our spirit is a complex organism composed of nine layers.

Before proceeding, it must be understood that what I was being shown was an esoteric understanding of our being, from a cultural perspective. Since I had a lot of confusion about the divinities. I had to separate the archetypes associated with these divisions in order to get a better understanding of the subject at hand. Upon doing so I saw that these divisions existed within all of us and was able to get a more profound understanding about the human being. It was through this association that I was shown that according to ancient Kamitic thought the number 1 is "True" Knowledge because it corresponds to the highest and our innermost division of our spirit, that the ancient Kamites called the Ba. The number 2 is "True" Wisdom because it corresponds to the second highest and the next innermost division of our spirit, that the ancient Kamites called the Khu. The number 3 is "True" Understanding and corresponds to our third highest division, and so on, all the way to our outermost being.

Nine Divisions of the Spirit

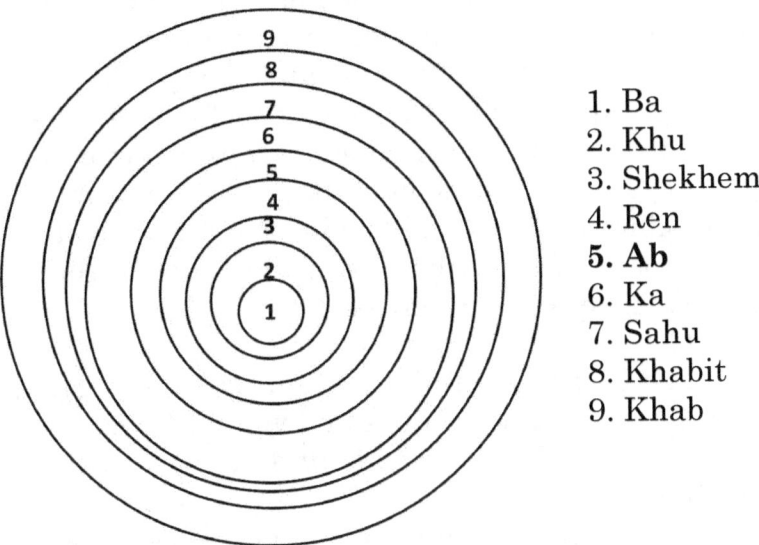

1. Ba
2. Khu
3. Shekhem
4. Ren
5. **Ab**
6. Ka
7. Sahu
8. Khabit
9. Khab

What this meant to me was that, while we all have access to these divisions of the spirit that exists within our being., most men and women in the world choose to function from divisions 6 through 9 (with 10 being strictly external influences), meaning most men and women are concerned exclusively about their physical wellbeing (money, clothes, houses, cars, alcohol, drugs, etc.) and will do whatever it physically takes (even if it means harming themselves and others) to get these things. "True" Knowledge and everything else comes from within.

Now, a lot of authors I have read talk about how everything comes from within but provide no real tangible examples of what this means. So, I decided to test this theory by creating a plan on something that I truly wanted and how to go about getting it, like some money to pay some bills. For instance, I had a $265 car payment, which wasn't much but when I became temporarily unable to work, it was an added expense that was hurting our funds. So, I wrote down every feasible way that I could get some money to pay this bill on paper. I wrote down every possible way that I could think of in order to exhaust and expose my physical limitations to me. Then when I found all the best possible ways that I could generate some money in order to pay some of the bills that I had, I put my list of possibilities away and tried not to think about my desire at all. That's when I saw the magic or the power of God work within my being.

When I stopped thinking about how I was going to get the money for a few days and when I finally picked my list up, I discovered a different and easier way of obtaining the money that I needed in order to pay the car bill. It was truly amazing because it was like out of the clear blue sky a solution to my problems came to me. Shortly after, while talking to the bank attendant about my account, she mentioned that because I was on temporary disability there was temporary disability insurance on my car note. This basically meant that my insurance would make payments on my car until I was able to return back to work. This made me realize that the Divine is definitely within our being and that when we allow "It" to play an active role in our life. We will find different routes and solutions to obtaining what we want.

What this taught me was that we all need the same things. We all need money, clothes, a house, etc. (natural resources) in order to physically exist, so in this regard we are all the same. God doesn't favor one individual, group of people, etc. over another. This also means that one group of people is not better than another or vice versa. Our children need to understand that certain groups of people are not smarter or better at performing certain skills like doing mathematics, while others are better at playing music, etc. God doesn't play favorites.

What distinguishes, us from one another are the choices that we make. The reason an individual or group of people are better at performing a particular task is that they choose to develop that skill by practicing and making all of the necessary sacrifices to do so. This means that what determines who we are and what will be are the choices that we make. In regards to the divisions of our spirit, this means we could either choose to try to accomplish our goals from the outside in (9 to 1) or from the inside out like a ripple effect (1 to 9). In other words, if we have to lie, cheat, steal, maim and murder to get the things that we want, we are doing things from the outside in and are no different from the beasts that live in the wild, surviving based upon their animal instincts. If we submit to the Spirit (1 to 9), It will show us the way.

What makes man and woman different from the animals is that we have an Ab, which is number 5 and corresponds to "True" Power. In other words, man and woman have a Power that animals do not have and that power is the power of choice. It is because of man and woman's power of choice or free will that we can choose to live like an animal or live like a god or goddess. In order for us to live like a god or goddess we have to access the higher divisions of our spirit. It is because of our Ab that when our loved ones die we wish them peace in the afterlife, because we sense that there is something else after death. It is our Ab that makes us feel guilty for committing a crime because we can sense that we are harming others by our ill actions.

The Divisions of the Spirit	Levels of the Spirit	Esoteric Level of the Spirit	Story of Osar
Khab (9) Khabit (8) Sahu (7) Ka (6)	Lower Divisions, Lower Level of the Spirit, Lower Kamit -(limited possibilites)	TASETT	Set (Set-an, Setanel, the Devil, devils, ghost, etc.)
Ab (5)	Four Moments of the Sun	Amun RA, KhepeRA, RA and RA Atum	Hru (Son of Osar, Child of God)
Ren (4) Shekhem (3) Khu (2) Ba (1)	Upper Divisions, Upper Level of the Spirit, Upper Kamit – unlimited possibilities	KAMTA	Osar (The Ancestors, Jesus Christ, Guardian Angels, etc.)

Divisions of the Spirit and the Maa Aankh

When we do what is correct, it is our Ab that gives us the feeling that we will be justly rewarded or that justice will be served. All of this is because the Ab division of our spirit gives us the power to be whatever we choose to be. The Ab division of the spirit, standing in between the nine divisions, is what makes man and woman unique. When an individual decides to live and do what is right based upon my new understanding of Mathematics, that's when they gain access to the higher divisions of the spirit, numbers 1-4.

So, to simplify matters, the Ab division of the Spirit, which corresponds to number 5 gives man and woman the power, freedom and right to choose to either function from divisions 1-4 or 6-9[59]. Divisions 1-4 (Ba, Khu, Shekhem and Ren), from my understanding, became known as the Upper Divisions, Upper Level of the Spirit, and eventually Upper Kamit or the Black Lands[60] –KAMTA (signifying that it is a mystery). While divisions 6-9 (Ka, Sahu, Khabit and Khab) became known as the Lower Divisions, Lower Level of the Spirit and eventually the Red Lands – TASETT (to indicate that it is mundane).

Since energy cannot be created or destroyed but only changes and transforms, el Ab, which gives man and woman free will, corresponds to man and woman's awareness, consciousness, conscience, self and soul or power to choose and become. It is the part of our being that makes decisions based upon what it has learned or experienced. It is always aware, giving us the power to choose, because it is essentially free. To indicate that, God gives us an Ab, which is the right to choose and make decisions, the freedom to become whatever it is we want to be. The Ab is identified with the sun, which moves freely between the two great lands.

So, in order to gain access to the higher levels of the Spirit, KAMTA, the Ab, it appears based upon my research, has to be associated with Amun RA and KhepeRA. When the Ab is at the RA and RA Atum positions, it is at the lower division o the Spirit or

---

[59] Keeping in mind that 10 correspond to the physical realm.

[60] The Black Lands are the fertile lands of our ancient ancestors.

TASETT; meaning when one moves their Ab (awareness, conscious, heart, will, etc.) to the Amun RA (midnight) position they gain access to divisions 1-4, which also puts in check divisions 6-9. When they move their Ab to the RA (midday) position, they only will have access to divisions 6-9.

When I compared what I found with the *Story of Osar*, I found that when we approach life from our ancient ancestors' or ancient cultural perspective, besides revealing that the ancient Kamitic (and other traditional African) systems are not mere superstitious arts and practices but actually practices based upon the observation of natural sciences, we have the ability to become whatever it is that we choose to be. Our failures, past experience, affiliations, background, etc. don't determine who we will be, because our Ab is essentially free to become whatever we choose to be.

Of course, similar themes can be found in various cultures. In fact, it is commonly stated that, "I can do all things through Christ who strengthens me," but when it is understood from a metaphorical perspective who the Christ really is, we get a deeper understanding of the Spirit of God and our connection to the Divine. You see, when it is understood from the ancient Kamitic perspective that the Power of God lies within us and that the only thing keeping us from experiencing the full power of God's grace are the choices that we make, it should become clear that it is impossible for us to rise out of poverty and the other social ills as mere human beings, but for an individual that has re-connected (religion) back to the higher parts of God's Power (symbolized as Osar, The Ancestors, Jesus Christ, those consumed by whiteness-purity, knowledge, wisdom, spiritual power, conscience, etc.), nothing is impossible. All they have to do is put their mind to it.

The deeper one goes within or the more introverted one becomes the more powerful they become. Whereas the more extroverted an individual becomes the more they depend upon their physical senses and the less powerful they become. This is not a magical pill, but when we impress what we want upon our spirit. The spirit will show us how to accomplish and achieve the desired goal.

So, returning to the *Story of Osar*, Hru was able to defeat Set (the lower divisions of the Spirit of God) and win the war (overcome the trials, tribulations and other problems in TASETT) because he surrendered his will to Osar (the higher divisions of the Spirit of God) and reclaimed the throne (knowledge, wisdom, peace, prosperity, which reside in KAMTA), thus revealing that the righteous really do not die (spiritually or physically) but they are reborn. As Jill Scott sings, now I can *Breathe*.[61]

Chillout Baby

I began to see that when I surrendered my will or Ab to the higher divisions of the spirit, that's when I was in my most receptive, powerful and purest state of being, because that's when my Ab is at the Amun RA point, the moment of renewal. When my Ab is at this moment in time, I am closest to KAMTA, which gives me direct access to my aakhu and netcharu. I noticed

---

[61] The reader will recall that at the Rã and Rã Atum moments there is excitement, a sense of emergency circulating around, signified by a shortness of breath.

at this particular moment we also receive most of our dreams.

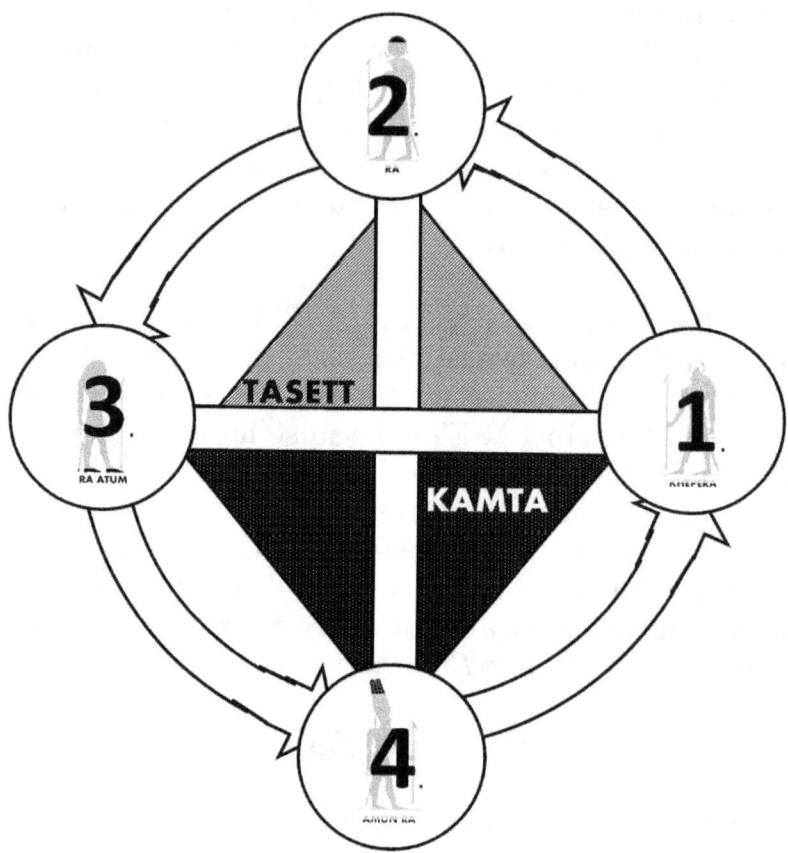

Figure 14: Maa Aankh and the Cycle of Life

1. KHEPERA
The sunrise (6AM), the East, birth, the beginning, awaken conscious (from sleep), Spring, the symbol of emergence from nothing, physical conscious-ness, the color black, which is KALA in Ki-Kongo.

2. RA
The midday (12PM), the North, masculinity, life, waking conscious (Solar as the Eye of God or the Left Aakhut), the

peak of male physical strength, emotional consciousness, warning, the color red, which is TUKULA in Ki-Kongo.

3. RA ATUM
The sunset (6PM), the West, death, descent, loss of conscious, Fall, symbol of the elders associated with those close to the death, mental consciousness, symbolized as an aging man. The color white, which is LUVEMBA in Ki-Kongo.

4. AMUN RA
The midnight (12AM), the South, femininity, rebirth, peak of female receptivity, the dreaming conscious (Lunar Eye of God or the Right Aabit), spiritual consciousness, the color yellow, brilliance, which is MUSONI in Ki-Kongo.

When I began to make comparisons between what I saw in nature the maa aankh, the above observances were discovered.

At that moment, the summer 1990-1991 hit by the green-eyed bandit Erick Sermon and Parrish Smith Making Dollars, aka EPMD, came to mind loud and clear that, *You Gots to Chill.*

Hru dwelling in the land of his uncle I imagined was more than just tough. It was horrible because it was hot. Things most likely never went right. Life was not fair. It was full of problems and trial and error. I could imagine it being a living hell. I could imagine him being frustrated, upset and angry a lot because he probably felt like he was fighting a losing battle, but when he *chilled* (relaxed his mind), that's when the part of his being that has the power to do kicked in.

What this meant to me was that the battle is

not mine. The battle has been and always will be between Osar and Set, so I shouldn't take it personal. It is my job rotating as the sun around these two lands to be, according to John 7:14–15, "in the world, but not of the world", or 93,000,000 miles away from everything[62]. In other words, I have to live in the world –TASETT (lower divisions of the Spirit), but our actions, behaviors, speech, etc. should be based upon KAMTA (the higher divisions of the Spirit). I should not be living my life as Set had, by the seat of my pants, full of anger, envy, resentfulness, disgust, excessive passion, wild and chaotic. This way of life eventually leads to complete desolation and isolation, symbolized as the desert land. I should be striving to live our life as Osar had done, by "**working to help each other to achieve a common goal.**"[63] I should instead be encouraging, inspiring and optimistic. This of course got me thinking, and made me see that the Rau, in nature, moves from Amun RA to RA Atum. It made me realize that it was optimal for me to try and keep my Ab at (or at least) in between the Amun RA and KhepeRA moments, because this is the moment when the Rau energy is the highest.

    I noticed that when I moved my Ab (Consciousness/Will) between the Amun RA and KhepeRA moments of time, that Amun RA is also the state of perfection and KhepeRA as the mind of a child (innocent and worry free). This meant to me that when I impress suggestions of change at this meditative-

---

[62] The Sun is 93,000,000 miles away from the Earth.

[63] This doesn't mean go and break bread with your enemy nor doesn't it mean that your enemy is all of a sudden going to be your friend. It is all about spiritual evolution.

renewal mind state, by theory it should be very effective, because it is like planting a seed in the fertile lands of KAMTA. So, if I wanted real change to occur in my life, then it would be wise at first to do the spiritual work –KAMTA– followed by physical work – TASETT. By doing the spiritual work one is able to plant the seed and establish firm roots that will eventually bear physical fruit. Keeping in mind that the Rau is divine energy and matter, which manifests itself as our emotions (energy) and matter (our physical beings, etc.), made me realize that there are numerous ways to impress upon the Rau to initiate physical change.

One of the most common ways of impressing a goal upon the Rau is through repetition, which is how habits are formed. Just then I remembered when I was in school during my youth getting those 1,000 sentence writing assignments that "I will not do _____."

There are of course other ways to impress what one wants upon the Rau as well, such as symbolic action. For instance, if one was to take a small stone and toss it over their shoulder, it would symbolize them getting rid of a problem. Another symbolic action would be burning a letter or something that one wants to rid them selves of completely, such as a negative habit. It was from this understanding that I began to see why I was taught by Ms. B not to cross myself and by Papá Raúl not to lay with my feet pointed towards the entrance door, because this is how the dead are carried out. This explained the purpose of certain superstitious beliefs and practices.

Another practice I found used by religious circles is the use of candles. By burning a candle one can impress upon the Rau the type of change they want, by simply suggesting that when the candle burns all the way to the socket it would be implanted into the KAMTA.

There are numerous ways to plant a seed into KAMTA, because the Rau, being composed of energy and matter, loves movement, and movement means rhythm. Rhythm exists in music, singing, drumming and dancing, which explain why cultures that have a high regard for spirituality also have a complex and vast musical, song and dance tradition.

The other thing that I learned is that because in KAMTA, logically, everything doesn't make sense but exists in allegorical, metaphorical and symbolic terms, this is the reason why logically speaking our dreams do not make sense, but when we understand the meaning of the symbols in the dreams the message becomes clear. It is because things in KAMTA are grouped together by association. This is the reason why the mere mention of the color red will trigger images of a fire, hot, red fire truck, flashing lights, etc., along with some emotional responses as well.

It was this understanding that taught me how to communicate and how to interpret messages from the invisible world. I can now firmly say that God answers all the prayers. The problem is that we haven't learned how to listen and interpret the signs that God gives us. When I learned how to observe nature with my spiritual senses, that's when I saw God's fingerprints everywhere, which led me to conclude that Rau is moved by repetition, rhythm, symbolic action, strange yet meaningful allegories and symbolic association.

It was this observation due to me moving my Ab in between the Amun RA to KhepeRA moments that allowed me to see that opposite of Amun RA was RA, which is depicted as the midday sun. The netchar associated with the midday sun was Hruaakhuti, the warrior spirit that first challenged Set. Hruaakhuti wears the mask of a hawk, emphasizing by association that he is a hardcore fighter and worker, hence the midday sun. It was after making this realization that Hruaakhuti appeared to me as the spirit that issues warning to us by trying to prevent catastrophes from occurring. He is the netchar that teaches us about the dangers of fire by rushing to our aide to avert and deter us from making a disastrous decision. Catastrophe and disaster, I saw, was definitely Set, signifying that one has entered the danger zone and is approaching death –RA and RA Atum. This zone is where everything is at the extreme. Panic! *Everything from Amun RA to KhepeRA is the safe zone.*

It became apparent to me that when we approach RA and RA Atum our Ab is entering Set's realm. This is the realm where our choices and decisions are influenced by low energy and low spirits. It is here, I noticed based upon my experience, that I had negative thoughts and feelings of being overwhelmed, anger, frustration, resentment, depression, etc. I could see that when I became worrisome and saddened by my physical situation, that's when I began to do desperate things. Desperate decisions aren't normally well thought out, which makes them even more dangerous, catapulting us into an even worse scenario.

Shortly after making this realization, I spoke with my mother on how she beat cancer, and she confirmed for me that one has to keep a positive state of mind. *Keep your Ab between Amun RA and KhepeRA.* My mother's remedy for beating this cancerous spirit was to thank God daily for her healing, maintain the same daily routine, take her medication, and read her Bible.

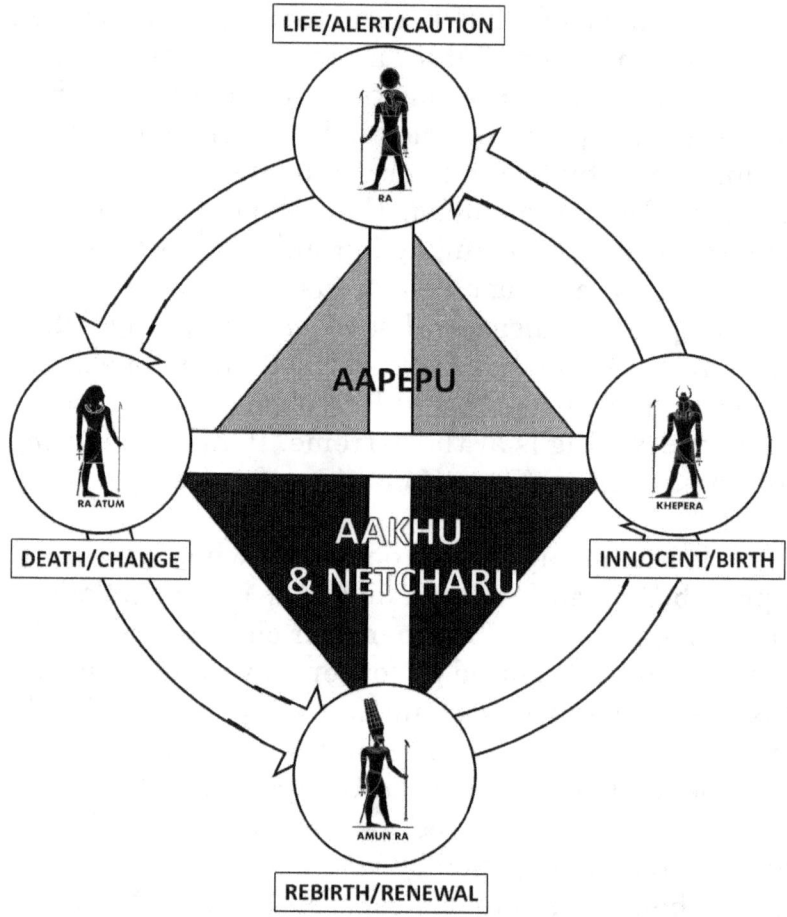

Figure 15: Maa Aankh and the Flow of Rau

    I never thought about it until I saw Hruaakhuti prior to speaking to her, and I realized that he manifested himself through her to beat the cancer. My mother, I noticed, wasn't cussing and fussing, but she was strong and resilient like a calm samurai warrior.

She told me that she didn't dwell on what the doctors' said but put her faith in God. It was through the conversation I had with my mother that I learned that Hruaakhuti doesn't just appear when it comes to life and death situations, but he is always near, patrolling the perimeters of our spirit like a dedicated soldier.

When I put it all together, I understood the Rau is the Holy Ghost, the Power or Spirit of God that journeys between the two lands (spirit/physical, enegy/matter, etc.) and can be manipulated, tricked, subject to attack, etc. because it is the fiery, encircling serpent. The head of Rau is near the Amun RA and KhepeRA moments of time. The tail of Rau is near RA and RA Atum. It was all beginning to make sense as I was plunged deeper into the esoteric understanding of things —particularly Deuteromony 28, which talks about blessings for obedience and curses for disobedience. In brief, those that follow the commandments of the Lord (Rau) will be blessed and their offspring blessed and prosperous because of the oath they have taken to live upright given to them by the ancestors. They will be made the head and not the tail. If one, however, failed to live according to the commandments given by the Lord (Rau), they will suffer abundantly, live in constant fear, dread both the day and night, be stricken with uncurable illnesses, and become slave to others' wills and wants. Others will be made the head and one will become the tail because of disobedience to the Lord (Rau). It was all an allusion of not being in control of one's spirit and being a slave to one's lower nature.

The message was clear. My time had come. It was my time to put what I learned into practice and decides if I wanted to be either at the head or at the tail end of the Rau —God's power.

Netcharu: The Inhabitants of KAMTA

Now, I had met the netcharu or had been formally introduced to them previously, but now I was beginning to really see these guardian angels surrounding me. I began to see them when I stopped thinking of these spirits as being archetypes and started to see them as energies. It was this perspective that led me to see how these spirits manifest themselves and how to establish a personal bond with these guardian angels that protect me.

Keep in mind what was said about the Rau being energy/matter and how allegories, metaphors, stories, symbols, rhythm, music, repetition, associations, etc. are all viable ways of communicating with the Spirit of God because they are unusual (non rational) methods. By using these methods I was able to improve and increase my ability to learn, retain and retrieve information from the higher divisions of the Spirit or KAMTA[64], which is where the netcharu our guardian angels reside.

Osar (Ausar, Asar, Osiris)

Osar, the heroic king that unified Kamit by introducing ethics, law and morality to the people, as well as bringing peace and prosperity to the land. But his jealous brother murdered him and later his body was hacked into pieces. After eventually being mummified and given a proper burial, Osar became

---

[64] It should now become clear why the ancient Kamitic and other traditional African and non-Western cultures continued to use unusual symbols to express their thoughts, ideas and beliefs.

the model ancestor for the ancient Kamitic people, governing the Underworld. He is a cool, calm, collective but very strong. It is because of Osar that all the netcharu have strong, courageous, ethical, moral and charitable characteristics. Osar, naturally, because he set the standard, has more of these characteristics (or light) than others, but this is the defining point that sets them drastically apart from the aapepu.

His colors are white and silver, white and blue, white and gold, white and green or simply all white. He corresponds to Jehovah Shalom, which means, "The Lord is our Peace", and symbols sacred to him are objects of stability like backbones and mountains. He has no special number and is the patron of mystics, dreamers and idealists. Osares are fond of all white things and white foods, but they are never to be given alcoholic beverages.

Djahuti (Tahuti, Tehuti, Thouth)

The faithful and trustworthy friend of Osar, who assisted the Lord in the unification of Kamit, is the only one that Set truly feared. Djahuti is the spirit of secrets and mysteries that corresponds to Jehovah Ezer – The Lord is our Helper[65] (Problem Solver). Djahuti's color is white and indigo, and his symbols are anything symbolizing wisdom including (but not limited to) cranes, ibises, owls, etc. Djahuti's special number is eight and he is the patron of diviners, high priest/esses, scribes and shamans.

---

[65] Jehovah Ezer, technically speaking, is not one of the classic Names of God in the Hebrew language. The biblical writers did however declare that the Lord is their Helper, just like they said the Lord is their Shepherd.

Oset (Auset, Iset, Euset, Isis)

The devoted wife of Osar, patroness of all children and mothers, is considered the mother of all and mother of revolutionary change. Oset was responsible for teaching Osar how to cultivate cereals for food, thus becoming the mother of all. When she heard the news that Osar was dead, she, despite the threat to her own life, sought out the body of the deceased king in order to given him an heir. Oset's defiance, from a political perspective, signified her attempt to restore dignity and greatness, thus making her the initiator of revolution.

Had it not been for her courage, devotion, love and desire to give birth to an heir, evil would never had been challenged and defeated. For this reason Oset corresponds to Jehovah Shammah, which means, "The Lord is There". Oset's colors are blue and white, and her special number is the number seven. Osets are fond of perfumes and lustrous objects like pearls and silvers. Her symbols: fish, seashells, seeds, etc. reflect her love for family, power of healing, and protection of wealth.

Npu-Kozo (Anpu, Enpu, Anubis)

Legends claim that Oset found Npu hidden in the marshes of Lower Kamit when she was searching for Osar's body in the marshes in Lower Kamit. Afterwards she adopted the child, who acted as a guardian for her and assisted her in finding the body of Osar.

Npu is one of the most famous of the netcharu, appearing in numerous movies and various comic books, because Npus are the young spiritual messengers with the jackal mask. Npus watch over crossroads, crosswalks, and all roads, and govern all forms of communication. Npus wear the head of a jackal or dog[66] to symbolize their childish, playful and curious ability to always find the truth, no matter how well one tries to hide it from them. For this reason, Npus are responsible for leading hunting expeditions and searching out lost things. The first child of Osar abandoned in the marshes is always, following the aakhu, appeased first, so that one does not get lost along the way. Npu, simply put, helps us to find things, which includes finding our way to a safely to our destination and back. Npu's colors are red, black and white and his special numbers are three and multiples of it. Npus are fond of sweets, candies, liquors, cigars, toys, dangerous/risky objects (like cutlasses, knifes, weapons, etc.) and walking sticks or canes.

A bit tricky and playful, Npu reminds one to be careful what one asks for and must be told specifically what one's intentions are. He is the patron of lawyers, technicians, servicemen, shamans, and anyone that acts as a bridge between two worlds. A faithful and protective guide, Npu corresponds to Jehovah Rohi, which means, "The Lord is our Shepherd", but if offended will allow one to wander in the dark like the Childrn of Israel, alone like a lost sheep with no guide, because quiet as kept Npu is the Kamitic Moses.

Nebhet (Nebt-het, Nephthys)

---

[66] Some believe that the jackal or dog mask is given to Npu to hide a deformity due to him being conceived from the drunken Osar. Others believe the dog mask is an actual deformed head, again because of Osar's drunkenness.

Nebhet, whose name means "Lady of the House", is the patroness of beauty, entertainment (musicians, artists, etc.), wealth (since entertainment is big business in contemporary times), eroticism and the esoteric arts, especially love magic. Legends state that Nebhet was originally married to Set but was in love with Osar, so much so that she either disguised herself as Oset or made the Lord drunk with ale and conceived a child with him. As a result of their union, Npu was born, but when Set murdered Osar and usurped the throne, out of fear that he would murder her child, the young mother abandoned the child soon after he was born[67]. Later, disgusted by Set's rage, she left her tyrannical husband and assisted Oset in finding and resurrecting the Kingdom of Osar.

Nebhet's colors are yellow or gold and her special number is five. She is fond of all beautiful and shiny things like jewelry. Her symbols are all things of beauty as well as kites, which she once transformed Oset and herself into as they mourned over the corpse of Osar. In the same way the deceased where identified in various areas of traditional Africa with kites or flags. For this reason she corresponds to the Jehovah Nissi, which means, "The Lord is our Banner (of Love)".

Hruaakhuti (Hru Khuti, Harakhte)

Hru-Ur (Hru the Elder), also known as Hru Behdet and Hruaakhuti, is a strong, no-nonsense, protective, old warrior spirit that championed for Ra before Hru-

---

[67] This story was later adopted and modified by the ancient Hebrews and became the origin of the biblical Moses.

oset (Hru Son of Oset) was born. Hru-Ur's main centre was at Edfu in Upper Kamit, but it was in Behdet where clansmen first shaped tools into weapons and fought off invaders led by Set in both Upper and Lower Kamit. As a reward for his prowess he was given the title Hru Behdet, Hru Edfu and Hruaakhuti.

The title Hruaakhuti, which means "Hru of the Two Horizons", is a reminder that the valuable metals that Hru-Ur shaped can be used as tools or weapons. In other words, like anything they can be used to create or to destroy, to defend or offend, to protect or harm, therefore hard work and responsibility are required.

It was Hruaakhuti that taught me a very valuable lesson about our ancestral spiritual traditions, which is that it is harder to obtain than maintain the things we want in life. In other words, it is easier to maintain and protect something that you have versus trying to obtain something that you want. It was this change of perspective that made me see how Hruaakhuti protects us from dangers seen and unseen by trying to keep us from moving to the midday sun.

Hruaakhuti's color is blood red and his symbols are all sharp objects (cutlasses, daggers, knives, spears, etc.) and tools. His special numbers are three and four. He is the patron of all that work with sharp instruments and tools, such as mechanics, guards, military personnel, EMS (emergency medical staff) personnel, firemen, surgeons, etc. He corresponds to Jehovah Jireh, which means, "The Lord is our Provider".

Maat (Ma 'At)

Maat is another famous netcharu due to the concept and principles of the same name Maa, which means balance, order, law, justice, reciprocity, etc. Some legends claim that she is the wife of Djahuti; others claim that she is the wife of Hruaakhuti. My experience led me to discover that she is neither. She is, however, closely associated with several of the netcharu, and acts more like a guardian, by bringing balance between the living and the Underworld. She shows one how to live for tomorrow by doing what is right today and helps us to obtain balance. She is the guardian of the sane, who can easily tilt the scales and make one insane.

Like many female spirits, I have found my Maat to be fond of shiny things but that she finds beauty in what is considered by most odd things, such as precious gems, stones, crystals and metals. But she is not a dainty oddity. After Set usurped the throne, I was shown that it was Maat who fought to restore and maintain balance, law and order. With one foot in the physical world and the other in the spiritual world, she sees both sides of the picture and therefore is the patroness of seers, philosophers, scientists and those that work to restore and maintain balance and order, such as honest policemen and judges. An ancient gypsy[68], she enjoys water, rum, dark wines, moist

---

[68] Coincidentally, I discovered later that the word gypsy according to the Oxford English Dictionary is derived from the word Egyptian, which was initially written Egipcian, Egypcian, 'gipcian, 'gypcian, to gitano (in Spanish), gitan (in French) and gypsy (in English) to mean wandering people that fit the European image of the dark-skinned Egyptians that were skilled in esoteric practices.

fruits like pears, nuts, as well as crystal balls, scales, etc. A very classy yet mysterious spirit, Maat corresponds to Jehovah Zidkenu, which means, "The Lord is our Righteousness", and her colors are sky or powder blue and yellow. Her special numbers are two and four.

Hru (Hra, Horus)

Hru, the Son of Osar and Oset, the true heir to the throne, is a very fiery and hot spirit that rules over justice. The child of Osar, believed to have acquired some of his talents from RA, rules over fire, thunder and lightning, which he uses to punish those who have escaped justice. Hru is famously remembered for two paths, one as Hrupakhart –"Hru the Child"– in which he is a very arrogant, opinionated, rash, hot tempered, borderlining tyrant, and Hru Maa Khru –"Hru True of Voice"– where he is fiery, hot, bold warrior with a high libido, yet he is mild mannered, fearless, reserved in speech and can often appear to be conceited and even mean, when in truth, it is just that he is truly above pettiness.

Hru is the patron of athletes, captains, managers, chemists, rulers, generals, heroes, leaders, public speakers and all those that have a competitive, heroic and leadership spirit. He governs success and his special colors are red and white. He is fond of red objects, strong foods like strong ales, stout beers, and strong coffees. He likes things that express their maleness or masculinity and distinct, unique smelling fragrances. He corresponds to Jehovah Sabaoth, which means, "The Lord is our Commander or Host", and his special number is six.

Sokar (Seker, Soqqar)

While Maat rules the gateway to the cemetery, it is Sokār that rules over the cemetery, and the influence of rebirth and renewal. It is during our visit to the cemetery that one learns about Sokār. As one buries their sorrows it is hoped that when they leave they are refreshed and renewed. Death is necessary in order for life to exist. Therefore, just like the burying of a seed in fertile soil, it is hoped that new life will soon emerge. This new life can be recovery from a bad habit, an addiction and debilitating illness, a dying relationship, etc.

Sokār is the patron of derelicts, beggars, the homeless, those afflicted with illness, disabilities and the less fortunate, and reminds one to be humble and thankful and to remember that God has the power to tear down any wall.

Sokār is fond of rum, cigars, dark flat ales, perfumes and colognes. He likes simple foods like beans, rice, corn, seeds and grains. He is a blessing in disguise. He is associated with the prodigal son and corresponds to Jehovah Rapha, which means, "The Lord is our Healer (to the original state of being)". Sokār's colors are white, indigo and yellow; and his number is 13.

Aapepu: The Inhabitants of TASETT

Just as Osar set the standard on what the netcharu are, Set[69] set the standard on what the aapepu will be.

---

[69] It is not known if Set was an actual foreigner that settled along the Nile after the other clans settled or not. I was shown however that Set was pretty

Set for the most part is uncontrollable, raw, sensual power. When power is not balanced, controlled, or managed properly it is chaotic, disastrous, destructive, unpredictable and wild. For this reason, storms, tornadoes and other forms of natural disasters were seen as signs of this malevolent and mischievious spirit. Also, accidents, arguments, problems, trials, tribulations and war were also attributed to Set since he disrupts and disturbs the order of things.

Now that I understood how this energy "thing" worked, I could see how Set, the ruler of this northern territory, became Setan and Satan. Through my research I learned that the mystic Bonaventure also associated the north with Hell, which is the realm of the Beast in the orthodox kabalah tradition. But no one ever explained what all of this meant and usually, when people talk about hell and the devil, they become frightened and spooked with thoughts of going to hell. It is the lack of details in understanding who and what the devil or Set is, I found, what gives him so much power in most people's lives. My mother would say all of the time, "They say the devil is the author of confusion," and what's the best way confusion enters into our mind? It is through doubt. When you are not certain on what it is that you are doing and why, you begin to doubt, and that's when Set leads you astray.

So, when I took a closer look at Set and really tried to understand who and what he is, I learned of course that he is associated with the bad seed of

---

popular in ancient times and once called Setanel or Satanel, which I found to be interesting because "El" is ancient Hebrew meaning God. Thus indicating that even amongst the ancient Hebrews he had a divine status as an angel of God that was kicked out of heaven.

humankind. But, just to call him the devil and run in fear does us a disservice because it doesn't reveal how Set manifests himself in our life. It is only when I began to see that Set, is Setan, Satan, Satanel, also called St. Nick, the jolly king of the North Pole, Santa Claus, that it became clear why Set is called the spirit of extreme sensuality and unpredictability. It is because Set's main weapons are the guilt and addiction, which he uses through misuse and perversions of pleasure. This is why Hru cut the seat of Set's pants, but also explains why Santa Claus is offered food and drink in exchange for gifts[70].

You see, the Kamau said that Set was the ruler of the desert lands because they associated excess pleasure and sensuality (emotions) with the extreme heat of a drying desert (the flesh). Thousands of years later, the poet Dante (1265-1321) did the same thing by associating the fall of Lucifer from the south of Jerusalem causing the land to dry and retreat north. This is why the Kamau called the northern territory TASETT, because the Kamau saw that our emotions are basically what we call the Devil's Playground. This is where we are the weakest and why we have so many problems. It is here we have all of our trials and tribulations.

---

[70] People can argue all they want about if Santa Claus is real or not, but most children know that he is, which is why all over the world. Children with no chimneys offer him cookies (sweets) and drink. No, he doesn't physically consume these offerings meant to sway his judgment but he does absorb the essence of the offerings given to him. And, just to think, people have the audacity to call individuals that venerate their ancestors focused on bringing peace idol worshippers and pagans. I mean anyone that tells their child to believe in Santa Claus has no right to accuse anyone of idol worshipping.

Set the Kamau doesn't just play tricks but he and those who follow him, it must be understood, sow seeds of chaos, destruction, and discord through the pleasures of the flesh. This is why the initiates stated, when they recited the *42 Declarations of Maa*, that they "have not" done a particular act or behavior, because the Kamau understood that anything that causes chaos, destruction, discord, etc. was an invitation for Set to bring his destructive change, which eventually leads to death. This is why the Kamau tried to erase all memory of Akhenaten from record, because, in their eyes, what he did almost brought complete ruin to their nation. That being said, it must be noted that certain actions and behaviors such as sexual perversions may have been done in the Kamitic and other traditional African society, but they were not approved, excused or tolerated for this very reason.

When I began to truly understand the details about Set and see that we are dealing with an energy or a spirit. It made perfect sense why there is a spike in depression, suicides and other calamities during the Christmas season. It is because this is the time when the spirit of the north descends to spread his version of joy. Right! If people don't understand and aren't careful, this unpredictable spirit will bring chaos into one's life.

This means the real demons or devils are not those people that dress up in black and bow down before a half goat-half man image. The real Set worshippers or Setians are those people engaged in any act or behavior that brings calamity, chaos, destruction, discord, etc. This is why those spirits associated with Set or who followed in his footsteps were called aapepu. Aapepu are symbolized as vicious snakes or worms because these animals are known to rob and suck the life out of their living host for their own survival. They are parasitic spiritual creatures that vampirize others, which is why the ancient Kamites claimed that they attack our RA daily.

When we think about the things that attack us on a daily basis, from the deceitful, dishonest, double-dealing, fork-tongue, fraudulent energies some of us have to cross everyday to the eye catching, mesmerizing illusions of grandeur that offer negative escapes through sex, drugs and other vices, it becomes quite easy to see that the aapepu are what our African American ancestors called hags, haints and hants, because they are cruel, malevolent, trickster spirits sung about in the old blues song.

Like the netcharu, the aapepu can also be found in nature. When an individual, for instance, finds them self attracted or drawn to some odd, malicious or chaotic disturbances, it is a sign that the aapepu is trying to capture their attention. They can be found in the alleys, slithering along desolate roads and lurking around in other places, inspiring chaos and disorder and spreading grief. Interesting, as I write this I remember my grandfather telling me when I was younger, whenever you see a fight or some other disturbance avoid it and walk the other way. This is because, as I understand it now, the aapepu are responsible for people getting hurt due to them being in the "wrong place at the wrong time".

The aapepu are responsible for inspiring the living to engage in negative habits, do evil and commit heinous acts like the ones that they did in their lifetime. For instance, like all of a sudden start hanging around the wrong crowd, drinking excessive alcohol and experimenting with other substances.

Specifically speaking, these spirits are the spirits that inspire feelings that don't empower us, such as anger, lying, cheating, deceitfulness, depression, discouragement, criticism, guilt, resentment, etc. They are also responsible for inspiring illness, unhealthiness and disease, since every physical manifestation has a spiritual beginning. Some of the common signs that one has been bitten or is being ridden by aapepu are anger, boredom, confusion, crying fits, depression, insomnia, and sadness. Based upon my wife's deceased grandmother, who was a curandera, I also believe that *susto* (fright illness) is also probably influenced by the aapepu.

Have you ever felt like someone is behind you but no one is there, or that someone is in your house but it is empty? Have you ever seen silhouettes in the dark and felt like someone is standing or sitting in front of you? Have you ever had your hair stand up on your neck? Or you wake up feeling restless as if your have been running a race. These are all signs that some aapepu are definitely near you, riding you or attached to you. My brush with a few aapepu in the hospital convinced me that TASETT is a real spiritual desert, and that this hell must be hot in the daytime and cold at night, because I have gotten goose bumps whenever the aapepu were near me.

While the aapepu are considered to be evil by most, I was shown many of them are not evil spirits at all. What makes them dangerous, however, is that a number of them are simply misguided spirits because they had no guidance in their lifetime. As a result, many of these spirits simply gave up on life and went down the wrong path, which led to them dying either a sudden, violent, horrible and/or dishonorable death. These misguided spirits shouldn't be feared, but they need to be recognized for who they are. The aapepu make us question our motives and reasons for our actions, which in return forces us deeper within. I understood this now because, had I not undergone my little experience, I would not have been here today to talk about it. I am for certain now that it was definitely because of my aakhu, my Npu and the mercy of Maat that kept me on the right path. Had it not been for Maat, I am sure that I would have lost my balance a long time ago. It was through Maat I came to understand that this whole evil/good dichotomy is all about balance and moderation.

Anyway, the Spirit showed me that when someone gives up on life it is like a student giving up and refusing to learn. What happens is that they cheat off of others to pass his or her class, cause disturbances or take an even more dangerous route that causes problems for all. This is what the aapepu have done. This is why no one wants to be around them in life and no one wants to remember them in death. It is tempting to pity them, but you must remember that we have a job to do, just as they did. It is best to encourage the aapepu to accept their fate and be committed to learn their lessons, just as you are doing, instead of being angry and envious and blaming others for their fall.

Fortunately, if one has a good rapport with their aakhu and netcharu, meaning one's Ab is in the Amun RA and KhepeRA zone, most aapepu won't even bother about mettling in our affairs, because it would take more energy to attack us than they would be able to retrieve from our being. Like their physical counterparts, the aapepu most of the time target easy victims who are confused, ill or vulnerable.

To dispel most aapepu, as I learned in the hospital, one simply has to change the energy of the environment that that they are in. Inspirational and motivational music is a very powerful way of dispelling aapepu, as well as high resonating sounds like bells and tambourines. Certain incenses, like frankincense and myrrh, which are mentioned in the Bible, are very good in dispelling negative energy. Another very good herb is tobacco, which is one of the reasons why Native American referred to it as a sacred plant. The cologne known as Florida Water is also a good dispelling agent, as well as blessed water and blessed olive oil[71].

Another simple way of dispelling aapepu and having them return back to TASETT is by jabbing at the spirit with a sharp instrument and forcing it to return peacefully wherever it came from. Sweeping, fanning with a fan, sudden movements like throwing cold water in the corners and yelling at the aapepu are also very effective. To prevent aapepu from entering one's home it is best to spiritually clean your home on a weekly basis.

Now, it must be understood that all of the above suggestions are merely cosmetic and temporary fixes. They will keep and prevent most negative spirits from entering your space, but if your mind is not right they will return. Like attracts like. If you focus on doing ill, then you will attract ill in your life. The best way to keep these energies from returning is, as stated in the

---

[71] See appendix.

Bible, "Keep your mind on Jesus", which, you all should know by now, is keeping your mind focused on the ethics of Osar (our honorable ancestors).

Just a tidbit: it is extremely difficult for spirits to learn without a physical body, because the purpose of a physical body is to experience life. But the aapepu, like any reptile, can be cultivated, elevated and mastered. Notice I say reptile to metaphorically indicate that these spirits, like reptiles, have a small brain, which means it can be done but it is best to leave this task for spiritual masters. It is only a suggestion, because of my bout with them in the hospital. As a result, I have learned that one has to definitely have a lot of light to even deal with these low essences on that level. This is why it is best for the most part to just leave them alone.

Trying the Spirit

The distinct difference I noticed between the netcharu and the aapepu is that the netcharu are mild mannered, while the latter are chaotic and wild. In simple terms, what this meant was that when we allow our emotions to run wild we are giving in to the Set and allowing our Ab (heart/conscious) to dwell in TASETT. Our kingdom will never be united when we do this, but when we exercise self-discipline and control, like the calm samurai or wise warrior, we are able to make conscientious and precise decisions, because we have allowed our Ab to move to its calm and most receptive states, Amun RA and KhepeRA. Here we are able to make best use of the power within our being. Just then I could see how one is able to ignore pain and suffering for a greater good. How a mother is able to go through hell to save her children, which made me see that the netcharu are truly guardians (warriors). Set, on the other hand, is a punk because he chose to go the easy way. *He couldn't handle real heat, the heat of truth within.*

Now, this was all theory of course, so I wanted to put it to the test. I was reminded to "try the spirit", so, astounded by what I had discovered, I decided to put the maa aankh to the test. When my body became ill I had to relearn how to do a lot of things, like getting in and out of the car, standing in the shower by myself and so on. One of the activities I had to relearn how to do was go up and down stairs. After spending several months of not going up or down a set of stairs because of pain in my joints, I had decided that the time was now and that I was not going to be denied this ability. When I began my road to recovery, I didn't think about how I was going to walk down the stairs again. I simply focused upon walking up and down the stairs. I didn't spend hours upon hours thinking about go up and down the stairs, I would just really imagine walking or being downstairs. One day, I remember, all of a sudden I got the urge to dance and I did just that, I danced. Then, I would practice one day at a time walking up and walking down the stairs.

Then the funniest thing happened one day. The toilet in the house kept running and tired of hearing it, I decided that I was going to fix it, so I shut off the water valves to the toilet and proceeded to fix the stopper, only to discover that the valve was not completely shut off so I had to turn off the main water valve, which was down stairs. Without "thinking" I was downstairs turning off the main water valve, because the bathroom, by this time, was practically flooded. It wasn't until after I had changed the toilet parts out that I realized, "Hey, I ran down stairs!"

Of course, when I thought about it, there was a part of me that didn't believe that I actually accomplished that feat. In fact, when I went back and tried to do it again, I could sense a fear of some sort of not walking down the stairs. Where was this fear coming from? How did I accomplish this feat? I thought.

It is said that what prevents God from fully blessing us is not God but our belief in God, which made me realize that this fear was definitely coming from my own personal experience. It was the lower division of the spirit or the TASETT, which, remember, is ruled by Set and the aapepu. It became apparent from an esoteric perspective that Set is the spirit that inspires us full of negative ideas and beliefs. Set is the one that reminds us of our past and tells us what we can't do based his limited perception of reality. This is where all of our discouraging thoughts, thoughts of failure, concern, worry and fear come from, which explains why one has to surrender their Ab to Osar, in other words, move their Ab to KAMTA. This is the only way one can look beyond and past what the Buddhist call maya, which are the illusions and lies of Set. This is why Hru had to flee to Djahuti to get his eye repaired. Later, in order to win the war, Hru had to have Osar intercede on his behalf.

So, to ensure that I was on the right track, I decided to test the maa aankh again. This time, since my healing wasn't going to come from taking medication alone but from a combination of things such as diet, music, dancing, etc., I decided to do a healing ritual and impress upon the Rau or plant a seed in KAMTA that I was being healed. Keeping in mind that when a candle is fully burned down it symbolizes that the idea (objective) has been firmly impressed or that the seed has been planted in KAMTA, I burned several glass-encased candles for my healing request. But two of the candles, a blue and a white candle, mysteriously did not burn completely down, as if someone had blown these candles out. To me, this signified that the rite was partially successful but that I needed to do something else in order to make the rite a true success.

I didn't know what I needed to do but I wasn't going to rationalize and think about it either, so I just laid it upon the Rau to show me what I needed to do. Then, one morning upon awakening, I kept thinking about a fish. Now, I didn't know what a fish had to do with my healing, so I vaguely thought about it. Then, the image of the Catholic saint Our Lady of Miraculous Medals popped into my awareness. Now, I didn't know anything about this saint, and in the past I would have dismissed the image from my awareness, but I didn't because I was beginning to understand that the religious history of African American spirituality was the religious history of my ancestry, since I had learned that the religious history of my aakhu was composed of traditional African beliefs, Roman Catholicism, Native American influences, as well as the various Protestant influences –Methodist, Baptist, Spiritism, Holiness, Pentecostalism, etc. It was this understanding that helped me to overcome all of my prejudices (ethnic, racial and spiritual) influenced by American social standards. I took the image of the saint that came to me as a sign from God communicating to the netcharu through my aakhu.

Further investigation led me to discover that the message was coming from the netchar Oset, because her colors were blue and white, the same colors as the saint. Other signs that it was Oset speaking to me through the saint were that another name for the saint was Our Lady of Medals of the Immaculate Conception, the candles that mysterious stopped burning were blue and white, not to mention the fish that opened the way for the saint to appear into my awareness. The other thing was that Our Lady of Miraculous Medals was depicted standing upon a snake, which is the symbol of aapepu (negative spirits in regards to illness). When I put all of these pieces of this puzzle together, what Oset was telling me was that she was the one that started this revolution within me and that God heard my request and she was initiating the change. A number of days later, it really hit me that, just like Oset had grafted a serpent to make RA ill in the *Story of RA and Oset*, in order to realize his divine name, Oset had apparently done the same to me, in order for me to realize my hidden name, an allusion to Amun RA. In other words, she did what she had to help me realize my divinity. After she made this realization to me, I promised to purchase Oset a statue of Our Lady of Miraculous Medals, because I identified it as being this ancient *basimbi* or netcharu in my life now.

Assistance from Npu

Of course, now I am a believer, but it still took a little while to walk this walk and not get discouraged. Again, when people heard of my situation they would issue this grave apology, as if I was dying or already dead. This, I noticed, can have a very devastating effect upon the psyche if one is not careful. Not only that, all of the negative ideas and thoughts that are broadcasted through the radio and television can also have a negative effect as well. It is not that I think people purposely choose to broadcast negative energy through the airwaves, but when they have no understanding about the Spirit, these images, ideas, etc. lead people into thinking and thinking, or thoughts are energy because they inspire movement.

I began to notice that I had to be more than just optimistic in order to get through this. I had to be oozing with so much "POSITIVITINESS" (I know it is not a word, smile) that it affected others who are negative in their track from affecting me with their energy. I needed God to guide me, shield me and walk with me wherever I went. I needed Npu.

As previously mentioned, I briefly met all of the netcharu –our personal guardian angels– but I didn't have a real rapport with them, because part of me refused to see them as being living and intelligent forces that exists within and outside of our being. It was only when I temporarily suspended thinking that I was able to see them as being real beings and realize that they had always been around. I, simply put, had to move my Ab beyond the moment of reasoning into the higher plane of consciousness in order to truly see. It was by doing this I was able to establish a genuine bond with them.

Now, I had seen Npu before in my life. He had gotten me out of a number of binds and jams before, and when not properly attended to I saw that he allowed me to wander around in the dark into a number of jams. This time, I needed him to assist me in finding a way for my recovery, but I had no idea how to establish a true connection with him, because African Americans had established a *sin regla* system –traditional system with no order or rules. In other words, there were no exact recipes, structure, rules, tradition, etc. to follow. This meant that in order to establish a true bond with Npu I would have to making direct one-to-one spiritual contact with him through my aakhu.

Calling upon God, my aakhu and following my intuition, Npu, I was shown, had a headdress of a dog to remind people that it is the Spirit of God that will finds a way for us to achieve a goal or find a solution, just like a hunting dog finds its mark by following the scent of its game or a guide dog leads its master to safety. It was revealed to me that Npu is in both lands. Shortly after being shown that, the image of Npu came to me along with that of the legendary Harriet Tubman[72], the heroine that led approximately 300[73] escaped slaves to freedom through the Underground Railroad. Npu and Ms. Tubman are both symbols that deal with opening the way and leading one to freedom. Freedom was away from the slave master's sight, from Set's control, and into the marshes, in the fields, into the dark night, into KAMTA.

Interestingly, after making this direct spiritual connection, I found a poster of Harriet Tubman carrying a rifle, wearing white, red and an almost black jacket. White, I was reminded, symbolizes the powers of the white realm – purity, wisdom, the honorable dead. The color black signifies the mysteries, the color of the night, the cover of night the slaves used to escape to freedom through the

---

[72] Harriet Tubman (born Araminta Ross) is the famous leader of the Underground Railroad that guided slaves to free states or even to Canada. Harriet Tubman, also called Moses after the biblical Moses that led the Jews of the Bible out of bondage, served as a nurse, scout and spy for the Union army, fought for women's rights and helped the elderly.

[73] The number 300 was a sign that it was Npu communicating this to me.

Underground Railroad, and KAMTA. I was amazed because KAMTA had taken on another meaning according to my spirits and became the Land of Freedom, while the color red symbolized mediation, alertness, danger and TASETT.

To work with this netchar (energy) I obtained an image of Npu and painted his image red, black (colors of the two lands) and white (allegiance to Osar), as well as the poster of Ms. Tubman. Guided by the maa aankh, my aakhu, Npu and Ms. Tubman, I added and subtracted items from Npu's sacred space in a personal corner near one of my doorways, as inspired. I noticed that, just like working with my aakhu, I would get sudden ideas or inspirations to just do something, like go to the store and get things for him. I knew it was Npu because of the colors or his special number, three or multiples of it, all the way to 21. For instance, I was once inspired to give him a black handled knife that I found, obviously signifying spiritual protection and defense. Another time I was inspired to give him a flashlight that had a red handle trimmed in black. Then, while walking in the backyard of my home, I found, a red, black and white chrome toy SUV. *This Npu likes to travel in style.*

Spirituality, as Papá Raúl once said, is supposed to be interesting and fun, but I was noticing that when I didn't worry about things it wasn't difficult but a natural process. I just really had to surrender my will and allow my Spirit to lead. I had to remind myself that this was not a deity or idol but that the netcharu were our guardian angels or guardian spirits that work with God. When candles, food, drink, etc. are set before them, it is not an act of worship but offering of thanks.

Only God is worthy to be worshipped and praised. Offerings that are given to the aakhu and netcharu are simple ritualistic acts of thanks designed to increase one faith in God and invite the benevolent spirits around us to take a more active role in our lives. Through this ritualistic actions and practices I discovered that, over a period of time, one will feel like they are blessed, guarded, guided and protected by God, especially when they began to receive messages in their dreams and waking state, as I had, like people did during the biblical times.

Now, as I began to trust my intuition more and more, I began to have fun, and noticed that the way my aakhu would say maa aankh sounded more and more like "My Unk". The more I began to say "My Unk" the way they did, two things came to mind. One of them was that "My Unk" was a funny way of saying the Ki-Kongo word Nkisi, which meant charm or medicine. That's when it was revealed to me that the maa aankh, the way they were using it, was also the name of the altar.

The other thing I was shown by them saying "My Unk" was that it was a play on the phrase "My Uncle", which is a pun referring back to the *Story of Osar* indicating that Set usurped the throne of Osar and stole Hru's birthright. When Hru defeated Set and reclaimed his birthright, but refused to rename it in order to remind all of his descendants so that it would never happen again, the maa aankh was called "My Unk's" (My Uncles) to indicate that Hru's heritage was stolen and retrieved.

The *flash* from this revelation engulfed me with a mystical fire. I felt my body get warm as my senses just tingled. All I could say was thank you God because I knew that it was truly God that was blessing me to make such discoveries.

I laid it upon Npu and Ms. Tubman to open the way for my healing. Again, I didn't focus upon how the spirit was going to show me how to heal my body; I just asked it to open the way. After doing so, I noticed various changes occurring to my body. I was getting stronger and definitely feeling a lot healthier. I still had some aches and pains, but overall I could see that it was getting better. My attitude also began to change. I became more optimistic and positive, as if waiting for a package in the mail. The more I welcomed this change, the more grateful I noticed that I became as well.

On Saturday, immediately after praying to God and asking that God strengthen my aakhu, after asking my aakhu to strengthen me with their wisdom, I honor Npu with a little rum (not too much), a thin cigar, a little candy (not too much) and light. Since he stands guard perfectly and is alert, I have to approach him cautiously by telling him what I am giving him. I noticed that when he is in need or wants something, just like a child, he would continue to ask for something (some would interpret it as nagging at our psyche). This was one of Npu's ways of alerting and informing me ahead of time that an intrusion was near and to protect my Ab of the negative influences.

For example, I now have my own rendering of the bar story that was once told to me by Papá Raúl, based upon my personal experience. One night, my wife and I went to a quincañera[74], and anyone that has ever been to one of these celebrations for young 15-year-old girls approaching womanhood knows that there is a lot of drinking involved by the adult attendees, because it is a big party, usually with around 75 people or more. I am always cautious going to any event where there is alcohol served, because I remember how Osar lost his life. So, we're at this quincañera with some of my wife's friends and afterwards, because the people we were with haven't seen us in a while due to the illness, we decided to hang out with them for a little bit longer at an after party.

    While at the after party there were three women (two sisters and a friend) that got into an altercation. It began with the friend trying to explain to one of the sisters how they play and joke around with each other. (I should have taken that as a hint because, remember, Npu can be a bit of a prankster and his sacred number is three.) A few minutes later, the discussion led to an argument and accusations about hatred and jealousy between two sisters and their best friends. When one of the husbands of the women involved saw what was going on and he tried to get them to drop the subject completely before it went too far, too late! The next thing I know, the argument went to arguing about childhood experiences, abandonment and manipulation and eventually broke into a fight between the two sisters with several people trying to break it up. It ended with one of the sisters running off into the cold night and the other

---

[74] A Latin American coming of age ceremony held for girls turning 15 years old. It is similar to the Jewish Bat Miztvah for girls.

expressing her hurt and pain for their sibling and love for her closest friends, who were like sisters.

Several hours later (I had not planned to be out this late –shaking my head, smile), when it was all said and done, my wife and I returned back home. I dressed for bed and, as usual, spoke to God while looking at the darkness of my bedroom. I thanked God that the situation didn't get worse, because it could have easily turned into something truly volatile. I thanked God for blessing my wife and I to return back home safely. Then, that's when Npu revealed himself to me. It was Npu that helped us to find our way out of the situation and home safely.

Then it came to me that it was Npu, through his curiosity that finds the smallest things to pick at and just like the discussion that led to a full-blown fight. Npu's curiosity can start off as a small piece of hanging thread and lead to the unraveling of a full sweater. This experience taught me that Npu is not bad, evil or a troublemaker, as some believe most psychopomps[75] are, but when Npu is around Set is not too far away. This is because it is an allusion to the fact that it is through our curiosity we try to find things to better ourselves. We look for things to better ourselves and make us feel better but sometimes, as the saying goes, curiosity can kill the cat, or the dog in our case (pun intended).

---

[75] Angels, spirits and certain animals (dogs, foxes, coyotes, cats (black cats/black panthers), owls, crows, leopards, vultures, etc.) whose job in religious lore is to guide souls into the afterlife. Like Npu of the Kamitic tradition, Eshu or Ellegua in the Yoruba tradition, in the Christian tradition, the angel Azarael or St. Peter who is believed to be at heaven's gates.

I am reminded by my aakhu to remember that Npu was abandoned in the marshes (TASETT region) and found by Oset, who raised him as her own. So, who knows what our DOG may have found and dug up (uncovered) while he was alone before Oset found him? Who knows what our DOG may have found before we were saved? I was really starting to see the benefit of familiarizing myself with the various symbols. Had I just meditated or prayed with no focus, I would have surely missed all of these signs.

The Battle Has Just Begun, Baby

It was through Npu that I saw that there are definitely a lot of negative ideas and images that influence our spirit. I mean, I saw these negative influences when I was in the hospital, but as I began my road to recovery, I began to see how the walls of despair and hopelessness truly existed in the world. From the numerous advertisements on the television and billboards promoting new drugs with (as I said before) 1,001 side effects, to the war torn, famine stricken, natural disaster countries all over the world. The world, according to the media, is definitely on its way to hell in a wicker-basket, with lighter fluid and gasoline bottles on its side to help send it away.

I was reminded that this is nothing new. I had been here before in a situation where I was expected not to live. *That's right, the 1980s.* The media had painted this picture before but somehow, out of nowhere, many of us survived.

I remembered, after going through that experience, that a lot of people tried to escape those rough times through music and other forms of artistic expression. Unfortunately, some of us tried to escape through the use of alcohol and drugs and lost their lives. All of these methods were temporary fixes to the ills that we faced back in the day, which I remember was the reason why I became depressed at a young age. It wasn't until I began to dig into my ancestral past that I was able to subdue the pain and suffering around me with peace. It was in no time I had almost forgot that I was even depressed, and when I looked up it was time for me to graduate from high school. It was at that moment I was shown again that this was the power of cultural traditions.

The planet is full of despair and sorrow because this is what they advertise all around the globe. The old expression "misery loves company" is true because in TASETT misery is big business. Very rarely is it shown people celebrating life and rebirth because, generally speaking, there is no money made for things that are positive and life bringing in nature. People aren't celebrating life-bringing events because they don't want to. It is because many people have lost the meaning of their cultural traditions, so they have lost how. As a result, we are bombarded with a host of negative energies and they keep getting stronger.

To help me to break through this wall of negativity and have my own wall, Hruaakhuti appeared to me, reminding me that his purpose is to protect and shield me from evil. I was then reminded by my aakhu of the biblical scripture Ephesians 6:10-18 which states:

"Be strong in the Lord and in the power of His might. Put on the whole armor of God, that you may be able to stand against the wiles of the devil. For we do not wrestle against flesh and blood, but against principalities, against powers, against the rulers of the

darkness of this age, against spiritual hosts of wickedness in the heavenly places.

"Therefore take up the whole armor of God, that you may be able to withstand in the evil day, and having done all, to stand. Stand therefore, having girded your waist with truth, having put on the breastplate of righteousness, and having shod your feet with the preparation of the gospel of peace; above all, taking the shield of faith with which you will be able to quench all the fiery darts of the wicked one.

"And take the helmet of salvation, and the sword of the Spirit, which is the word of God; praying always with all prayer and supplication in the Spirit, being watchful to this end with all perseverance and supplication for all the saints...."

So, I proceeded to get a belt (of truth), a symbol for the breastplate (of righteousness), sandals or boots (of peace), a shield (of faith), and a sword, actually a machete (of the Spirit of God). I had an image of Malcolm X standing guard with his AK and recalled reading about the legendary Afro-Brazilian Zumbi of Palmares whose spirit lives on in Capoeira. Then the image of St. George came to me, of him killing the dragon. I took all of these curious items that a warrior of God would need and want and placed them in an old iron pot. Inspired by both Hruaakhuti and Malcolm, I painted a red X[76] on the iron pot.

---

[76] The life of Malcolm X has been a cultural inspiration to people all over the globe, but when Spike Lee tried to promote his movie by advertising the "X" symbol, the "X" symbol became a popular icon worn by people that have never read or knew anything about Malcolm's life or the principles that he

Keeping in mind that this is a mental war, the song *Waging War* by Cece Winans came to mind, but I heard an aakhu say that this was not strong enough because Hruaakhuti doesn't start wars, Set does. Then the old song *Drive Old Satan Away* popped into my head. Standing in front of my Armor of God, my Hruaakhuti, I prayed to God my protector

Lord God, thank you for revealing yourself to me. You who are above me, beneath me and on all four sides, thank you for the blessings that you have bestowed upon me. Thank you for everything. I ask Father that you bless this Hruaakhuti. Bless this Hruaakhuti to protect me, shield me from danger, and chase away negative thoughts and the vile ways of the enemy. Do not my God let me be consumed by the enemy.

Hruaakhuti! Anoint me and cover me from head to toe with your amour. Protect me! Do not let the enemy defeat me! Bind the beast with your iron chain and restrict his movements from harming me, bless me, confront this enemy and defeat him, so that I can claim the victory. Amen.

I put some blessed oil (the symbolic blood of a ram)[77] in my hands and with my hands raised to God I rubbed it around. Then I anointed my head, crossed my arms and anointed my throat, chest, shoulders, arms and hands. I anointed the back of my neck and as far as I could reach my upper and lower back. Then I moved to my backside, down my thighs, my knees and finally

---

lived by. It wasn't long after that one could find people engaged in criminal activities wearing an "X" hat or shirt, disrespecting Malcolm's legacy.

[77] See Appendix on how to make blessed oil, waters and rums.

my feet. I repeated this prayer several times until it resonated with me.

Since that time my Hruaakhuti has grown and adaptations have been made, but on more than one occasion I have seen my Hruaakhuti work for me. One of the lessons he taught me was that part of the reason I wasn't progressing the way I wanted was because I was living for tomorrow and not for today. When I asked him to explain, my wife and I was invited to visit a church. At the church, this minister preached that people are living in fear because they are worried about tomorrow. Coincidence? I think not.

Anyway, Hruaakhuti was showing me that my diet in the past was not based upon living healthy. It was based upon living so that I wouldn't become ill, have hypertension, get diabetes or some of the other illnesses that affect people because eating unhealthy. A lot of people in the past according to photos were basically agrarians before the food industry became so "mechanized". They weren't sedentary and everything was cooked from scratch. Trying to eat food so that one doesn't become ill, I was shown, is psychologically eating out of fear. This made me adopt a more wholesome agrarian-type diet, like my ancestors had, consisting of 60-70% carbohydrates (composed of fruits, whole grains and vegetable), 5-10% of fats and 20% of protein.

Hruaakhuti explained to me that the purpose of pain is to simply signify, like when I moved my Ab to the RA moment, that I was approaching danger. It didn't mean that one should fear it and flee from it. It simply means that if one is going to go through the fire that they have to be prepared. Hruaakhuti told me that today households, neighborhoods and communities are being overran and destroyed because people refuse to stand up for God out of fear of what's going to happen to them physically. People today simply have greater respect for Set than they do for Osar and God because they don't understand that if they do what is right, God, the ancestors and the spirits will protect them. I was shown that when we go to a park, we should be asking God to empower it and bless the area so that the children playing are protected from the forces of evil. When we go down a street and see something that is shady, we should be praying to bless the street with peace and protect the inhabitants on it. We are Children of God and we shouldn't be living in fear. I was told that I needed to stop being reactive and learn to be proactive. If I live proactive by not worrying about what tomorrow is going to bring but focus on today, I would be blessed, because God is Justice and true Justice is Love, so do what's right for all.

A Visit from the King of Whiteness

Now, I heard what Hruaakhuti was telling me, but "seeing is believing" so, again, I decided to try the spirit. Since I was slow getting back to work due to the illness, and by this time most of my funds had been depleted, our utilities and now medicals bills started to mount up. Naturally, Set and the aapepu brought doubt, worry and fear of how things were going to get paid, but I refused to give in. Instead, following what my spirits taught me, I relaxed my Ab and took it to the Amun RA and KhepeRA moments of time. There, in a calm and relax state, we (my wife and I) paid what we could and calmly explained to the bill collectors the situation and moved on. It felt so weird, because in the past, when bill collectors would call, I would go into a frenzy and yell back at them over the phone where they could go. This time I didn't, I simply told them what I was able to do and that was it. I told them calmly what I was going to pay for, such as our rent, car, utilities and food, and if there was anything left over they might get some money.

After telling the bill collectors this, some of them threatened about how high the interest was going to be and all that other jazz, but after seeing that I was unmoved they simply accepted our terms. A number of them helped to make arrangements with us by giving us a settlement amount, which was less than what I would have been paying. Quite a few of them did this to clear their books. It was just beautiful and it all came from believing and trusting that God will make a way. It was proof that despite the tragedy that I had undergone, all would be taken care of and I would be reborn. I would acquire the peace and wisdom of the white crown if I just surrendered my will.

Then, one day, my father-in-law called, and after talking to my wife, asked how we were doing on money and paying our bills. After my wife explained to him that we did our best to pay what we could, he, along with my mother-in-law and parents, decided to organize a Ms. Becue fundraiser on my behalf, even though I don't eat pork, mind you.

After a couple of months of planning, flyers were posted everywhere. The event was even broadcasted on several radio stations. Of course, I felt like it was "Save Ferris Day" from the 1980s' movie *Ferris Bueller's' Day Off* for people that didn't really know what was going on with me, because mysteriously they saw that I was healthy, then I disappeared and was very sickly-looking. Then, suddenly as before, Set and aapepu came to my awareness with their doubt and worry that people wouldn't show up, that the event would be a waste of money and a complete failure.

Refusing to give in to the negative suggestions made, keeping in mind the old gospel song that *Jesus Can Work It Out*, remembering that since God is unimaginable and indefinable, Jesus is a merely a symbol used to help one their attention on the Spirit (Jesus is the Christian Osar), having no clue how things were going to work out, I lit a Seven African Powers candle (since it was multi-colored) and gave all doubt to the Spirit. Telling the Spirit that I didn't know how things were going to work but I was not going to worry about it and leave it in God's hands, refusing to give in to doubt and worry and ponder on things out of my hands, made me really see how Set and the aapepu try to eclipse our sun. Instead of focusing on what Set stated I simply cast my doubts away as the candle burned away. In the end, the event was a success.

It was interesting to see how God and the spirits work. What made it so fascinating was that that, based upon all of the events that my wife and I had attended and supported, from birthdays, quincañeras, weddings, wedding receptions, fundraisers, etc., we expected certain people to show up in support. That was not even the case. The people that showed the most support besides my family were the people that I had least expected. I mean people that I thought that were my friends or would show didn't, whereas those whom I definitely thought were my enemies attended and pitched in by making contributions and donations, like my wife's ex. That's right, my wife's ex! No one can tell me that God and the spirits don't exist and don't help the righteous. When I look at it now, I see that I easily could have messed that up if I had did things based upon what I "thought and believed".

I had to swallow my pride and tell my wife's ex thank you, which he accepted. When I tried to speak to him after the event, he gave me the same old smuck response I was used to receiving from him in the past, which was a clear sign that it was the spirits influencing him. I could just imagine him saying, "Just because I helped you doesn't make us friends. I am not inhumane, I just don't like you." I had to laugh, say okay and move on.

The lesson that was learned was that, first of all, you can't depend upon people, because they are "wishy-washy" and unstable. When you put your faith and trust in humankind, that's when they let you down the most. Instead you can only rely on one individual and that is God. *Build your hopes on things eternal. Hold on God's Unchanging Hand.*

The second lesson that I learned from this little experience was that you can't please people either, for the same reason. People change all the time and really don't know what they want, like or need. This is the reason why a person can be a star one day and in two weeks be as broke as a cobble-stoned street with potholes. So many lives have been ruined because of people trying to please man and woman and cater to their likes and dislikes. So, do it for God and to please your ancestors. Live your life from the end, based upon how you want to be remembered. I don't want, when I pass into the next life, to hear that "He was a son-of-a-gun, kept up a lot of mess, had this issue, etc." No, I want to be known and remembered as one that did right, strove to do right, etc., like my grandparents were when they passed. I'm living my life to be a star in God's memory.

That's when I got a glimpse of the kingdom that Osar had built. For a few fleeting moment, Osar's kingdom was resurrected as people from various walks of life (many whom I didn't even know) came together to assist my wife and I financially. Some people didn't even purchase a dinner but just gave to the cause. The interesting thing was that in a few hours a little over a $1000 was raised. Finally, I got it!

Two Eyes Are Better Than One

Finally, I got it, and the only way I could explain it was that the maa aankh, as I understood it, is a cosmogram inspired by the Kongo yowa cross but based upon the Kamitic concepts and principles. The facts are that Kamit became a powerful civilization because the Kamau believed that their country was divided into two lands due to the way the Nile River flowed. These two lands were called Lower Kamit, the northernmost of the two regions, and Upper Kamit, the southernmost region.

Lower Kamit, due to its close proximity to the Mediterranean Sea, was basically a desert shrub land, consisting of wild grasses and all types of plant life. This undeveloped region, because it was basically unsuitable for most human life, is what the Kamau termed as wild. An analysis of the Kamitic history will reveal that most of the foreign invaders came from the north of the entire country. So, the early Kamau represented this region with a red crown called the Deshret and called it TASETT –The Red Lands.

Upper Kamit, which lay further south of Lower Kamit, due to the fertile soil produced by the inundation of the Nile River, was basically a developed region. An analysis of the Kamitic history will reveal that, because of the inundation of the Nile River, not only were the country's basic needs taken care of, but also they were able to establish trade and thus become a prosperous nation. It was the inundation of the Nile that inspired the early Kamau to see this region as being a developed, dependable or stable territory, which was a direct opposite of Lower Kamit. As a result, the early Kamau represented this region with a white crown called the Hedjet and called this region KAMTA –The Black Lands.

Since both lands were derived from the Nile River, the early Kamau concluded that the inundation of the Nile was due to the movement of the sun (although technically speaking it was the Dog Star Sirius that indicated when the Nile would soon be flooding). It was the Kamau's observation of the sun what led to them creating the most accurate calendar of ancient times, because, unlike other cultures, the Kamau calendar was based upon the sun and the stars rather than on the moon. With the sun calendar, the Kamau were able to make accurate estimates of when the Nile would flood and therefore determine the best times to plant their crops. It is because of the Kamitic calendar there have always been seven days in a week and twelve months in a year. The sun, the Kamau observed, rose at sunrise, peaked at midday, fell at sunset and was somehow mysteriously reborn to begin anew.

It was after observing that at around six in the morning, when the sun begins to rise, "things" become awake; at around noon, when the sun peaks, "things" are active; when the sun sets, around six in the evening, "things" seems to sleep or die; and then, during the darkness of the night, "things" are miraculously reborn, the Kamau realized, thousands of years before Einstein was born, that everything that exists is composed of energy, and that matter is simply energy in its densest form.

Based upon these observable facts, the Kamau created their cultural way of life, because they realized that everything that occurred in nature also occurred within them.

Since the Nile flowed through both lands, which meant that the same possibilities and potential existed to both, the Kamau, inspired by the Nile, called it the sea of nothingness, the source of all life and beginnings, nyun.

Nyun, metaphorically speaking, is what divided and distinguished the two lands from each other. Understanding that everything is energy and that matter is the densest form of energy led to the understanding that from nothing comes something, from the invisible comes the visible, from the unseen world comes the seen world. In other words, it is our thoughts, ideas, beliefs, etc. what leads to the creation of physical objects and things. The physical world is a mere reflection of the spiritual world and vice versa. So the Kamau believed that out of nyun came the principle maã, which established the balance, law, order and reciprocity throughout the universe. It is the righteous road that one has to walk, the road that leads to eternal life.

As a result, KAMTA –The Black Lands– also came to symbolize the invisible realm; the spiritual world; the world of ideas, thoughts and beliefs; the Upper Land; the older region, the more stable region (hence the Kamitic word for stability is djet, symbolized by a backbone); and, last but not least, the land of the ancestors (or whiteness), represented by the legendary king Osar.

TASETT –The Red Lands–, on the other hand, came to symbolize the physical realm; the visible world; the world of physical "things"; the Lower Land; the younger region; the more wild (or uncivilized) area; and, last but not least, the land of the living (red), represented by Set (the first red man of the north before St. Nick or Santa Claus), the young, wild and envious brother of Osar.

Again, understand that this was all based upon energy and that what occurred in the universe also occurred within the human being. The four moments of the sun were identified as different attributes and manipulations of the energy, Chi, Ki, life force or Holy Ghost, that the Kamau called the RA or Rau. The first position, represented by the sun at sunrise, was called KhepeRA (the Coming RA). The midday position was called RA (the Ruling "Visible" RA). The sunset position was called RA Atum (The Complete RA), and the final, or actually beginning, position was called Amun RA (The Hidden or "Invisible" RA).

These concepts and principles is what I was informed were called the maa aankh, which is the

Kamitic cultural way of life. The maa aankh is composed of the Kamitic words "maã", which means to be true, to be upright, truthful, real, actual and veritable; and the word "aankh", which means eternal life, to live and to swear an oath. It roughly translates as **_"To swear an oath to live upright, truthful and veritable."_** It means that a true ruler, leader, warrior, Child of God, etc. is basically a shaman, because they are one that has walked through the land of the Living (or Living Hell) and the land of the Dead (or the Land of the Ancestors) in order to be reborn and acquire eternal life.

Proof that they had been reborn can be seen in their actions, words and deeds, because their physical life is a reflection of their spiritual well-being. Since they know that God will take care of everything, because nyun is the source of everything and everything that exists ascends out of the nyun from KAMTA into TASETT, the true Hru, like a brave, calm and peaceful warrior (like Jesus, Buddha, and various other holy figures and saints throughout history), rests his or her will at the Amun RA moment of time. It is at this moment of time that one sees the Light (symbolized by the two Eyes of RA), witnesses true miracles/magic and meets the true dwellers of KAMTA, the netcharu and their ancestors, the aakhu.

Who Called Me?

Like many African American families, my extended family has a yearly family reunion, usually a week or so before the fall school session begins, but, because of my health condition, my wife and I had planned not to attend this year, also because we were short on funds. But my extended family all around the country wanted to see me and make sure that I was doing fine.

Especially considering since the last time they saw me, they saw how sickly my body had become. Now, I don't know how it was done, but a way was made and, thanks to my wife and parents, we were able to attend our family reunion, hosted by my great aunt and uncle in Portsmouth, Virginia.

While in Virginia, parents, nieces, nephew, my wife and I were able to visit the Jamestown settlement, where I discovered that everything that I had learned prior to this experience regarding slavery and African Americans was true and confirmed by archeologists, curators and historians. Such as St. Augustine, Florida being the first settlement in North America. The first enslaved Africans to arrive on the shores of North America were from the Kongo-Angolan basin and these people, due to the Portuguese merchants, had knowledge of Christianity prior to being enslaved.

I can't even begin to explain how good and overwhelmed with joy I felt to hear all of this and have it confirmed by historians. I was taken to a higher level of ecstasy when my father, after reading and discussing some of my research, saw that what I was writing about coincided with the findings of the educated community. In other words, he realized that I wasn't crazy! (Laugh) But, when we both saw an ancient Kongo rosary that had skulls on it, which had been carved out of what looked like precious stone, and where the image of Jesus normally stood, the image of the fearless and legendary Queen Nzingha (also known as Ana de Sousa Nzingha Mbande 1583 – 1663), who fought against slavery in her homeland in Africa, replaced it... And, to hear my father ask, "The skulls are for the ancestors, right?"

I was in total blissfulness, because it verified that African Americans weren't Christianized, it was Christianity that was Africanized, but somewhere along the way we lost sight of the path. We became ashamed of our culture, of our history, and began to believe all of the lies and stereotypes that the oppressors told us. The very tools that we created for the upliftment of humanity were abandoned, as we became spooked by the mere mention of the word ritual. We became afraid of our sciences, so much so that we condemned and ridiculed the children for their natural curiosity into themselves. Our lack of understanding about whom we are and hatred for religion made us forget the very thing we detest. Our heroes, heroines and martyrs have used these same things as tools of empowerment.

That's when it became apparent, that all of this work (research, studying, practicing, etc.) was not just for my benefit. The reason I had to walk this path was to heal my soul and the souls of my ancestors of the evil brought about through slavery. It was important for me to walk this path in order to heal myself of negative conditionings so that I could help others. As I continued to look at the Kongo rosary, that's when I got confirmation that my ancestors were healed and pleased with my work, when I heard a voice whisper in my ear, as I looked upon the Kongo rosary in awe, *"Job, well done"*. At that moment, I knew that I had finally ascended and been reborn (healed) from this experience. That is when I finally stopped running and accepted my calling to become a preacher/shaman.

Appendix A:
Making Maa aankh With the Aakhu & Netcharu

The Africans (Yorubas, Dahomeans, etc.) that believed in one God and numerous divinities that were taken to North America during slavery were not able to retain all of their religious practices, as the Africans that were taken to the Caribbean and South America had done, mainly because they were outnumbered by white Anglo-Saxon Protestants. Those Africans, on the other hand, from the Kongo-Angolan region, who believed in one God, three major types of spirits and numerous icons that could be used as charms, were however able to retain, adapt and modify their spiritual beliefs and practices, in order to create a new type of religion and use it as a tool for their survival. These creative Africans, however, were not able to retain all of their religious theology. As a result, with no clear understanding of certain spiritual practices, it is my belief that a lot of the social ills that plague our families, communities and society exist because there are no strong cultural traditions in place.

A thorough analysis of history reveals that, when there is a lack of strong cultural traditions, people have the tendency to engage in all sorts of acts and behaviors. The reason is that cultural traditions act as a guide and a model to instruct people on how they should live and aspire to reach their highest potentials. Cultural traditions are also very powerful because they not only unite people together based upon their ethnicity and heritage, but they also give people strength to overcome change. Cultural traditions also have the ability to reconnect one back to their ancestral past, which is why ancestor veneration is such a powerful practice.

In the Afro-Diaspora, it is believed that the ancestors are physically dead (meaning they have no physical body), but they are not dead spiritually because their spirit (and memories) continues to live on. Just like a moment of silence is used to remember the dead, in the Afro-Diaspora this moment is used to reflect back upon the lives of those that are deceased. It is during this time that communication with the ancestors is established and strengthened.

Although ancestor veneration is incorrectly called ancestor worship and is mistaken as being a religious practice, the true purpose of honoring the ancestors is to strengthen family loyalty, cultivate cultural values and remember the sacrifices made by ancestors in order for one to live today. Ancestors are not worshipped. They are called upon for two reasons. The first reason is that it is believed that, since they are spirits, they are closest to God then their living descendants. The second reason is that it is believed that the ancestors are still interested in the lives of their descendants and those whom they cared for when they physically were alive.

There are many ways to honor one's ancestors. The simplest way, commonly practiced throughout West, is by having a moment of silence. In some memorial services for veterans that I have participlated in, I have seen an empty plate and a turned over glass, placed on a table, to symbolize that the dead cannot partake in food and drink with the living. In the Afro-Diaspora we understand that the ancestors cannot physically consume food and drink but they can absorb and be strengthened by the essence of these earthly substances. For this reason, food (with no salt) and drink (like water, coffee, liquor, etc.) are symbolically offered for the ancestors to consume. This is done around or at a small table that has been syncretized with African ancestor veneration and Spirist practices, called a bóveda or vault in English. Historically speaking, from my understanding, the bóveda was used only to honor one's guardian spirits, but since it can also be used as a sacred place of reflection (spirit communication), the bóveda became a place to venerate one's ancestors as well.

The bóveda, for the most part, goes by the way one feels. This feeling or following one's intuition is believed to be influence and inspiration given to the practitioner by the ancestors. That being said, contrary to popular belief, there is no right or wrong way to set up a bóveda and honor one's ancestors. There are only two rules that must be followed when it comes to working with the bóveda. The first is that it must be attended to faithfully. This means the waters must be refreshed, a white candle offered and the surface cleaned (at least) on a weekly basis. The second rule is that, since it is an altar for honoring the deceased, only photos of the deceased are to be placed upon it.

Since the bóveda is a multi-purpose altar that can help one develop meditative and mediumistic abilities, by bringing the ancestors and other spirits back into one's awareness, one is free to set-up the bóveda as they feel.

Now, this spiritual practice in general is based upon syncretism between the African American spiritual experience and Caribbean Spiritism. It has taken a number of years to develop because it is composed, based upon my understanding, of Afro-American (people of African descent throughout the

Afro-Diaspora) history, culture, language and mysticism. It is not something that I created based upon my intellectual observation. It was given to me, or rather I was born into it. That being said, I caution against creating practices just because they appeal to one's intellect. Spirituality is not just based upon what one thinks but on their interaction with the spiritual realm. To create a tradition without having this understanding will lead to a lot of mental anguish and will produce disastrous results.

It should be noted that this spiritual path is unique to the Afro-American experience and rooted in ancient African American shamanistic beliefs, with the main intent focused upon healing. It is not going to appeal to everyone because it is not "the only way". It is presented here to help others on a similar path to discover and embrace their roots in order to bring "whiteness or blessings of the ancestors" back into their lives.

Now, my bóveda symbolizes the land of the ancestors, the mystical KAMTA that Osar rules where the Great Hall of Judgment rests. It is designed to honor our aakhu (biological and cultural ancestor memory) as well as the netcharu (archetypical spirits/energies) that they are associated with or work under. It consists basically of nine glasses (eight small glasses and one large glass) of cool water. Each of the glasses symbolizes a particular netchar or class of spirits called clans or tribes in order to strengthen the familial connotation of this path. The largest glass is dedicated my Osarian spirits. The remaining eight follow no particular order because they have been subjected to change. (These spirits simply refuse to be pigeonholed). So, four glasses are placed on the left (representing Djahuti, Hruaakhuti, Npu and Hru), overseen by an old black man figurine (on my left) to symbolize the Right Eye. The remaining four glasses are placed on the right (representing Sokãr, Maat, Nebhet, Oset) and are overseen by an old black woman (to my right) to symbolize the Left Eye. This old black couple symbolizes the eldest of my paternal and maternal ancestors.

Standing in between these figurines is a white cross, symbolizing the maa aankh and representing the divine order. The maa aankh is placed on the altar to symbolize that the righteous souls do not die, but evolve and are reborn. Overlooking the entire bóveda is a white painted rooster that is anointed with frankincense oil, to keep it charmed and prevent the aapepu from entering the space. If you choose to use another oil do so, I simply alternate between frankincense, myrrh or Van Van or however way the spirits lead me. The white rooster is symbolic of Osar and the ancestor's protective purity. The symbology is simple: since cocks are fighters and they eat worms (some fight snakes), the white painted rooster chases away the negative aapepu.

Surrounding the bóveda are photos of my ancestors in silver frames (symbolic of the stars in my life), alone with other figurines symbolizing aakhu I do not know, such as my Native American ancestry, but whose presence I know is near.

At the bóveda I thank God for my aakhu and netcharu and ask that they be blessed with wisdom, power, strength, etc. so that they can in return assist and guide me in life. Afterwards, the aakhu and netcharu are called upon to assist me in my life by guiding and sharing their wisdom, power, and strength with me. The aakhu are offered light, cologne

(Florida Water), white rum (not too much so that they don't become drunk), cigar smoke (for protection and to help them to make the journey from the spirit realm to the physical realm), and strong black coffee with no sugar to keep them alert.

Besides developing the death awareness, the bóveda is also very useful in attracting positive influences and dispelling negative energies. For instance, one day I was feeling down. I had made the mistake of going to sleep upset about a disagreement with my wife, so naturally I awoke with that same energy but even stronger. Anyway, I got up and made breakfast as usual, but this negative energy was riding me. I forgot that the aapepu bring feelings and thoughts of anger, depression, guilt, resentment, etc. So, without thinking, I went to go get something and it was in front of my bóveda. The next thing I know, I was inspired to put on Pharoahe Monch's *Push*. That's when it "dawned" on me that there were aapepu near. I was reminded, as I looked at my bóveda, that one couldn't pass the Judgment if their Ab is heavier than a feather of truth. What weighs our Ab (heart, conscious, etc.) down and makes it feel heavy are all of the inspirations (anger, despair, resentment, guilt, depression, etc.) of the aapepu. The visual trigger made me change the way I was thinking and talk about the issue with my wife. After doing so, we both felt better and the issue was resolved. This is just one of the simplest ways the aakhu can intercede on our behalf.

Establishing Communication with the Netcharu

While many of us may find it easy to believe that we have guardian angels or guardian spirits that watch over and protect us, engaging in conversation or dialogue with our guardians would appear to be very strange for most of us because many western societies shun such practices. If our shamanistic practices had not fallen into obscurity, speaking and receiving messages from our guardians would be a common occurrence, similar to the people in biblical days. Again, just think how different Christianity would have been if Mary were not told that she would conceive a child. Think about all of the other incidences in which spiritual entities interceded in the Bible and other holy books.

It must be remembered that the greatest trick that the devil ever played was convincing people that he didn't exist. In fact, he did such a great job that he convinced many that spiritual entities don't exist at all because you can't measure (physically touch, smell, see, taste or hear) any of them. Entities are called angels, spirits, etc. because they are composed of energy and although they cannot be physically seen their presence can be experienced. Energy is just the higher form of physical matter, which means even if you can't physically measure it, it will manifest itself physically. Thus we have that good-natured spirits will manifest or inspire good-natured results (character, personality traits, etc.). Negative or bad natured spirits will manifest or inspire negative-results, and so on.

This is not to say that people are not responsible for their own actions and deeds, because we are. But the fact of the matter is what we manifest in the spirit becomes a physical reality, which is why it is important to be able to communicate with the netcharu, our spiritual guardians.

The easiest and simplest way to engage in dialogue with our netcharu is similar to meeting a new business contact. If you have an image of the netcharu or sign, place this before you. Begin by first introducing yourself to them (even though they know who you are) and explain to them what you need them to do for you. Next, allow them to go to work and try not to think about it. Once they have helped you, don't offend them; give them a small offering of appreciation. Usually, you will get a hunch what the netchar desires. The key is that you treat them like ordinary people.

For instance, if you need help finding something, Npu, the finder of lost things, would be the one you would approach. If this is your first encounter with Npu, you might begin by introducing yourself to him. Next, you would tell him, "Npu, help me to find _____." Then, you go about your business. Usually, if you do something completely opposite of what you requested, do not worry about it and just relax. You will get a hunch to look in a certain place. This is Npu responding to your request. It is the old axiom that if you weren't looking for something you would find it, but the day you start looking for something you can never find it.

Anyway, when you find what you are looking for, offer Npu a few pieces of candy, a little rum, a little incense, tobacco or whatever to show your appreciation. These things, including flowers, food, water, etc., are not consumed by the spirits, but help give them energy and strength to further assist you. It should also be noted that occasionally you might get a hunch to obtain a particular item for a spirit. Don't be alarmed. Usually, when a spirit does this, they are working directly with your aakhu and trying to obtain something to further assist you. When this happens it is best to try and understand why the spirit is requesting this particular item. Remember, it does you no good just to follow your intution and do something on gut impulse without having a clear reason why it is done. This is how a lot of good intentions became bad ideas, because of zealous believers. The aakhu, understanding how things can easily become misconstrued, have no problem explaining to their living descendants the purpose behind their intentions. If you find a spirit is not willing to share this information with you, it most likely is an aapepu.

For instance, once upon a time I got the hunch to purchase a couple of flashlights for one of my netcharu. The idea behind it, according to my aakhu, was so that this particular netchar could magically see and find things that were hidden from my physical eyes.

Working with the spirits is a great experience because they will help you to become a stronger and wiser individual by teaching you lessons that were believed to be lost due to Death. As you can see from the previous examples given, it is important to first establish communication with your aakhu, because they are the foundation. Our aakhu are the ones that first made oath with God to fulfill a particular task, according to some legends, which is why they hold such a high position in the psyche of people of African descent. They are the djett (the backbone) of Afro-American spirituality and expect us to live a certain way. This means that if this book found its way into your hands and you are reading it, it is not a coincidence. Your aakhu had something to do with it. The warning, however, is that you cannot engage in malicious work due to impulses from TASETT. If you choose to do evil, the spirits have a great way of teaching you so that you will not engage the practice ever again. With that, I wish you peace and blessings on this path.

Appendix B: The 42 Declarations of Maa

1. I have not done wrong.
2. I have not violently stolen from others.
3. I have not stolen.
4. I have not murdered any man or woman.
5. I have not swindled offerings.
6. I have not diminished obligations.
7. I have not stolen from God.
8. I have not spoken falsehoods.
9. I have not uttered evil words.
10. I have not caused anyone pain.
11. I have not fornicated.
12. I have not caused the shedding of tears.
13. I have not dealt deceitfully.
14. I have not misbehaved.
15. I have not acted deceitfully.
16. I have not wasted ploughed land.
17. I have not been an eavesdropper.
18. I have not set my lips in motion (against any man or woman).
19. I have not been wrathful except for a just cause.
20. I have not dishonored the wife of any man (or the husbad of any woman).
21. I have not dishonored the wife of any man (or the husbad of any woman).
22. I have not polluted myself.
23. I have not caused terror.
24. I have not misbehaved.
25. I have not stopped my ears against the words of Right and Truth.
26. I have not worked in grief.
27. I have not acted with rudeness.
28. I have not stirred up trouble.
29. I have not hastily judged.
30. I have not sought for distinctions.
31. I have not been an eavesdropper.
32. I have not multiplied my words exceedingly.
33. I have not done harm or ill.
34. I have never cursed the ruler of the land (or the law of the land).
35. I have never fouled the water.
36. I have not spoken scornfully.
37. I have never cursed God.
38. I have not stolen.

39. I have not cheated God.
40. I have not stolen the offerings of the ancestors.
41. I have not mistreated children, nor have I desecrated the holy places of God.
42. I have not killed with evil intent the cattle (or creations) of God.

The *42 Declarations of Maa* are a set of statements that were pronounced by the deceased Kamau (the Ancient Africans of Egypt) on the Day of Judgment. These statements, erroneously called the 42 Negative Confessions or the 42 Laws of Maat, are believed to be the inspiration behind the famed *Ten Commandments*. But, unlike the *Ten Commandments*, all of the historical records that have been recovered indicate that the Kamau never went around quoting the *42 Declarations of Maa* as laws. The reason why the Kamau never did this, it appears per an analysis of their history, is that they understood the dilemma that would be created through the creation of commandments. For instance, to make a commandment that one should not kill would put an individual (especially a soldier) in a spiritual predicament, where they would have to question if it is right or wrong to kill in order to defend and protect themselves, their fellow soldiers, civilians, countrymen, etc. To remedy this problem from ever occurring, the *42 Declarations of Maa* were created as a guide suggesting what **"<u>should be</u> the correct and ideal action and/or behavior"** in order to maintain peace and harmony throughout the Kamitic society, which consisted of 42 nomes (22 city-states in Upper Egypt and 20 city-states in Lower Egypt).

That being said, evil and/or sin, also called taboos from the Ancient African perspective, is any action and/or behavior that caused, inspired or motivated abnormality, arguments, chaos, confusion, destruction, deviation, disorder, disunity or war, in one's home, community, neighborhood, etc. These actions and behaviors were considered evil, sinful or taboos because they were all signs of the jealous one, Set, which eventually lead to degradation, death and the fall of humankind.

Appendix C:
The Precious Blood of the Ram (Lamb)

The ancient Hebrews, I was reminded, were instructed to perform this rite so that the angel of death would pass over their home. The Spirit revealed to me that this was an adaptation of an old Amun RA rite performed in ancient Kamit, whereas, instead of a sacred lamb, a sacred ram was used. Early African Americans, after learning the story the Spirit told me, familiar with the symbology, substituted red brick dust to symbolize the sacred blood. Others simply painted their front porch steps red to make a permanent deterrent against death and other negative spirits. Those refusing to be accused of practicing superstitious beliefs chose to symbolize the blood with that of blessed olive oil or water.

Blessed oil, water, colognes and rums are simply mundane and ordinary objects that have been prayed upon. These mundane objects that have been made sacred are not powerful within themselves. They are simply tools. A lot of people prefer to use blessed oil and/or blessed water that have been blessed by a clergyman or woman, but you can make your own. Papá Raúl taught me that all that is required is that you say a sincere to God to bless the substance to be used for general conditions, healing, protection or whatever. If you believe it is sacred, it becomes powerful and sacred. If you have to pray over it numerous times or have someone else you respect pray over it, do whatever it takes, so long as it becomes a powerful tool for you.

Blessed oil is usually virgin olive oil that has been prayed over. To protect the integrity and sacredness of this substance, it should be distinguished from other oils used in your household. I have heard of people cooking with blessed oil, which I can't comment upon as being right or wrong. It is something that I will not do because virgin olive oil is too strong for my taste, which is why it is a great oil for blessing and protection for me. Simply experiment and trust your intuition.

Blessed or Holy water is usually bottled spring water that has been prayed over by a minister, that can be drank, cooked with, as well as bathed in. It can also be used as eyewash to bring clarity and as a sprinkle to get rid of negative forces.

Peace Water is water consisting of white rose petals, basil and talcum powder. Once prayed over, it can be used to bring peace to a hostile environment.

Ocean water is water collected from an ocean. It represents the boundary where land and ocean meet. Since it is related to KAMTA, thus beginning, a little of it can be added to bathwater to help one conceive. It also is helpful in developing one's spiritual gifts and talents.

River Water is water collected from a river. Mixed with a little cinnamon and prayed over, it can be used for financial blessings.

Bay rum is a cologne consisting of bay leaves steeped in rum, after which it is prayed over and used similarly to blessed oil but for more general purposes.

Tobacco rum is also a type of cologne that consists of rum that has been steeped with either strong cigars or chewing tobacco. After the desired scent is obtained, it is strained and the liquid is prayed over and used for strong protection.

Some other fragrances that can be found in most grocery stores or retail stores catering to Caribbean and Latin Americans are:

Florida Water is a floral alcohol fragrance used for general purposes.

Rose Water, a perfume commonly used for love.

To personalize these items, simply add a bit of your saliva or urine to them, and/or your personal cologne, which makes it so that these items can only be used for you.

Appendix D: Bibliomancy

In African American Spirituality, the Bible is held in very high regard and is viewed by many as being the Word of God[78]. As such, many people from all over the world turn to it in times of indecision and use it as a tool of divination to receive counsel and inspiration from it, which is called the art of bibliomancy.

Now, before proceeding: a lot of misinformed people will tell you that divination is evil and it is the work of the devil. They will also say that the Bible speaks against divination and all sorts of psychic phenomena regarding it, which is totally untrue. Most of these people that say this will claim to be Bible scholars, but examples of oracles can be found all throughout the Bible. The most popular oracle was called the Urim and Thummim. Here is a partial listing of some of those examples: Numbers 27:21, Joshua 7:14, I Samuel 10:20, I Samuel 23, II Samuel 5:23-25, Acts 1:24-26, and Acts 19:12. Contrary to popular belief, the lots spoken of in the Bible is not a vote but an oracle system based upon sortilege. Talks and support of the practice can be found in Leviticus 16:8 and Ezekiel 21:12. Divination was basically used by early Judeo-Christians to learn of God's will.

The purpose of using oracles is that you have the right to know certain particulars about your life, the impact you make upon the lives of others and the impact others have upon you and those whom you care for. The reason oracles are looked upon as being evil or

---

[78] For many non-Christians the Koran or other holy books are viewed as the mouthpiece of God.

tools of manipulation is that many have misused them for their own selfish purposes[79], because people are ignorant as to what these tools truly are. When it is understood what an oracle is and its purpose, it becomes easier to recognize a true diviner from a charlatan. It becomes easy to see as well that oracles are not meant to tell you who is bad and who is not. They are meant to help you to develop spiritually and understand the Divine Plan.

I first learned of this practice by observing how preachers prepare for sermon. Many times most good preachers do not know what they are going to say before a congregation. From what I have seen, they do not follow a pre-written script, but instead they pray and ask for God to show them or give them a message as to what they should tell the congregation that they are going to speak before. Following this prayer, they follow their intuition and wherever it leads them. Most of the time the preacher's intuition leads them to open their Bible to a particular book, scripture or verse in the Bible. It is from this book, scripture or verse that the preacher gets the message of what they are supposed to preach about. It was from observing preachers and this practice that led me to use it so many years ago.

To consult the Bible, one first prays to God and asks for a solution to their problem or whatever troubles them. Any legitimate question can be asked if asked in the proper manner, but I have found that it is best to ask "how to do", "should I do", "what to do" and

---

[79] This was part of the reason why I was taken advantage of in my past relationship.

non-judgmental questions, because God is concerned with your spiritual development and the skills that you need to develop in order to properly get what you want out of life. For instance, instead of asking, is it right/wrong to do buy this car? Ask, "Speak (Lord/God) upon me purchasing car?" Instead of "Should I go to this function or to my aunt's house?" ask separate questions, like, "Should I go to this function?", "Should I go to my aunt's house?"

With the Bible closed and your eyes closed, place your hand (follow your intuition) upon the Bible and ask your question. You may want to breathe your question onto the Bible. Next, with your eyes closed (or without looking), open the Bible wherever you feel the urge or feel guided to open it at. Open your eyes, read the passage and think about how it relates to your question. Your ancestors and spirit guides will assist you in trying to interpret the meaning.

An example of a reading using bibliomancy: One day I wasn't feeling as upbeat as normal. I wasn't down or anything, but I just felt a blah feeling, almost as if I was waiting for something. Anyway, I didn't particularly care for the feeling and it made me wonder why I felt this way and how can I prevent myself from feeling this way. So, I followed the procedure given above and opened the Bible to Psalms 61.

The interpretation that I got was that, even though I had a change of heart, I was still a little troubled or having difficulty encouraging and motivating myself daily. The solution was to look at the blessings and the truth that have come into my life, which will be motivation enough for me to perform my daily works.

This is one of the ways to trust God. It will take a little practice and a little getting used to to perform this practice, because of the society that most of us are born in that tell us to trust in what we see and physically can control. But, as we allow the Spirit to be our guide, we will find that it will all pay off and everything will be worthwhile. I hope this simple divination will help you in your life and serve you well.

Appendix E:
Glossary of Terms

42 Declarations of Maa: a set of 42 affirmatives, believed to be recited after death during Judgment in order for the deceased to ascent into the heavens. The 42 Declarations of Maa also sometimes referred to as the *42 Negative Confessions,* believed to be the inspiration behind the *Ten Commandments.*

Aakhu: are the souls of deceased relatives that continue to exist after death. The aakhu are believed to dwell in heaven and act as intermediaries between God and man. They act as moral guardians and represent particular aspects of our conscience. Their spiritual efficacy can be seen in their practical wisdom. The aakhu are also considered to be spirit guides and the souls of children that have died prematurely.

Aapepu: negative, destructive spirits that inspire chaotic and destructive behavior amongst the living. When alive, these spirits are believed to have been no-good-doers that most people tried to avoid in life, that hung around alleys, street corners and in other unsavory places. In death they are the same no-good-doers, offering the same unwise advice leading to accidents,

	problems and other major dilemmas. Some times referred to in old blues songs as the *blues* that one had to protect themselves from. Believed to be the Kamitic equivalent of the bankuyu, associated with Set.
Abakwa:	a secret Cuban society of men believed to be derived from the Ekpe Society in the Cross River region of Africa.
Amen:	believed to be derived from the Kamitic words amun and amon, which mean "to hide, to conceal, to make mysterious, to fortify, to make firm", it is a declaration of affirmation following Jewish and Christian prayers. The common translation of the word is "So, be it" and "Let it be".
Amun RA:	is the regenerative, feminine and rebirthing aspects of the self. Amun RA represents the self's ability to be reborn, rebirth and restored back to one's original state of being. Symbolized a young man with plumes on his head that sits or stands victorious because he has been purified and renewed. It corresponds to the winter sun RA-sherå. Another popular symbol was that of a ram (sheep) which also symbolized the return.
Bakulu:	KiKongo term form ancestral spirits.
Bankuyu:	KiKongo term for trickster spirits.
Basimbi:	KiKongo term for mysterious benevolent spirits.

Cuban son:	described by Ned Sublette in his book *Cuba and Its Music: From the First Drums to the Mambo* as "a Cuban synthesis: Bantu percussion, melodic rhythm, and call-and-response singing, melding with the Spanish peasant's guitar and language."
Deshret:	is the red crown of Lower Kamit, the northern region that symbolizes the desert area called TASETT. Spiritually speaking, the Deshret represents aggression, selfishness, arrogance, ungratefulness and all of the other impurities acquired while trying to survive in the physical world.
Devil:	see Set and Aapepu.
Four Moments of the Sun:	sunrise, midday, sunset and midnight.
Four Stages of Life:	birth, growth to maturity (adulthood), death and rebirth.
Hedjet:	is the white crown of Upper Kamit, the southern region that symbolizes the lush, fertile lands called KAMTA. Spiritually speaking, the Hedjet represents knowledge, wisdom, patience, purity, etc. acquired by God and one's ancestors in order to live an eternal life.
Holy Ghost:	the Holy Ghost, also called God's Power, the Divine Spirit symbolized as a dove in the old testament of the Bible, is Rau in the Kamitic tradition. It is the Power of God that that comforts, guides, teaches, convinces, etc., which can also be

Hru: lost according to Christian tradition. the hero of the story in the Story of Osar that the Kamitic initiates of old identified themselves with.

Kamitic: the name the Ancient Africans of Egypt called themselves and the name given to them, according to a biblical table of nations, incorrectly translated and spelled as Ham, but should be Kam. Also believed by modern scholars, the name used to refer to all people of color. To make a distinction between ancient inhabitants and their spiritually influenced descendents, ancient Kamitic is used to refer to the Kamitic civilization, while Kamitic is used to refer to those in contemporary times inspired by them.

KAMTA: the lush and fertile land of the south, also called Upper Kamit, represented by the white Hedjet crown. Symbolized on the maa aankh as the mysterious realm, the spirit world, the hidden world, the land of the dead and the land of the great ancestor Osar.

KhepeRA: is the creative and youthful aspects of the self. Symbolized as a scarab beetle or opening lotus bud to represent the beginning and birth. Since "KH" doesn't really exist in the Kamitic language, it should actually be spelled KEPERA.

Kongo Cross: see Yowa Cross.

La Madama: is a cultural icon found throughout

	Latin America, that represents the old African matriarch ancestors brought to the Americas. Commonly ridiculed and depicted as Aunt Jeminina in the United States, in Latin America the image is highly regarded and respected.
Maa:	the vertical line on the maa aankh that brings the material (secular) and spiritual world together, or makes that which is above below and vice versa. Maa commonly translates to mean order, law, truth, balance and reciprocity. In ancient times it was the primeval mound that God stood upon before bringing things into being; it later came to represent the road to resurrection or into the afterlife. It is only through the Maa that one is able to ascend past the horizon and receive peace, freedom, joy, love, success, etc. in life and death.
Maa aankh:	a cosmogram inspired by the Kongo Cross, based upon the Kamitic (Ancient Egyptian) principles, that illustrates the cycle of life, the four seasons, the four directions, the four stages of life, evolution of the soul and the crossroad between the two lands (material and spiritual worlds).
Maa Khru:	(pronounced maa'sha-roo) the Kamitic term that translates to mean "true of voice" but is the Kamitic equivalent of "being born" or "saved", since the initiate

professes it after being purified of impurities.

Nebertcher: is the Kamitic name for God, which translates to mean *Lord of Everything*.

Netcharu: commonly defined as Kamitic deities, are believed to be ancient founders of the Kamitic people that later became nature spirits, equivalent to saints and angels. Recognized as guardian spirits. These benevolent spirits are believed to be the first followers of God that assisted the legendary Osar in uniting the Kamitic kingdom and initiating the ancestral culture that exists throughout the Afro-Diaspora.

Nyun: the sacred, primeval waters of life believed to be the source of the Nile, represented on the maa aankh as the horizontal line that separates the two Great Lands.

Nzambi Mpungu: is the Kongo-Angolan name for God.

Orishás: also called Orixas, believed by some to be African angels, guardian spirits, deities and/or ancestral founders of a people derived from the Yoruba tradition of Nigeria.

Osar: Viewed through the maa aankh as the great ancestral king in the Story of Osar that saved his people by giving them laws, teaching them how to grow grain and giving them religious instructions. Symbolizes one's ancestors and spirit guides and is a perfect spirit model, similar to Jesus Christ. Also spelled Osiris, Asar and Ausar.

Oset: Viewed through the maa aankh as the heroic matriarch in the Story of Osar that despite the threat on her life searched out for the body parts of Osar, thereby rekindling hope for the return of greatness. Also spelled Isis, Aset and Auset.

Palo Mayombe: a Congolese (Bantu) religion practiced in Cuba and parts of the Caribbean. It is believed that Palo (for short) is closely related to the African American folk tradition known as hoodoo.

Pert em Hru: a one hundred-chapter book of funerary text, called the Book of Coming Forth by Light, incorrectly called the Egyptian Book of Dead.

RA: is the active, aggressive, aware aspect of the self, symbolized as a hawk; corresponds to the north direction, maleness and the summer. It symbolizes Life.

RA Atum: is the dying or transformative aspect of the self. Symbolized as an old man due to the elders' ability to transform one's life through wisdom. Associated with the west and the autumn season. It symbolizes Death.

RA Tem Kheper: the spiritual trinity supporting the land of the living.

Rau: are the numerous forms of RA or the collective that make up the Holy Spirit or Holy Ghost. It is the power, intelligence and will of God that gives people the power to move, clap their hands, stomp their feet, live right, act right and do the right thing.

Religion: a set of beliefs and practices as it pertains to some Divinity.

Santería: a syncretic religion practiced primarily in Cuba and various parts of the Caribbean, consisting of Yoruba religious beliefs combined with Roman Catholicism. Also called Regla de Ocha or Lukumi.

Set: the envious brother of Osar in the Story of Osar that created all types of chaos throughout the land. Early Christians identifying with this force changed his name from Set to Set-an and later Satan. Set symbolizes the destructive and negative spiritual forces that inspire chaos and evil.

Spirituality: the tendency to make meaning through a sense of relatedness to God, oneself, and/or others that transcends the self in such as way that it empowers and does not devalue the individual.

Story of RA and Oset: is a cornerstone of Kamitic religious thinking, where RA clearly states that he is not the sun, sun god or God, but in so many words reveals that he is the *Spirit of God* that comes as KhepeRA in the morning,

	RA at noon and Tmu (RA Atum) in the evening.
TASETT:	the desert, northern region of Kamit, also called Lower Kemet, represented by the red Deshret crown. Symbolized on the maa aankh as the city or village, physical realm, the world where things go awry, the material world and the land of the living.
Yowa Cross:	also called the Dikenga, Tendwa Nza Kongo or Kongo Cross, is a cosmogram signifying the meeting of two worlds, the living and the dead (ancestors). One of the inspirations behind the Maa aankh.

Appendix F:
Selected Bibliography & Recommended Reading

Books with an asterisk (*) besides them are highly recommended by the author.

Amen, Ra Un Nefer. *Metu Neter Vol. 1: The Great Oracle of Tehuti and the Egyptian System of Spiritual Cultivation*. Khamit Media Trans Visions Inc, 1990.

Ashanti, Kwabena F. *Rootwork and Voodoo: In Mental Health*. Tone Books, 1987.

Battle, Michael. *The Black Church in America: African American Christian Spirituality*. Wiley-Blackwell, 2006.

*Bockie, Simon. *Death and the Invisible Powers: The World of Kongo Belief*. Indiana University Press, 1993.

Bolling, John L. "Guinea across the Water: The African-American Approach to Death and Dying." *A Cross-Cultural Look at Death, Dying, and Religion*. Eds. Joan K. Parry and Angela Shen Ryan. Nelson-Hall, 1995. 145-59.

*Bridges, Flora Wilson. *Resurrection Song: African-American Spirituality*. (The Bishop Henry McNeal Turner/Sojourner Truth Series in Black Religion) Orbis Books, 2001.

*Browder, Anthony T. *From the Browder File: 22 Essays on the African American Experience*. Institute of Karmic Guidance, 1989.

*Browder, Anthony T. *Nile Valley Contributions to Civilization*. Institute of Karmic Guidance, 1992.

Budge, E.A. Wallis. *An Egyptian Hieroglyphic Dictionary Vol. I and II.* New York: Dover Publication, 1978.

Budge, E.A. Wallis. *Osiris & The Egyptian Resurrection, vols. 1 & 2.* Dover Publications, 1973.

Carruthers, Jacob H. *The Irritated Genie: An Essay on the Haitian Revolution.* Kemetic Institute, 1985.

Courlander, Harold. *A Treasury of Afro-American Folklore: The Oral Literature, Traditions, Recollections, Legends, Tales, Songs, Religious Beliefs, Customs, Sayings and Humor of Peoples of African Descent in the Americas.* New York: Marlove and Company, 1976.

Diop, Cheikh Anta. *The African Origin of Civilization: Myth or Reality.* Lawrence Hill Books, 1989.

*Doumbia, Adama and Naomi Doumbia. *The Way of the Elders: West African Spirituality & Tradition.* Llewellyn Publications, 2004.

Dossey M.D., Larry. *Recovering the Soul: A Scientific and Spiritual Approach.* Bantam, 1st ed. 1989.

Dundes, Alan. *Interpreting Folklore.* Indiana University Press, 1980.

Fatunmbi, Falokun. *Iwa-Pele: Ifa Quest the Search for the Source of Santeria and Lucumi.* Original Publications, 1991.

Fett, Sharla M. *Working Cures: Healing, Health, and Power on Southern Slave Plantations.* University of North Carolina, 2002.

*Fu-Kiau, K. Kia Bunseki. *African Cosmology of the Bantu-Kongo: Principles of Life & Living*. Athelia Henrietta Press, 2001.

Gadalla, Moustafa. *Egyptian Cosmology: The Animated Universe*. Tehuti Research Foundation; 2nd. ed. 2001.

Gomez, Michael. A: *Exchanging Our Country Marks: The Transformation of African Identities in the Colonial and Antebellum South*. The University of North Carolina Press, 1998.

Grillo, Evelio. *Black Cuban, Black American: A Memoir*. Arte Publico Press; 1st ed. 2000.

*Hall, James. Sangoma: My Odyssey Into the Spirit World of Africa. Jeremy P. Tarcher, 1994.

Hollenweger, W. J. *The Pentecostals: The Charismatic Movement in the Churches*. Augsburg Publishing House, 1972.

Hurston, Zora Neale. *Moses: Man of the Mountain*. University of Illinois Press, 1984.

Ions, Veronica. *Egyptian Mythology: Library of the World's Myths and Legends*. Peter Bedrick Books; Rev Sub ed., 1983.

James, George G. M. *Stolen Legacy: The Greeks were not the authors of Greek philosophy, but the people of North Africa, commonly called the Egyptians*. Julian Richardson Associates, 1988.

Jacobs, Claude F. and Andrew J. Kaslow. *The Spiritual Churches of New Orleans: Origins, Beliefs *and Rituals of an African-American Religion*. The University of Tennessee Press, 1991.

*MacGaffey, Wyatt. *Custom and Government in the Lower Congo*. University of California Press, 1970.

*MacGaffey, Wyatt. *Religion and Society in Central Africa: The BaKongo of Lower Zaire*. The University of Chicago Press, 1986.

*Mbiti, John S. *Introduction to African Religion*. Heinemann, 1991.

*Mbiti, John S. *African Religions & Philosophy*. Heinemann, 1992.

McQuillar, Tayannah Lee. *Rootwork: Using the Folk Magick of Black America for Love, Money and Success*. Fireside, 2003.

Murphy, Joseph M. *Working the Spirit: Ceremonies of the African Diaspora*. Beacon Press, 1995.

Paris, Peter J. *The Spirituality of African Peoples*. Augsburg Fortress Publishers, 1994.

Puckett, Newbill Niles, *Magic & Folk Beliefs of the Southern Negro*. Dover Publication, 1969.

*Raboteau, Albert J. *Slave Religion: The "Invisible Institution" in the Antebellum South*. Oxford University Press, 1978.

Shafton, Anthony, *Dream-Singers: The African American Way with Dreams*. John Wiley & Sons, Publishers, 2001.

Smith, Theophus H. *Conjuring Culture: Biblical Formations of Black America.* Oxford University Press, 1994.

Some, Malidoma Patrice. *The Healing Wisdom of Africa: Finding Life Purpose Through Nature, Ritual and Community.* New York: Jeremy P. Tarcher/Putnam, 1998.

Sublette, Ned. *Cuba and Its Music: From the First Drums to the Mambo.* Chicago Review Press, 2007.

Sullivan, Martha Adams. "May the Circle Be Unbroken: The African-American Experience of Death, Dying and Spirituality." *A Cross-Cultural Look at Death, Dying, and Religion.* Eds. Joan K. Parry and Angela Shen Ryan. Chicago, IL: Nelson-Hall, 1995. 160-71.

Synan, Vinson. *The Holiness-Pentecostal Movement in the United States.* William B. Eerdmans Publishing Company, 1971.

Teish, Luisah. *Jambalya: The Natural Woman's Book of Personal Charms and Practical Rituals.* San Francisco: Harper and Row, 1985.

*Thompson, Robert Farris. *Flash of the Spirit: African and Afro-American Art and Philosophy.* Random House, 1983.

*Thompson, Robert Farris. *Face of the Gods: Art and Altars of Africa and the African Americas.* Prestel, 1993.

Thorton, John. *Africa and Africans in the Making of the Atlantic World, 1400-1800*. Cambridge University Press; 2 ed., 1998.

Williams, Chancellor. *Destruction of Black Civilization: Great Issues of a Race from 4500 B.C to 2000 A.D*. Third World Press, 1987.

Young, James T. *Rituals of Resistance: African Atlantic Religion in Kongo and the Lowcountry South in the Era of Slavery*. Louisiana State University Press, 2007.

Index

42 Declarations of Maa, 32, 300

ãakhu, 151, 157, 160, 161, 162, 163, 168, 169, 170, 173, 175, 176, 186, 204, 217, 233, 243, 254, 259, 261, 262, 263, 264, 266, 268, 269, 300

Aakhut, 156

ãapepu, 151, 157, 163, 164, 167, 168, 175, 241, 249, 252, 253, 254, 255, 256, 258, 259, 272, 273

Abakwa, 65, 74, 301

Afonso I, 109, 110

Allan Kardec. *See* Spiritism

Amun Rã, 189, 193, 198, 202, 205, 230, 231, 233, 235, 237, 239, 254, 294

ancestors, vii, xii, 16, 21, 28, 66, 68, 73, 80, 90, 94, 98, 100, 104, 106, 107, 110, 127, 130, 134, 138, 151, 152, 160, 161, 162, 163, 165, 167, 168, 169, 183, 196, 200, 212, 214, 225, 229, 231, 252, 271, 275, 280, 299, 302, 303, 305, 307, *See* ãakhu

angels, xii, 77, 102, 109, 110, 149, 150, 163, 164, 189, 240, 241, 260, 263, 304, 305

Antonio Maceo, 92

archetype, 77

Armor of God, 269

Azuza Street, 122, 123, 124

bakulu, 109

bankuyu, 109

basimbi, 109, 260

bibliomancy, 15, 297, 299

Boukman, Dutty, 116

conscious mind, 141

Council of Foreign Plantations, 111

Deshret, 199, 301, 307

divination, 146, 147, 149, 297, 299

divisions of the Spirit, 224, 232, 235, 241

Djahuti, 164, 206, 209, 242, 246, 258

Genesis, 150, 191

God's Unchanging Hand, 6, 168, 274

gris-gris, 116

guardian angel, 110, 151, 240

Harriet Tubman, 81, 261, 262

Hedjet, 199, 200, 212, 302, 303

Holiness, 120, 121, 123, 124, 125, 126, 259, 312

Holy Ghost. See Rãu,

Hru, 164, 181, 192, 208, 209, 211, 212, 213, 214, 230, 232, 234, 245, 247, 248, 258, 263, 302, 305

Hruãakhuti, 237, 239, 245, 246, 268, 269, 270, 271, 272

HruKhti, 164, 271

HruUr, 164

Jesus, 14, 17, 93, 99, 102, 104, 134, 136, 150, 201, 207, 222, 230, 232, 273, 280, 305

Jung, 76, 77, 157, 159

KAMTA, 199, 200, 201, 214, 229, 232, 233, 235, 236, 237, 240, 241, 258, 262, 295, 302

KHEPERÃ, 191, 192, 233

maã ãankh, 195, 196, 201, 202, 205, 206, 214, 216, 217, 220, 234, 257, 258, 262, 263, 264, 275

maãkhru, 211

Maat, 41

Maãt, 164, 246, 247, 248

Malcolm X, 22, 23, 29, 67, 86, 150, 269

Martin L. King, 20, 22, 23, 29, 33, 132, 150

Nebertcher, 202, 304

Nebhet, 208, 244, 245

Nebthet, 164

netchar, 237, 259, 262

netcharu, 151, 157, 163, 164, 167, 175, 176, 233, 240, 241, 243, 246, 249, 252, 254, 259, 260, 263, 304

Npu, 164, 208, 243, 244, 260, 261, 262, 264, 265, 266, 267

Nut and Geb, 164

Nyu, 304

Nyu (Nu, Nun), 201

Nzabmi Mpungu, 110

Nzambi Mpungu, 109, 305

orisha, 41, 52, 76, 77, 89

Orishas, 305

Osar, 92, 164, 167, 201, 205, 206, 207, 208, 209, 210, 211, 212, 214, 222, 223, 230, 231, 232, 235, 241, 242, 243, 244, 245, 247, 249, 258, 262, 263, 265, 271, 273, 275, 302, 303, 304, 305, 306

Oset, 164, 177, 178, 179, 180, 181, 182, 188, 189, 190, 204, 207, 208, 209, 242, 243, 244, 245, 247, 259, 305, 306

Our Lady of Medals of the Immaculate Conception. See Oset

Palo Mayombe, 51, 89, 126, 133, 305

Pentecostalism, 120, 126, 259

Portuguese, 108, 110, 111, 280

prueba, 177, 218

Queen Nzingha, 280

quinceañera, 265

quinceañeras, 274

Rã, 177, 178, 179, 180, 181, 182, 188, 189, 190, 191, 192, 193, 194, 198, 202, 206, 208, 220, 230, 231, 232, 234, 235, 237, 239, 247, 252, 259, 271, 306

Rã Atum, 189, 192, 198, 230, 231, 232, 238, 239, 306

Rãu, 207, 218, 222, 223, 224, 230, 235, 236, 237, 240, 258

Santa Claus, 250

Santeria, 65, 92, 126, 306, 309

Satan, 200, 269, 306

Satanel, 200, 249

Second Great Awakening, 114

Seven African Powers candles, 273

Shu and Tefnut, 202, 203

Sokãr, 164, 220, 248, 249

Spiritism, 65, 117, 118, 119, 120, 166, 259

St. George. See HruKhuti

TASETT, 199, 200, 229, 232, 235, 236, 249, 253, 255, 258, 262, 268, 301, 307

Ten Commandments, 17, 32, 113, 128, 136, 300

Tubman, 264

unconscious mind, 141, 224

Vodu, 65, 115, 116, 126

voodoo, 116

Yowa Cross, 186, 187, 195, 303, 307

Zumbi of Palmares, 269

Maa:
A Guide to the Kamitic Way for Personal Transformation

Paperback: 204 pages   **ISBN-13:** 978-0985506704

Before the 42 Laws of Maat and the 10 Maat Virtues, the ancient philosophers of Kamit (Egypt) relied upon a set of shamanic principles that taught how to work the Ra (the Spirit of God), called the Seven Codes of Maa. Like most shamanic principles the 7 Codes allowed the Kamitic people to see science and magic as the same thing, and work them both. In this book you will learn how to discover your purpose in life, reconnect to your ancestral past, create sacred spaces, and foretell the future using ordinary objects found in nature in order to change your dreams into a reality.

Maa Aankh Vol. II:
Discovering the Power of I AM Using the Shamanic Principles of Ancient Egypt for Self-Empowerment and Personal Development

Paperback: 226 pages   **ISBN-13:** 978-0985506711

After learning that early African Americans in the Antebellum South followed the Kongo Cross, which the author used to discover the Maa Aankh, an Egyptian-style medicine wheel. Using this diagram as a guide revealed that the familiar physical reality we live in is limited, but beyond our five physical senses is a rich and unlimited spiritual dimension. Everything we desire – peace, prosperity, success, love, joy – can be found in this spiritual realm, because they are ethereal in nature. Most people have a problem obtaining these goals because they allow themselves to become disconnected from their Source. But, by learning how to stay connected to this invisible reality, you can overcome the physical problems you face. Included are practical exercises based upon shamanic traditions that will help you break away from the destructive beliefs and habits that disconnect you from the Source. As well as spiritual practices and rites that will help you maintain the connection to create the life that you want and deserve.

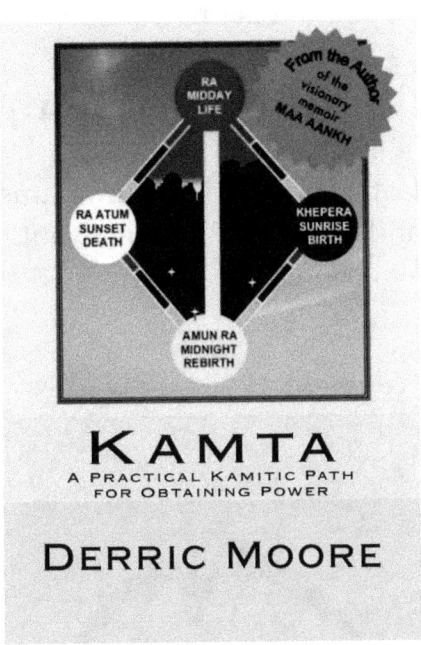

Kamta:
A Practical Kamitic Path for Obtaining Power

Paperback: 148 pages   ISBN-13: 978-0615468518

When Derric Moore became deathly ill due to the debilitating dis-ease lupus, the last thing he wanted to do, was to accept that it was "God's will." He needed something new and he needed something fast! So he appealed to God for help, and his ancestors and guardian spirits responded by giving him a spiritual system based upon Ancient Egyptian (Kamitic) theology and Afro-spiritual practices, which he used to improve his health. In this practical guide that approaches Kamitic philosophy from a shamanistic perspective, you'll learn how: - To tap into the Power of God within you – How to effectively pray and get your prayers answered - How we subconsciously make our bodies ill, but with a little effort can improve our overall health – How to change your dreams – Foretell the future through divination – Build sacred space to attract positive influences into your life – And, much, much more.

Visit us at:

1SoLAlliance.com

For Maa Aankh cosmograms and additional learning tools.

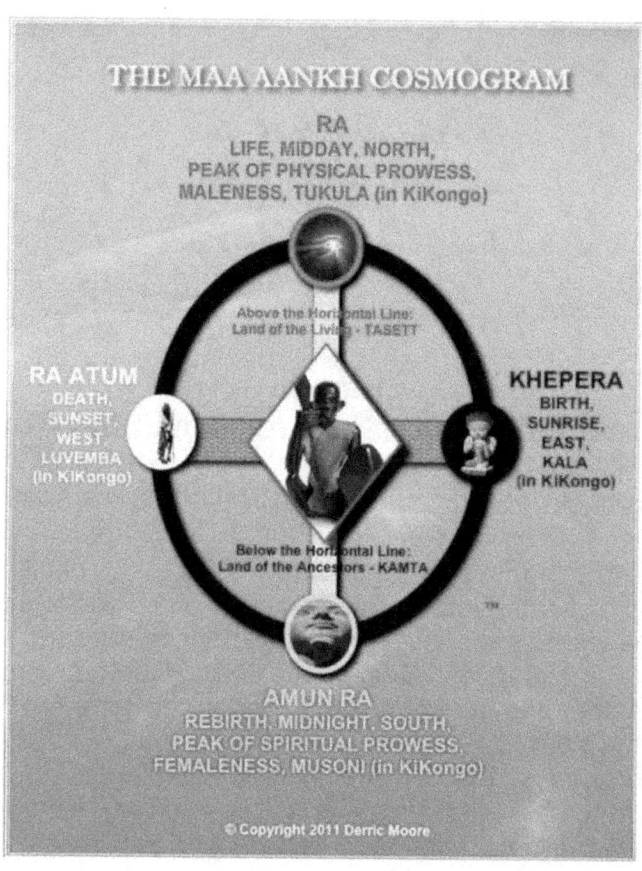

Maa Aankh Vol. III:
The Kamitic Shaman Way of Working the Superconscious Mind to Improve Memory, Solve Problems Intuitively and Spiritually Grow Through the Power of the Spirits

Paperback: 236 pages   **ISBN-13:** 978-0985506742

Our current state of affairs is proof that if you want change, it is not enough to say you believe in God. In order to create change and make miracles occur in your life. You have to "know" you are made in the image of God and act on it! Once again, refusing to conform to any academic, religious or philosophical doctrine because it constitutes blind obedience. By using the Seven Codes of Maa (the core concepts and principles of ancient Egyptian spirituality), Moore has once again eloquently laid out a practical and scientific approach to Kamitic spirituality that any novice or adept would appreciate but, this time. He has gone a step further by showing how to implement the concepts and principles as an Afro-American healing art. In this informative and illustrated book, you will learn: * How to use the Superconscious mind to improve your memory and create miracles. * How to use the Superconscious mind to foresee the future using simple divination techniques. * How to establish a connection between your superconscious mind and the spiritual realm. * How to build altars, spirit pots and alternative altars (for those limited by time, space, unforeseen circumstances, etc.). * And, much, much more. Discover how to wake up the Divine within you and improve your life today!

Help Get the Word Out!

I would like to personally thank you for purchasing the *Maa Aankh (2nd. Edition): Finding God the Afro-American Spiritual Way, by Honoring the Ancestors and Guardian Spirits* and reading it in its entirety. I hope that you enjoyed reading the strategies and techniques that I have shared with you in this book.

It would be immensely helpful to me if you could write a review for this book and publish it on Amazon.com.

To write a review:
1. Simply type in Amazon's search engine **Maa Aankh 2nd**
2. Scroll down to the reviews section.
3. And just write an honest review (good or bad) and give the book as many stars as you think it deserves.

Thank you in advance,

Derric "Rau Khu" Moore

www.ingramcontent.com/pod-product-compliance
Lightning Source LLC
Chambersburg PA
CBHW052141300426
44115CB00011B/1473